Economic Development in the World's Smallest Economies

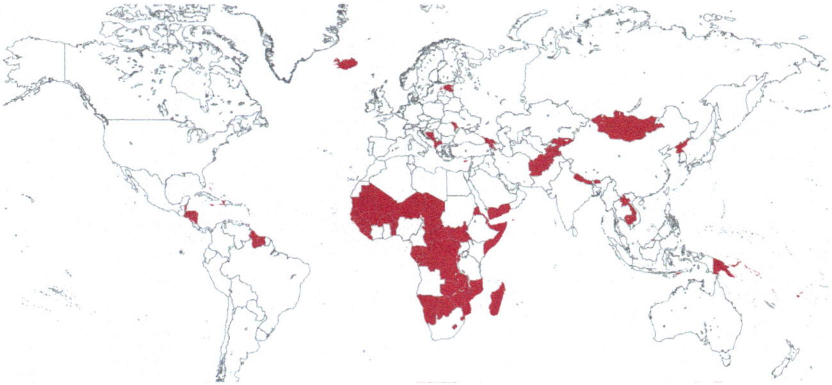

Aneta A. Teperek

Economic Development in the World's Smallest Economies

How Geography, Demographics, and Culture Define Economic Activity

palgrave
macmillan

Aneta A. Teperek
New York, USA
e-mail: aneta.teperek@osew.org

ISBN 978-3-031-63809-1 ISBN 978-3-031-63810-7 (eBook)
https://doi.org/10.1007/978-3-031-63810-7

This Palgrave Macmillan imprint is published by the registered company Springer Nature Switzerland AG.
The registered company address is: Gewerbestrasse 11, 6330 Cham, Switzerland

Contents

List of Figures

List of Tables

Introduction

Various typologies have been employed in the examination of the economic development of countries. They have been classified according to a number of different criteria, including population size, land area, location, and GDP per capita. Nevertheless, there has been no categorization based on the economic potential of the country that divides the 193 UN-recognized nations into three groups: the world's largest economies, the world's medium-sized economies, and the world's smallest economies. The last group of countries, collectively generating only 1% of global GDP, plays a minor role on the international stage because of its small economic potential. Meanwhile, the group of the world's smallest economies comprises as many as 93 countries, which represent nearly half of the total number of countries in the world. Moreover, the world's smallest economies possess significant potential in terms of resources, including youthful population and untapped human resources; unexploited mineral resources both on land and within their maritime Exclusive Economic Zone; their maritime exclusive economic zones; pristine environments; favorable coastal geographic locations; and rich indigenous cultural heritage. Nevertheless, these nations receive little attention in the literature; and attract little interest from scholars, politicians, and state leaders of larger economies. The media tends to focus on the world's smallest economies only when a significant event occurs in or involves them. However, shortly thereafter, the world tends to forget about them. This a major reason why the author became interested in this group and decided to examine the world's smallest economies (the WSE), focusing in this book on the geographic, demographic, and cultural conditions, as these factors are fundamental in influencing economic growth and development. The layout and structure of this book are subordinate to that objective.

Chapter 1 defines the group of the world's smallest economies and provides a general overview of the 93 countries classified into it. Chapter 2 presents the geographical locations of the countries under analysis in relation to the Earth's hemispheres, time zones, continents, and distance from the sea. The objective was to assess whether the location, closest neighborhood, and land area (i.e., size and shape) influence the economic growth and development of the world's smallest economies. Chapters 3 through 7 focus on the natural potential of the 93 countries under study, with Chap. 3 serving as an introduction to the following four chapters, which concentrate on specific components of the natural environment. Although the analyses of climate, flora, soils, terrain, and water resources are conducted separately, they form a single integrated system in which societies function and economies operate. Each component interacts with and is dependent on the others. Chapter 4 focuses on climate, a key element of physical geography. The classification of the world's smallest economies by climate zone and climate type was made to illustrate the significant impact of climate on national economies, with a particular focus on those countries whose primary economic sectors are highly vulnerable to climate conditions. The identification of natural plant formations allowed the selection of countries with the highest share of forests, which serves as a crucial foundation for their economies and development. The climatic and plant conditions exert a significant influence on the formation of soil structures, which are described in Chap. 5. The objective of this analysis was to assess the fertility of soils and their agricultural suitability. Additionally, the examination of the land use structure were conducted, with particular attention given to its economic applications. Land use is closely related to topography, discussed in Chap. 6. Landforms significantly affects the potential for agricultural development, a crucial sector for many of the world's smallest economies. It also impacts the development of land transportation and the associated costs. Over the course of centuries, geological processes have not only shaped the landforms, but have also led to the formation of valuable mineral resources, which serves a crucial source of income for many of the world's smallest economies. Chapter 7 addresses the final environmental component: water resources, both marine and inland. A substantial portion of this chapter is dedicated to the maritime Exclusive Economic Zone (EEZ), which offers many economic benefits to two-thirds of the world's smallest economies. And, the inland freshwaters, which are vital for agricultural and industrial expansion, also serve as a source of drinking water, a scarcity experienced by numerous of the world's smallest economies. The following chapters of the book, comprising Chaps. 8, 9, 10, 11, 12, and 13, focus on the demographic conditions of the world's smallest economies. Chapter 8 provides an introduction to the subsequent demographic chapters and elucidates the significance of humans in the economy. As both consumers and producers, people play a crucial role in shaping the economic opportunities and directions of economic growth. Chapter 9 presents an analysis of population changes in relation to changes in the economic potential of the world's smallest economies from 1970 to 2019. The countries exhibiting either accelerated or decelerated population growth in comparison to their economic growth were identified. This, in turn, reflected the economic development or underdevelopment of these economies, and thus determined their overall wealth and prosperity. Chapter 10 presents an overview of the distribution of the population residing in the world's smallest economies. From the perspective of the group, the proportion of the population living in the world's smallest economies, characterised by verying level of economic potential, including low, lower-middle, upper-middle, and high was determined. Furthermore, the urbanisation index was employed. Chapter 11 examines the population density of the world's smallest economies, which is influenced mainly by geographic, economic, and historical considerations. In Chap. 12, the fundamental factors affecting demographic potential are discussed, namely natural increase and migration. The natural increase, which is closely related to the level of economic development is shown in relation to the demographic phases in which the world's smallest economies currently find themselves. Population change is also influenced by migration, which is discussed in the second part of this chapter. The low level of economic development observed in the majority of the world's smallest economies results in a lack of employment opportunities. As a result, residents are forced to seek employment in more economically prosperous nations, which has led to a considerable rate of emigration. The economic development of the world's smallest economies is influenced not only by the dynamics of population growth but also by the demographic structure, as discussed in Chap. 13. In particular, the age structure is of great consequence, as it determines the labour pool and the demand for educational and social services. A comprehensive analysis was therefore conducted of the pre-working age, working age, and post-working age populations of the world's smallest economies. Additionally, indicators such as life expectancy, fertility (the average number of children born per woman of childbearing age), and infant mortality were examined in order to assess the impact of demographic factors on the economic development of the world's smallest economies. Chapters 14 through 17 presents an analysis of the cultural conditions that prevail in the world's smallest economies. The influence of culture on economic growth and development is substantial, alongside traditional factors, such as land, raw materials, labour, and capital. Chapter 14 provides a general definition of *culture*. Moreover, a typology of the 93 countries analysed was created based on religious, linguistic, and ethnic similarities. The countries were grouped into eight subgroups (African, Latin American, Islamic, Pacific, Slavic-Orthodox, Western (European), Buddhist, and Hindu). Chapter 15 provides an analysis of the dominant religions in the world's smallest economies, examining their impact on ethical and moral attitudes, which in turn affect not only populations but also economies and their long-term development. Chapter 16 introduces the second element of culture: languages, as communication in a common language facilitates economic ties with the world. Chapter 17 provides an overview of the eight primary cultures that are dominat in the world's smallest economies. It focuses on identifying the cultural characteristics that foster economic development and accelerate economic growth, as well as those that impede and hinder economic development in the analysed countries. The book concludes with a summary of the overarching insights into the influence of environmental, demographic, and cultural factors on the economic growth and development of the world's smallest economies.

The content presented in this book is the result of extensive research, supported by a range of sources, including specialised reports, statistical data used in many studies, national and international, specialised literature, media reports, and personal observations made during travels to most of the world's smallest economies. This publication has been written with the intention of providing valuable resource for researchers, students, policymakers, economists, and practitioners interested in this group of economies, which represents almost half of the countries in the world. It is crucial to acknowledge that the geographic, demographic, and cultural conditions represent merely a subset of the factors influencing the economic growth and development of the world's smallest economies. In addition to these, there are numerous other factors, such as historical, systemic, economic, political, and international, which, due to the extensive scope of the material, are not included in this publication.

CHAPTER 1

Specification of the World's Smallest Economies

In 2019, there were 193 countries in the world that were full members of the United Nations. These countries varied significantly in size, measured by the territorial area (ranging from 2 km^2 to 18 million km^2) and population (from 11,000 to 1.4 billion). Their economic potential, expressed in terms of gross domestic product (GDP) at constant prices, also varied widely (from US$ 45 million to more than US$ 20 trillion) due to numerous factors, with geographic, demographic, and cultural conditions being the most significant. In alignment with this perspective, it can be assumed that the impact of these factors was greatest in the world's largest economies, which form the core of the global economy. This leads to the question regarding the world's smallest economies, which represent the periphery of global economy and as a group, generated only 1% of the global GDP. Was the influence of geography, demography, and culture conditions on their economies the weakest? The answer to this question is important because the group includes as many as 93 countries, nearly half of the world's nations. In 2019, their individual economic potential ranged from US$ 45 million to US$ 29 billion (Table 1.1), and collectively, they produced a GDP of US$ 877.3 billion.

Accordingly, their economic potential—defined as the capacity of their economies[1] expressed in terms of gross domestic product (GDP)—was

[1] It can also be defined as the ability of an economy to produce goods and services in one year.

A. A. Teperek, *Economic Development in the World's Smallest Economies*, https://doi.org/10.1007/978-3-031-63810-7_1

Table 1.1 GDP of the world's smallest economies in 2019 (constant 2010, US$)

No	*The world's smallest economies*	*GDP*	*No*	*The world's smallest economies*	*GDP*
		USD			*USD*
1	Tuvalu	45,924,329	48	Malawi	9,754,076,228
2	Nauru	103,452,832	49	Moldova	9,887,013,490
3	Marshall Islands	185,601,020	50	Tajikistan	10,450,075,054
4	Kiribati	210,571,183	51	Bahamas	11,259,359,316
5	Palau	217,497,827	52	Rwanda	11,380,725,067
6	Saint Thomas and Príncipe	277,211,854	53	Nicaragua	11,541,046,299
7	Micronesia	307,352,260	54	Congo	11,654,686,638
8	Tonga	455,079,252	55	Northern Macedonia	11,719,729,961
9	Dominica	496,699,507	56	Guinea	11,760,762,589
10	Saint Vincent and the Grenadines	758,962,832	57	Equatorial Guinea	12,526,213,821
11	Samoa	762,625,023	58	Chad	12,976,290,262
12	Vanuatu	865,850,907	59	Niger	13,127,408,385
13	Saint Kitts and Nevis	913,748,421	60	Laos	13,195,413,135
14	Grenada	1,032,710,909	61	Madagascar	13,495,494,374
15	Solomon Islands	1,171,806,613	62	Mauritius	13,786,807,917
16	Comoros	1,190,720,115	63	Armenia	13,996,188,672
17	Guinea-Bissau	1,220,795,318	64	Brunei	14,006,979,905
18	East Timor	1,264,348,739	65	Haiti	14,022,671,611
19	Somalia	1,432,368,330	66	Mongolia	14,037,996,022
20	Seychelles	1,469,133,919	67	Jamaica	14,349,236,596
21	Antigua and Barbuda	1,525,166,900	68	Namibia	14,383,460,524
22	Belize	1,619,911,044	69	South Sudan	14,405,738,581
23	San Marino	1,708,644,214	70	Malta	14,564,729,002
24	Saint Lucia	1,709,223,245	71	Benin	14,867,185,273
25	Central African Republic	1,822,841,757	72	Albania	14,872,299,622
26	The Gambia	1,913,886,427	73	North Korea	15,102,180,391
27	Eritrea	1,918,515,447	74	Mali	15,562,204,140
28	Cape Verde	2,148,955,357	75	Burkina Faso	16,708,316,591
29	Burundi	2,399,222,285	76	Zimbabwe	17,327,035,948
30	Bhutan	2,489,357,935	77	Mozambique	17,875,790,909
31	Liberia	2,548,948,907	78	Yemen	18,415,400,223
32	Lesotho	2,874,585,679	79	Georgia	18,521,919,919
33	Andorra	3,539,838,261	80	Iceland	18,546,969,950

(*continued*)

Table 1.1 (continued)

No	*The world's smallest economies*	*GDP*	*No*	*The world's smallest economies*	*GDP*
		USD			*USD*
34	Sierra Leone	3,816,410,758	81	Botswana	18,643,744,000
35	Fiji	4,217,157,352	82	Gabon	19,938,879,843
36	Maldives	4,500,657,090	83	Bosnia and Herzegovina	20,808,476,283
37	Barbados	4,621,053,250	84	Cambodia	20,920,953,618
38	Suriname	4,678,196,480	85	Trinidad and Tobago	21,071,140,166
39	Djibouti	4,774,548,828	86	Afghanistan	21,808,863,988
40	Guyana	4,780,623,910	87	Honduras	21,843,374,259
41	Montenegro	5,343,969,842	88	Papua New Guinea	21,852,485,469
42	Eswatini	5,531,910,971	89	El Salvador	23,054,399,018
43	Togo	5,625,948,588	90	Nepal	24,575,559,443
44	Liechtenstein	6,755,911,742	91	Senegal	25,821,124,786
45	Kyrgyzstan	7,208,211,269	92	Estonia	27,667,385,533
46	Mauritania	7,947,658,539	93	Cyprus	28,678,431,658
47	Monaco	8,152,851,306			
The world's smallest economies in total					877,322,893,050

Source: Own compilation based on The World Bank

used as the criterion for selecting this group of countries. Although, GDP is sometimes criticized for not fully capturing the growth of national wealth and social welfare[2] (Maczynska, 2018; Sedlacek & Orrell, 2012), it remains the most popular and widely used economic indicator that measures economic potential, and thus was employed to distinguish the group of countries under examination (Coyle, 2015; Stieglitz et al., 2019).

Although the 93 smallest economies in the world (Table 1.1) generated only one-hundredth of global GDP—slightly less than the Netherlands—they were home to more than 32 times as many people, or 561.8 million, accounting for 7.3% of the world's population in 2019. The world's smallest economies collectively cover a land area of 17.5 million square kilometers, equivalent to the size of South America, representing 12.3% of the total area of all countries. Their maritime Exclusive Economic Zone span 30.7 million square kilometers, accounting for 22.7% of the global.

[2] GDP does not take into account the so-called soft values, such as trust or security, which is why it is sometimes referred to as a hard quantitative measure.

The world's individual smallest economies differ in almost every respect:

- Economic potential—from US$ 45.9 million GDP (Tuvalu) to US$ 28.6 billion GDP (Cyprus)
- Level of economic development—from US$ 93 per capita (Somalia) to US$ 209,241 per capita (Monaco)
- Level of socio-economic development, expressed in HDI (Human Development Index)—from 0.384 (Somalia) to 0.997 (Cyprus)
- Population—from 11,000 (Tuvalu) to nearly 38 million (Afghanistan)
- Land area—from 2 km^2 (Monaco) to 1.5 million km^2 (Mongolia)
- Climate—from circumpolar climate (Iceland) to equatorial (e.g., Congo, Equatorial Guinea, Gabon, Kiribati, Maldives, Saint Thomas and Principe, Somalia)
- Sea access—from 26 landlocked countries (e.g., Chad, Laos, Liechtenstein, Nepal), 32 continental countries with sea access (e.g., Belize, Bosnia and Herzegovina, El Salvador, Togo, Yemen) to 35 island countries (e.g., Cyprus, Dominica, East Timor, Samoa)
- Culture—from African (e.g., Benin, Botswana, Madagascar, Sierra Leone), Latin American (e.g., Dominica, Honduras, Saint Lucia), Islamic (i.e., Brunei, Djibouti, The Gambia, Kyrgyzstan Somalia), Pacific (e.g., Fiji, Nauru, Tonga), Slavic-Orthodox (e.g., Albania, Armenia, Georgia, North Macedonia), and Western European culture (e.g., Andorra, Malta, Monaco, San Marino), to Buddhist (e.g., Bhutan, Cambodia, Lao) and Hindu (i.e., Nepal) culture
- Religion—from Christian to Islamic, Hindu, Buddhist and tribal religions as the main faiths
- Statehood length—from countries that are long-estalished (San Marino) to those that are more recently formed (South Sudan, East Timor)
- Political system and regime—from monarchies (e.g., Bhutan, Brunei, Samoa) to republics (e.g., Kyrgyzstan, Micronesia) and from democratic (e.g., Estonia, Iceland, Malta) through democratic-authoritarian (e.g., Burkina Faso, The Gambia) to authoritarian (e.g., Eritrea, North Korea)

Despite the rich diversity and numerous attractions that the world's smallest economies have to offer, they have not been the subject of much interest from scholars, politicians and world leaders, or the media. They have received little attention in economic literature. They have also been overlooked by the global community. The small size of these economies was the reason why the world did not take much interest in them. On occasion, they attract attention due to their sporting achievements (e.g., Jamaica, Senegal), involvement in procedural violations and money laundering (e.g., Andorra, Cyprus, Monaco), natural disasters (e.g., Haiti, Nepal, Vanuatu), or conflicts that evoke public indignation (e.g., Eritrea, Yemen, Somalia, Zimbabwe). Additionally, they are noticed when their actions threaten the interests of global or regional powers (e.g., Afghanistan, Bosnia, and Herzegovina, North Korea). However, once these episodic events pass, the word's interest in the world's smallest economies fades. Meanwhile, they deserve attention, if only for demographic potential they possess accounting for 7.3% of the world's population, with more than one-third being yound and underutilized. The total land area of the world's smallest economies accounts for 12.3% of the global and is home to valuable mineral resources. Additionally, their maritime Exclusive Economic Zone, which covers 22% of the world's total, contains abundant marine resources. Most of the world's smallest economies enjoy a warm equatorial or subequatorial climate and favorable coastal geographic location with 35 countries situated on islands and 32 countries on continents. Many of them boast unique heritage influenced by African, Muslim, Western, Orthodox-Slavic, Buddhist, and Hindu traditions. All these natural, cultural, and demographic conditions, formed and modified over centuries, have shaped the economies of countries studied and contributed to their economic growth and development. To determine the extent of these influences, a detailed analysis of the world's smallest economies, hereafter referred to as the WSE, was conducted in terms of their natural, demographic, and cultural conditions.

Bibliography

Coyle, D. (2015). GDP: A Brief But Affectionate History Exciting History. *Princeton University Press*, 3–7.

Maczynska, E (2018). Refleksje na Kanvie Ksiazki Diane Coyle pt. PKB: Krotka Lecz Emocjoonujaca Historia. Builetyn PTE, No. 3(86), 65.

Sedlacek, T., & Orrell, D. (2012). *Zmierzch Homo Economicus, Rozmowa z R. Chlupatym*. Studio Emka.

Stieglitz, J. E., Fitoussi, J. P., & Durand, M. (2019). *Beyond GDP: Measuring What Counts for Economic and Social Performance*. OECD.

CHAPTER 2

The World's Smallest Economies in the Background of the World

2.1 Location

The WSE are scattered across the globe, occupying four hemispheres (Fig. 2.1) and spanning from 20° south latitude (Tonga) to 65° north latitude (Iceland), and from 175° west longitude (Tonga) to 178° east longitude (Tuvalu). The largest number of countries (69) are located in the northern hemisphere, while the southern hemisphere contains the remaining countries (24). The equator passes through the land area of five countries (Congo, Gabon, Kiribati, Maldives, Somalia). Similarly, the meridian that divides the Earth into eastern and western hemispheres (Burkina Faso, Fiji, Kiribati, Mali). In total, there are 62 of the WSE located on the eastern side of the Earth and 31 on the western side (Fig. 2.1).

From the perspective of the four hemispheres that divide the globe, almost half of the WSE (40 countries) are located in the northern and the eastern hemispheres (between the equator and 59°E). The latitude at which the analyzed countries are located is important, because it is related to the altitude of the sun's peak, and at the same time, to the different angles of the sun's rays, which consequently affects the climate of the WSE (including heating, day length, and occurrence of seasons) and their other natural conditions.

There is only one of the WSE and also the only country in the world that is located in all four hemispheres, and that is Kiribati. Because of its location, it is the first country in the world to welcome the New Year (14 hours earlier than London), and this is especially true of its

A. A. Teperek, *Economic Development in the World's Smallest Economies*, https://doi.org/10.1007/978-3-031-63810-7_2

Northern Hemisphere	
Western Latitude	**Eastern Longitude**
Iceland (65° 00' N, 18° 00' W)	Estonia (59° 00' N, 26° 00' E)
Bahamas (24° 15' N, 76° 00' W)	Liechtenstein (47° 16' N, 9° 32' E)
Mauritania (20° 00' N, 12° 00' W)	Moldova (47° 00' N, 29° 00' E)
Haiti (19° 00' N, 72° 25' W)	Mongolia (46° 00' N, 105° 00' E)
Jamaica (18° 15' N, 77° 30' W)	Bosnia and Herzegovina (44° 00' N, 18° 00' E)
Saint Kitts and Nevis (17° 20' N, 62° 45' W)	San Marino (43° 46' N, 12° 25' E)
Belize (17° 15' N, 88° 45' W)	Monaco (43° 44' N, 7° 24' E)
Antigua and Barbuda (17° 03' N, 61° 48' W)	Andorra (42° 30' N, 1° 30' E)
Mali (17° 00' N, 4° 00' W)	Montenegro (42° 30' N, 19° 18' E)
Cape Verde (16° 00' N, 24° 00' W)	Georgia (42° 00' N, 43° 30' E)
Dominica (15° 25' N, 61° 20' W)	North Macedonia (41° 50' N, 22° 00' E)
Honduras (15° 00' N, 86° 30' W)	Kyrgyzstan (41° 00' N, 75° 00' E)
Senegal (14° 00' N, 14° 00' W)	Albania (41° 00' N, 20° 00' E)
Saint Lucia (13° 53' N, 60° 58' W)	North Korea (40° 00' N, 127° 00' E)
El Salvador (13° 50' N, 88° 55' W)	Armenia (40° 00' N, 45° 00' E)
Gambia (13° 28' N, 16° 34' W)	Tajikistan (39° 00' N, 71° 00' E)
Saint Vincent and the Grenadines (13° 15' N, 61° 12' W)	Malta (35° 50' N, 14° 35' E)
Barbados (13° 10' N, 59° 32' W)	Cyprus (35° 00' N, 33° 00' E)
Nicaragua (13° 00' N, 85° 00' W)	Afghanistan (33 00 N, 65 00 E)
Grenada (12° 07' N, 61° 40' W)	Nepal (28° 00' N, 84° 00' E)
Burkina Faso (13° 00 N, 2° 00 W)	Bhutan (27° 30' N, 90° 30' E)
Guinea-Bissau (12° 00' N, 15° 00' W)	Laos (18° 00' N, 105° 00' E)
Trinidad and Tobago (11° 00' N, 61° 00' W)	Niger (16° 00' N, 8° 00' E)
Guinea (11° 00' N, 10° 00' W)	Yemen (15° 00' N, 48° 00' E)
Sierra Leone (8° 30' N, 11° 30' W)	Chad (15° 00' N, 19° 00' E)
Liberia (6° 30' N, 9° 30' W)	Eritrea (15° 00' N, 39° 00' E)
Guyana (5° 00' N, 59° 00' W)	Cambodia (13° 00' N, 105° 00' E)
Suriname (4° 00' N, 56° 00' W)	Djibouti (11° 30' N, 43° 00' E)
	Somalia (10° 00' N, 49° 00' E
	Benin (9° 30' N, 2° 15' E)
	Marshall Islands (9° 00' N, 168° 00 E)
	South Sudan (8° 00' N, 30° 00° E)
	Togo (8° 00' N, 1° 10' E)
	Palau (7° 30' N, 134° 30' E)
	Central African Republic (7° 00' N, 21° 00' E)
	Micronesia (6° 55' N, 158° 15' E)
	Brunei (4° 30' N, 114° 40' E)
	Maldives (3° 15' N, 73° 00' E)
	Equatorial Guinea (2° 00' N, 10° 00' E)
	Kiribati (1° 25' N, 173° 00' E)
	Saint Thomas and Principe (1° 00' N, 7° 00' E)
Southern Hemisphere	
Western Latitude	**Eastern Longitude**
Samoa (13° 35' S, 172° 20' W)	Nauru (0° 32' S, 166° 55' E)
Tonga (20° 00' S, 175° 00' W)	Gabon (1° 00' S, 11° 45' E)
	Congo (1° 00' S, 15° 00' E)
	Rwanda (2° 00' S, 30° 00' E)
	Burundi (3° 30' S, 30° 00' E)
	Seychelles (4° 35' S, 55° 40' E)
	Papua New Guinea (6° 00' S, 147° 00' E)
	Solomon Islands (8° 00' S, 159° 00' E)
	Tuvalu (8° 00' S, 178° 00' E)
	East Timor (8° 50' S, 125° 55' E)
	Comoros (12° 10' S, 44° 15' E)
	Malawi (13° 30' S, 34° 00' E)
	Vanuatu (16° 00' S, 167° 00' E)
	Fiji (18° 00' S, 175° 00' E)
	Mozambique (18° 15' S, 35° 00' E)
	Zimbabwe (20° 00' S, 30° 00' E)
	Madagascar (20° 00' S, 47° 00' E)
	Mauritius (20° 17' S, 57° 33' E)
	Namibia (22° 00' S, 17° 00' E)
	Botswana (22° 00' S, 24° 00' E)
	Eswatini (26° 30' S, 31° 30' E)
	Lesotho (29° 30' S, 28° 30' E)

Fig. 2.1 WSE by geographic coordinates and hemispheres. (Source: Own compilation based on CIA, The World Factbook)

easternmost region, that is, the Line Islands (the Christmas Islands). Consisting of 11 coral islands, the Line Islands are in the outermost time zone. Kiribati also has two more time zones: Gilbert Island time zone UTC +12:00, Phoenix Island time zone UTC +13:00, Line Island time zone UTC +14:00 (Fig. 2.1). The existence of three time zones in this country, very small in terms of total area (811 km^2), is related to the spatial dispersion of the 33 islands of Kiribati. They occupy an oceanic space of more than 3.5 million km^2, slightly less than the area of the entire European Union (4.2 km^2).

In addition to Kiribati, which leads in the number of time zones, Micronesia has two time zones (Chuuk Time Zone UTC +10:00 and Pohnpei Standard Time Zone UTC +11:00) and Mongolia (Hovd Standard Time Zone UTC +7:00 and Choibalsan Time Zone UTC +8:00). The state of Micronesia includes more than 600 islands that cover an area of 702 km^2, slightly smaller than Singapore. On the other hand, the oceanic space in which these islands are scattered reaches more than 7.4 million km^2, slightly less than the area of Australia (7.7 million km^2). Spatial dispersion dictates that Micronesia has two time zones. In the case of Mongolia, the two time zones are associated with a vast land area of more than 1.5 million km^2, making Mongolia the largest WSE.

The remaining 90 WSE have a single time zone (Table 2.1). The largest number of countries (26) are in +2:00 UTC time zone: Central European (i.e., Albania, Andorra, Bosnia and Herzegovina, Cyprus, Estonia, Iceland, Liechtenstein, Malta, Moldova, Monaco, Montenegro, North Macedonia, San Marino), Central African (i.e., Botswana, Burundi, Comoros, Equatorial Guinea, Gabon, Malawi, Mozambique, Namibia, Rwanda, South Sudan, Zimbabwe), and Southern African (e.g., Eswatini, Lesotho).

The assignment of the analyzed countries to different time zones is closely related to their location on continents. The WSE located in North and South America are in the time zone from UTC -06:00 to UTC -03:00; in Africa—from UTC 0:00 to UTC +4; in Europe—from UTC +2 to UTC +4; in Asia—from UTC +3:00 to UTC +9:00 and in Oceania—from UTC +9:00 to UTC +14:00 (Table 2.1).

From the point of view of location on the continents, the largest number, more than a third of the group (36 countries), are located in Africa (Table 2.2). They account for 68% of all countries located on the African continent (53 countries). In contrast, the fewest WSE are located in South America (2 countries). They represent only 15% of all South American

Table 2.1 WSE time zones

Time zone		*The world's smallest economies*
UTC -6:00	Central Standard Time	Belize, El Salvador, Honduras, Nicaragua
UTC -5:00	Eastern Standard Time	Jamaica, Haiti
UTC -4:00	Eastern Standard Time	Bahamas
	Atlantic Standard Time	Antigua and Barbuda, Barbados, Dominica, Grenada, Saint Kitts and Nevis, Saint Lucia, Saint Vincent and the Grenadines, Trinidad and Tobago
	Guyana Time	Guyana
UTC -3:00	Suriname Time	Suriname
UTC 0:00	Greenwich Mean Time	Burkina Faso, The Gambia, Guinea, Guinea-Bissau, Liberia, Mali, Mauritania, Saint Thomas and Principe, Senegal, Sierra Leone, Togo
UTC +1:00	Cape Verde Time	Cape Verde
	West Africa Standard Time	Benin, Central African Republic, Chad, Congo, Niger
UTC +2:00	Central African Time	Botswana, Burundi, Comoros, Equatorial Guinea, Gabon, Malawi, Mozambique, Namibia, Rwanda, South Sudan, Zimbabwe
	Central European Time	Albania, Andorra, Bosnia and Herzegovina, Cyprus, Estonia, Iceland, Montenegro, Liechtenstein, Malta, Moldova, Monaco, North Macedonia, San Marino
	South African Standard Time	Eswatini, Lesotho
UTC +3:00	Arabian Standard Time	Yemen
	East African Time	Djibouti, Eritrea, Madagascar, Somalia
UTC +4:00	Armenia Time	Armenia
	Georgia Time	Georgia
	Mauritius Time	Mauritius
	Seychelles Time	Seychelles
UTC +4:30	Afghanistan Time	Afghanistan
UTC +5:00	Tajikistan Time	Tajikistan
	Maldives Time	Maldives
UTC +5:45	Nepal Time	Nepal

(*continued*)

Table 2.1 (continued)

Time zone		*The world's smallest economies*
UTC +6:00	Kyrgyzstan Time	Kyrgyzstan
	Bhutan Time	Bhutan
UTC +7:00	Indochina Time	Cambodia, Laos
	Hovd Standard Time	Mongolia
UTC +8:00	Choibalsan Time	Mongolia
	Brunei Darussalm Time	Brunei
UTC +9:00	Korean Standard Time	North Korea
	Palau Time	Palau
	Eastern Indonesia Time	Papua New Guinea
	East Timor Time	East Timor
UTC +10:00	Chuuk Time	Micronesia
UTC +11:00	Pohnpei Standard Time	Micronesia
	Vanuatu Standard Time	Vanuatu
	Solomon Islands Time	Solomon Islands
UTC +12:00	Fiji Time	Fiji
	Marshall Islands Time	Marshall Islands
	Tuvalu Time	Tuvalu
	Nauru Time	Nauru
	Gilbert Island Time	Kiribati
UTC +13:00	Tonga Standard Time	Tonga
	Phoenix Island Time	Kiribati
UTC +14:00	West Samoa Time	Samoa
	Line Islands Time	Kiribati

Source: Own compilation based on CIA The World Factbook

countries (2 out of a total 13 countries). The remaining continents, that is, North America (including Central America), Europe, Asia, and Australia and Oceania, have between 12 and 15 WSE (Table 2.2).

The WSE in Africa (36 out of 93 countries) are located on both sides of the equator: in the northern hemisphere (21 countries) and in the southern hemisphere (15 countries). They are all in Sub-Saharan Africa, with the exception of Djibouti, which is classified in the North and Middle East regions. The remaining 35 countries are located in West, Central, East, and Southern Africa (Table 2.3). Of these, 13 are landlocked countries, 17 are continental countries with access to the sea and 6 are island countries located in the oceans bordering the continent: the Atlantic Ocean (e.g., Cape Verde and Saint Thomas and Príncipe) and the Indian Ocean (e.g., Comoros, Madagascar, Mauritius, and Seychelles).

Table 2.2 WSE by continents

Continent	*The world's smallest economies*	*Countries*		*WSE share of global countries*
		WSE	*World*	
		Quantity		*%*
Africa	Benin, Botswana, Burkina Faso, Burundi, Cape Verde, Central African Republic, Chad, Comoros, Congo, Djibouti, Equatorial Guinea, Eritrea, Eswatini, Gabon, The Gambia, Guinea, Guinea-Bissau, Lesotho, Liberia, Madagascar, Malawi, Mali, Mauritania, Mauritius, Mozambique, Namibia, Niger, Rwanda, Saint Thomas and Principe, Senegal, Seychelles, Sierra Leone, Somalia, South Sudan, Togo, Zimbabwe	36	53	68
North America	Antigua and Barbuda, Bahamas, Barbados, Belize, Dominica, El Salvador, Grenada, Haiti, Honduras, Jamaica, Nicaragua, Saint Kitts and Nevis, Saint Lucia, Saint Vincent and the Grenadines, Trinidad and Tobago	15	22	68
Europe	Albania, Armenia, Andorra, Bosnia and Herzegovina, Montenegro, Estonia, Georgia, Iceland, Liechtenstein, Malta, Moldova, Monaco, North Macedonia, San Marino	14	43	33
Asia	Afghanistan, Bhutan, Brunei, Cyprus, Cambodia, East Timor, Kyrgyzstan, Laos, Maldives, Mongolia, Nepal, North Korea, Tajikistan, Yemen	14	48	29
Australia and Oceania	Fiji, Kiribati, Marshall Islands, Micronesia, Nauru, Palau, Papua New Guinea, Samoa, Solomon Islands, Tonga, Tuvalu, Vanuatu	12	14	86
South America	Guyana, Suriname	2	13	15
WSE group in total:		93	193	48

Source: Own compilation

Table 2.3 Sub-Saharan WSE by regions

Sub-Saharan Africa's regions			
Western	*Central*	*Eastern*	*South*
Benin, Burkina Faso, Cape Verde, The Gambia, Guinea, Guinea-Bissau, Liberia, Mali, Mauritania, Niger, Senegal, Sierra Leone, Togo	Central African Republic, Chad, Congo, Gabon, Equatorial Guinea, Saint Thomas and Príncipe	Burundi, Eritrea, Comoros, Madagascar, Malawi, Mauritius, Mozambique, Rwanda, Seychelles, Somalia, South Sudan, Zimbabwe	Botswana, Eswatini, Lesotho, Namibia
13 countries	6 countries	12 countries	4 countries

Source: Own compilation

The land areas of the WSE located in North America (15 out of 93 countries) extend between 10°N and 26°N latitude and between 62°W and 95°W longitude, bordering the United States, Mexico, and South America. They are bordered by the Pacific Ocean to the west and by the Atlantic Ocean to the east. They include four mainland countries: Belize, El Salvador, Honduras, and Nicaragua, which are located on the Yucatan Peninsula, along the Central American Rift, which served as a bridge for Indigenous peoples to migrate from North America to South America in the past [1] The remaining WSE are island nations (11 countries) scattered throughout the Caribbean Sea, which connects to the Atlantic Ocean. The WSE of Guyana and Suriname are also on the Atlantic Ocean, but are part of South America.

The WSE located in Europe (14 out of 93 countries) with the exception of Iceland, which is near the northern Arctic Circle, and Estonia on the eastern coast of the North Sea are located in the southern part of the European continent, below the 47°N parallel. The land areas of five of them (Albania, Bosnia and Herzegovina, Malta, Monaco, Montenegro) lie on the Mediterranean coast or on seas directly connected to it. They are surrounded by landlocked microstates: Andorra, in the heart of the eastern Pyrenees; Liechtenstein—in the Alps, on the eastern side of the upper Rhine; the enclave of San Marino—in the Apennines, in the northern part

[1] As a result of colonization and the imposition of Spanish culture, the entire region came to be known as Latin America. The continent is called Central America, while the neighboring island nations to the east are called the West Indies.

of Italy, as well as states with a socialist past: Armenia, Georgia, Moldova, and North Macedonia.

Many of the WSE are located in Asia similar to Europe (14 out of 93 countries). Their territories span the northern hemisphere, with the exception of East Timor, which is 600 km from Australia's northern borders. The Maldives occupy the equatorial portion of the Indian Ocean. Also on the equator, heading west in the South China Sea and joining the Pacific Ocean, is Brunei, whose territory is part of the world's third largest island Borneo. Another island nation is Cyprus, surrounded by the waters of the Mediterranean Sea. The remaining countries occupy a continental area and only some of them have access to the sea (e.g., Cambodia, North Korea, and Yemen). Yemen's territory is on the Arabian Peninsula on the Red Sea; Cambodia's is on the Indochinese Peninsula on the South China Sea; and North Korea's is on the Korean Peninsula on the Yellow Sea and the Sea of Japan. The remaining 7 WSE are landlocked. Most of them, with the exception of Mongolia and Laos, have direct borders with each other, such as Kyrgyzstan with Tajikistan, Tajikistan with Afghanistan, and Bhutan with Nepal.

All the WSE in Oceania (12 countries) are island states (Fig. 2.2), scattered across the Pacific Ocean, in the eastern hemisphere (between the meridians 134°E and 173°E). Their territories extend into both the northern and southern hemispheres (between the parallels of 9°N and 20°S), from the northernmost Marshall Islands to Tonga, almost 3500 km to the south. With the exception of Papua New Guinea, which shares an island with Indonesia, the rest of the other WSE are occupied by single islands

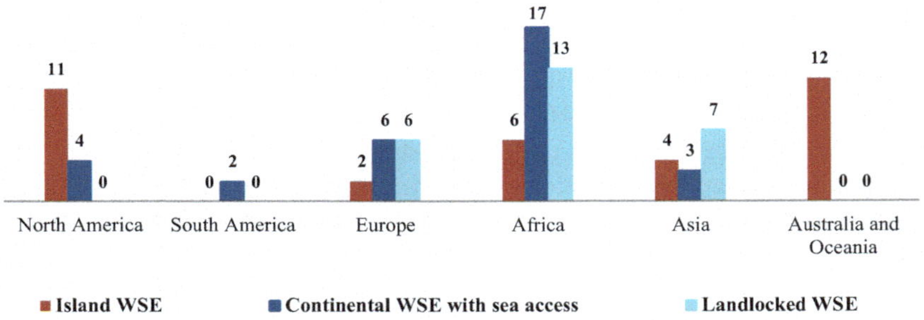

Fig. 2.2 WSE by sea access (number of countries). (Source: Own compilation)

(e.g., Nauru) or multiple islands (e.g., Tuvalu with 9 islands, Vanuatu with 13 islands, Kiribati with 33 islands, and Palau with over 320 islands). Most island nations are separated by hundreds or even thousands of kilometers. For example, the distance between Fiji and Tuvalu is more than 1000 km, Fiji and Vanuatu 1200 km, Micronesia and the Marshall Islands is more than 1400 km, Micronesia and Palau is more than 1700 km, Samoa and Tuvalu is 1550 km, Tonga and Samoa is 900 km.

Of the 93 WSE, 26 are landlocked countries (e.g., Afghanistan, Andorra, Chad, Laos, Liechtenstein, and Mongolia), located on only three continents: Africa, Asia, and Europe (Fig. 2.2). Another 32 countries are located on continents, but have access to the sea (e.g., Cambodia, Estonia, Georgia, Honduras, Mozambique, Namibia, North Korea, Suriname, and Yemen). Most are located in Africa on the Atlantic and Indian Oceans, and in Europe on inland seas. The remaining 35 countries are island islands, occupying a single island (e.g., Cyprus, Dominica, Iceland, Madagascar, Mauritius, Nauru) or many islands (e.g., Antigua and Barbuda, Kiribati, Maldives, Malta, Papua New Guinea, Tonga). They are mainly located in the Pacific Ocean in Oceania and in the Caribbean Sea in Central America (Fig. 2.2). It is worth noting that the island WSE account for as much as three-fourths of all island countries in the world (35 out of 47 countries). A more global conclusion is that the vast majority of the world's island states have the smallest GDP. This is probably due to geographical and spatial constraints.

2.2 Land Area

Land area is often defined as *a limited geographical space that determines its existence*. Some describe the land area as *the basic condition of its existence* (Otok, 2012), since *it constitutes the space for existence and the possibility of development for the society that occupies it* (Bachvarow & Suliborski, 2003). The territory, together with the population and public authority, is the basic constitutive component of the state, which is subject to the sovereign authority of the state. In colloquial language, *"territory"* is sometimes used interchangeably with the term *land*, although, in fact, it is one of the three components of *"territory"*, along with the coastal sea and the airspace over the land and sea parts of the *"territory"*—an interpretation from political science (Rykiel, 2006). The territory of a state includes land, together with inland and underground waters, defined by boundaries that mark the geographical location of the state.

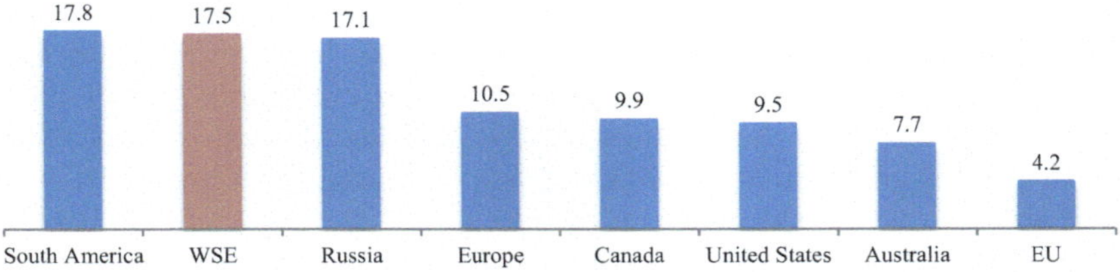

Fig. 2.3 WSE group land area in compared to selected countries and continents (million km^2). (Source: Own compilation based on The World Bank)

The Earth's land area is 148.9 million km^2, which is one-third of the Earth's total surface (excluding the oceans). For comparison, this is less than the area of the Pacific Ocean (155 million km^2). The countries of the world cover a total area of 130 million km^2. Nearly 12.3% of this area is occupied by the WSE group, with a total area of 17.5 million km^2 (Fig. 2.3). This is slightly less than the area of the entire South American continent (17.8 million km^2) and slightly more than the area of the largest country on Earth—Russia (17.1 million km^2).

The WSE group includes countries with very diverse land areas (Fig. 2.4), ranging from 2 km^2 (Monaco) to 1,564,116 km^2 (Mongolia). The difference between the smallest and the largest is enormous. The area of Monaco is 780,000 times smaller than that of Mongolia.

The largest countries in terms of land area of more than 1 million km^2 (five countries), that is, Chad, Mongolia, Niger, Mali, and Mauritania (Fig. 2.4) cover a total of 6386 thousand km^2, which accounts for more than 36.42% of the WSE group territory (Fig. 2.5).

The WSE with an area from 500,000 km^2 to 1,000,000 km^2 (9 countries), that is, Afghanistan, Botswana, Central African Republic, Madagascar, Mozambique, Namibia, Somalia, South Sudan, and Yemen, cover a total of 5,878,000 km^2 (33.52% of the WSE group area). Countries between 100,000 km^2 and 500,000 km^2 (22 countries), that is, Benin, Burkina Faso, Cambodia, Congo, Eritrea, Gabon, Guinea, Guyana, Honduras, Iceland, Kyrgyzstan, Laos, Liberia, Malawi, Nepal, Nicaragua, North Korea, Papua New Guinea, Senegal, Suriname, Tajikistan, and Zimbabwe cover a total of 4,395,000 km^2 (25.05% of the WSE group area). The largest subgroup with countries between 10,000 km^2 and 100,000 km^2 (28 countries), that is, Albania, Armenia, Bahamas, Belize, Bhutan, Bosnia and Herzegovina, Burundi, Djibouti, East Timor, El Salvador, Estonia, Eswatini, Equatorial Guinea, Fiji, The Gambia, Georgia,

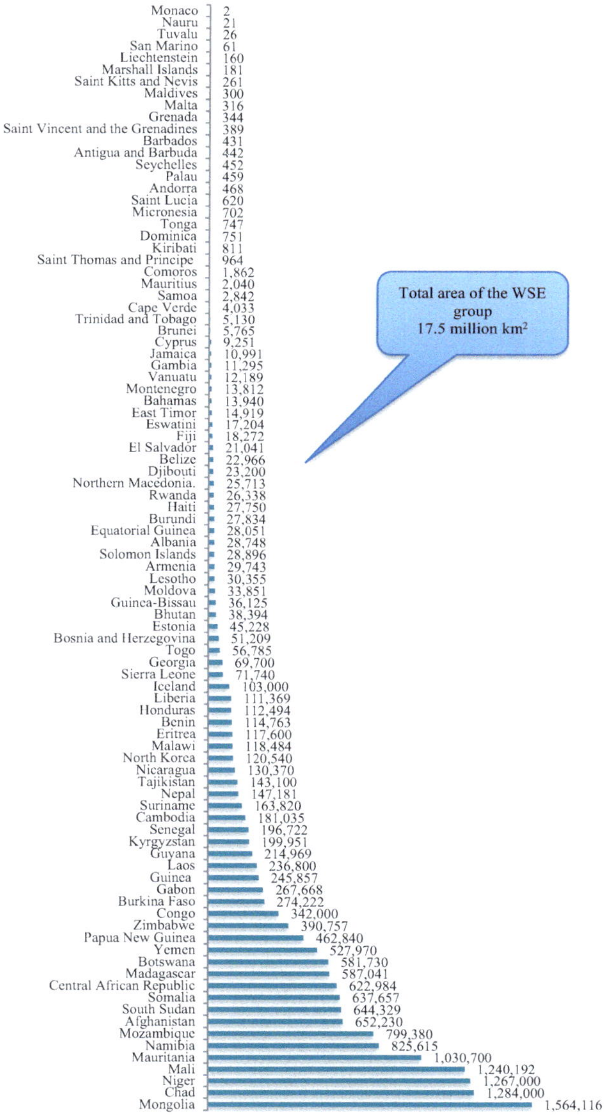

Fig. 2.4 WSE land area (km^2). (Source: Own compilation based on CIA The World Factbook)

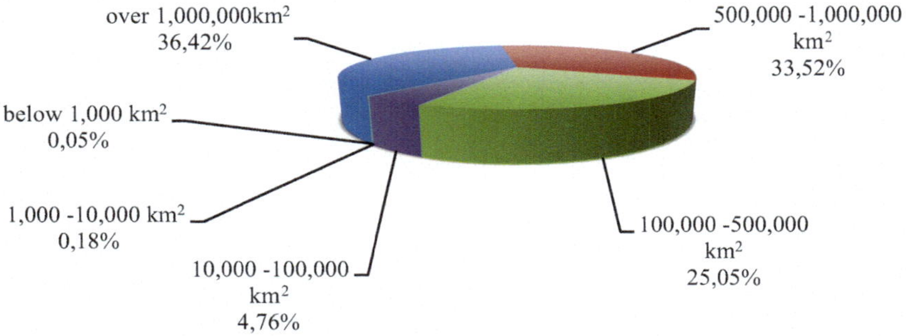

Fig. 2.5 WSE by land area as a share of WSE group (%). (Source: Own compilation based on CIA The World Factbook)

Guinea-Bissau, Haiti, Jamaica, Lesotho, Moldova, Montenegro, North Macedonia, Rwanda, Sierra Leone, Solomon Islands, Togo, and Vanuatu, covers an area of 836,000 km^2 (4.76% of the WSE group area). Countries between 1000 km^2 and 10,000 km^2 (8 countries), that is, Brunei, Cape Verde, Cyprus, Comoros, Mauritius, Samoa, and Trinidad and Tobago, cover 31,000 km^2 (0.18% of the WSE group area), and countries below 1000 km^2 (21 countries), that is, Andorra, Antigua and Barbuda, Barbados, Dominica, Grenada, Kiribati, Liechtenstein, Malta, Maldives, Marshall Islands, Micronesia, Monaco, Nauru, Palau, San Marino, Saint Thomas and Principe, Seychelles, Saint Kitts and Nevis, Saint Lucia, Saint Vincent and the Grenadines, Tonga, and Tuvalu, covering 8900 km^2 (0.05% of the WSE group area).

Analyzing the number of the WSE in each subgroup (Fig. 2.6), it can be seen that there are the fewest countries with an area of more than 1 million km^2 (five countries), and the most of countries with an area between 10,000 km^2 and 100,000 km^2 (28 countries) and from 100,000 km^2 to 500,000 km^2 (22 countries). It is worth noting that the situation is similar worldwide. The most numerous subgroups in the world are countries with areas between 10,000 km^2 and 100,000 km^2 (55 countries) and between 100,000 km^2 and 500,000 km^2 (55 countries).

In contrast, the WSE subgroup with the smallest areas (1000 km^2–10,000 km^2 and less than 1000 km^2) is almost identical to the world's (Fig. 2.6). This leads to the conclusion that almost all of the world's smallest countries in terms of area are also part of the WSE. This would suggest a correlation between country's small territory and its small

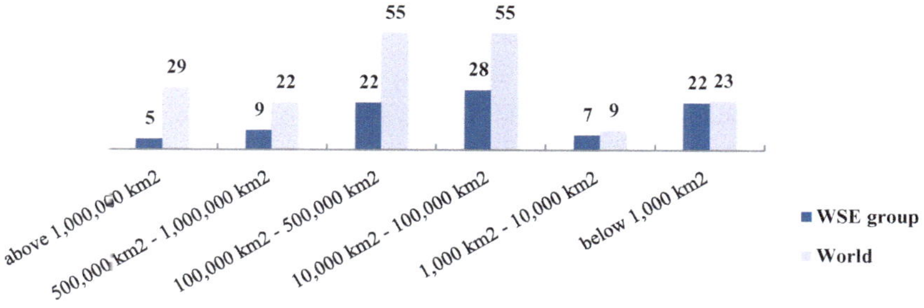

Fig. 2.6 WSE and global nations by land area (number of countries). (Source: Own compilation based on CIA The World Factbook)

economic potential, as well as the likely impact of a small territory on the economy. This is true for almost all countries in the world with less than 10,000 km^2, with the exception of Bahrain, Luxembourg, and Singapore. These countries have exceptionally large economic potential. For example, Singapore's GDP was US$ 335 billion in 2019, only 2.5 times less than that of the WSE group (US$ 877 billion GDP).

The size of a country's land area is also related to its shape. From an economic point of view, most of the WSE have a favorable shape that is conducive to government administration (e.g., Honduras, Suriname, and Yemen). Their compact and consolidated territories make it easier to maintain the intensity of internal links and communication with all parts of the country, as well as to exercise effective state control. On the other hand, countries with extensive territories, such as Benin, The Gambia, and Togo, are difficult to manage. In the event of an external conflict, such countries are more difficult to defend. Transportation costs are higher. The WSE with territories containing branches, such as peninsulas, that extend beyond the main territory, such as Congo, Kyrgyzstan, and Namibia, also have administrative problems. Unfavorable shape is associated with fragmented territories, consisting of scattered parts separated by sea waters, as in the case of the insular Bahamas, Kiribati, Maldives, Palau, Papua New Guinea, Seychelles, and Vanuatu. Fragmentation hinders state governance and control, as well as the interaction of communities living in the extreme parts/islands, often leading to the disappearance of national unity.

The WSE with highly fragmented territories have longer borders (Fig. 2.7) For example, the total length of Estonia's land and

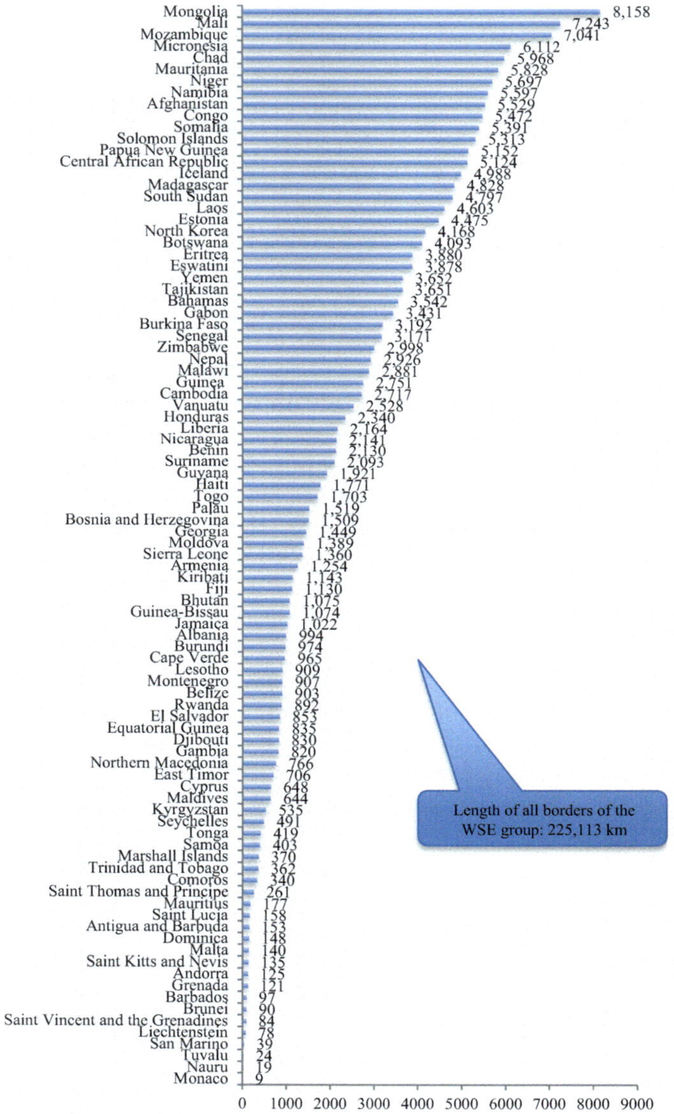

Fig. 2.7 WSE borders in total (km). (Source: Own compilation based on CIA The World Factbook)

maritimeborder is 4451 km, which is only half the length of Mongolia's borders (8082 km), despite the fact that Mongolia's land area is more than 34 times that of Estonia. Such a long total Estonian border is mainly due to the fragmentation of its maritime border. This is because it consists of the maritime continental border and the borders of the islands belonging to it (1520 islands). Estonia's maritime border accounts for more than 85% of its total borders. Another example is Micronesia, one of the smallest WSE in terms of area (702 km^2), but with one of the longest borders in the WSE group (fourth place). Their length (more than 6112 km) is similar to that of Chad. However, Chad is 210 times larger in land area than Micronesia, whose borders are so long because of the number of islands (more than 600) that make up this small country.

In 2019, the total length of the WSE group's borders was 225,113 km (Fig. 2.7), more than four times that of Russia, which has a similar land area (17.5 million km^2). The length of the group's land borders accounted for 67% of all borders (151,616 km). Landlocked countries, such as Mongolia (8082 km) and Mali (7908 km), have the longest borders (Table 2.4). Mongolia borders Russia (3457 km) and China (4630 km), while Mali has as many as seven land neighbors: Senegal (489 km), Côte d'Ivoire (599 km), Niger (838 km), Guinea (1062 km), Burkina Faso (1325 km), Algeria (1359 km), Mauritania (2236 km). The length of land borders and the larger number of neighbors are usually associated with a larger area of the country, as in the cases of Chad (6404 km; 1284 thousand km^2), which borders with six countries, Niger (5920 km; 1267 km^2), which borders with seven countries, South Sudan (6018 km; 644 thousand km^2) and Central African Republic (5920 km; 622 km^2), which border with six countries.

In contrast, the shortest land borders have the smallest landlocked WSE (Table 2.4) with one or two neighboring countries, such as enclave of San Marino (37 km, 61 km^2) surrounded by the Italian territory; Liechtenstein (75 km, 160 km^2) with Austria and Switzerland; Andorra (118 km, 468 km^2) with France and Spain, or Eswatini (546 km, 17,364 km^2) with Mozambique and South Africa as neighbors (Table 2.4).

The land borders of the continental WSE located on the sea or ocean (32 countries) vary in length. Their share in the total length of borders (Table 2.5) ranges from 15% (Estonia) to 90% (Benin, Bosnia and Herzegovina, Congo, The Gambia, Guinea, Togo). The longest land borders are Congo (5540 km), Mauritania (5002 km), Mozambique (4783 km), Namibia (4220 km), and Guinea (4046 km).

Table 2.4 Landlocked WSE, land area and borders

No	*WSE*	*Land area*	*Border length*	*WSE bordering countries and borders length*
		km²	*km*	
1	Mongolia	1,564,116	8082	Russia (3452 km), China (4630 km)
2	Mali	1,240,192	7908	Senegal (489 km), Côte d'Ivoire (599 km), Niger (838 km), Guinea (1062 km), Burkina Faso (1325 km), Algeria (1359 km), Mauritania (2236 km)
3	Chad	1,284,000	6406	Nigeria (85 km), Liberia (1050 km), Cameroon (1116 km), Niger (1196 km), Central African Republic (1556 km), Sudan (1403 km)
4	South Sudan	644,329	6018	Kenya (317 km), Uganda (475 km), Democratic Republic of Congo (714 km), Central African Republic (1055 km), Ethiopia (1299 km), Sudan (2158 km)
5	Afghanistan	652,230	5987	China (91 km), Uzbekistan (144 km), Turkmenistan (807 km), Iran (921 km), Tajikistan (1257 km), Pakistan (2670 km)
6	Central African Republic	622,984	5920	Congo (487 km), Sudan (174 km), South Sudan (1055 km), Cameroon (901 km), Chad (1556 km), Democratic Republic of Congo (1747 km)
7	Niger	1,267,000	5834	Benin (277 km), Libya (342 km), Burkina Faso (622 km), Mali (838 km), Algeria (951 km), Chad (1199 km), Nigeria (1608 km).
8	Laos	236,800	5274	Burma (238 km), China (475 km), Cambodia (555 km), Vietnam (2161 km), Thailand (1845 km)
9	Kyrgyzstan	199,951	4573	Tajikistan (984 km), China (1063 km), Kazakhstan (1212 km), Uzbekistan (1314 km)
10	Botswana	581,730	4347	Zambia (0.15 km), Zimbabwe (834 km), Namibia (1544 km), South Africa (1969 km)

(*continued*)

Table 2.4 (continued)

No	*WSE*	*Land area*	*Border length*	*WSE bordering countries and borders length*
		km²	*km*	
11	Tajikistan	144,100	4130	China (477 km), Kyrgyzstan (984 km), Uzbekistan (1312 km), Afghanistan (1357 km)
12	Burkina Faso	274,220	3611	Togo (131 km), Benin (386 km), Ghana (602 km), Ivory Coast (545 km), Niger (622 km), Mali (1325 km)
13	Zimbabwe	390,757	3229	South Africa (230 km), Zambia (763 km), Botswana (834 km), Mozambique (1402 km)
14	Nepal	147,181	3159	China (1389 km), India (1770 km)
15	Malawi	118,484	2857	Tanzania (512 km), Zambia (847 km), Mozambique (1498 km).
16	Moldova	33,851	1885	Romania (683 km), Ukraine (1202 km)
17	Armenia	29,743	1570	Iran (44 km), Georgia (219 km), Turkey (311 km), Azerbaijan (996 km)
18	Burundi	27,830	1140	Democratic Republic of Congo (236 km), Rwanda (315 km), Tanzania (589 km)
19	Bhutan	38,394	1136	China (477 km), India (659 km)
20	Lesotho	30,355	1106	South Africa (1106 km)
21	Rwanda	26,338	930	Uganda (172 km), Democratic Republic of Congo (221 km), Tanzania (222 km), Burundi (315 km)
22	Northern Macedonia	25,713	838	Serbia (101 km), Kosovo (160 km), Bulgaria (162 km), Albania (181 km), Greece (234 km)
23	Eswatini	17,364	546	Mozambique (108 km), South Africa (438 km)
24	Andorra	468	118	France (55 km), Spain (63 km)
25	Liechtenstein	160	75	Austria (34 km), Switzerland (41 km)
26	San Marino	61	37	Italy (37 km)
The landlocked WSE in total		9,598,351	86,716	–

Source: Own compilation based on CIA The Factbook

Table 2.5 Continental WSE with sea access, bordering countries

No	*WSE*	*Area*	*Border length*			*WSE bordering countries and borders length*
			Total	*Land*	*Sea*	
		km²		*Km*		
1	Mozambique	799,380	7523	4783	2740	Eswatini (108 km), Zambia (439 km), South Africa (496), Tanzania (840 km), Zimbabwe (1402 km), Malawi (1498 km)
2	Namibia	824,292	5792	4220	1572	Zambia (244 km), South Africa (1005 km), Botswana (1544 km), Angola (1427 km)
3	Mauritania	1,030,700	5756	5002	754	Algeria (460 km), Senegal (742 km), Morocco (1564 km), Mali (2236 km)
4	Congo	342,000	5709	5540	169	Angola (231 km), Central African Republic (487 km), Cameroon (494 km), Democratic Republic of Congo (1175 km), Gabon (2567 km)
5	Somalia	637,657	5410	2385	3025	Djibouti (61 km), Kenya (684 km), Ethiopia (1640 km)
6	Estonia	45,228	4451	657	3794	Russia (324 km), Latvia (333 km)
7	Guinea	245,857	4366	4046	320	Senegal (363 km), Guinea-Bissau (421 km), Liberia (590 km), Ivory Coast (816 km), Sierra Leone (794 km), Mali (1062 km)
8	Eritrea	117,600	4174	1840	2334	Djibouti (125 km), Sudan (682 km), Ethiopia (1033 km)
9	Gabon	267,667	4146	3261	885	Cameroon (349 km), Equatorial Guinea (345 km), Congo (2567 km)
10	North Korea	120,538	4102	1607	2495	Russia (18 km), South Korea (237 km), China (1352 km)

(*continued*)

Table 2.5 (continued)

No	*WSE*	*Area*	*Border length*			*WSE bordering countries and borders length*
			Total	*Land*	*Sea*	
		km²	*Km*			
11	Yemen	527,970	3507	1601	1906	Oman (294 km), Saudi Arabia (1307 km)
12	Guyana	214,969	3392	2933	459	Venezuela (789 km), Suriname (836 km), Brazil (1308 km)
13	Senegal	196,722	3214	2683	531	Guinea-Bissau (341 km), Guinea (363 km), Mali (489 km), Mauritania (742 km), The Gambia (749 km)
14	Cambodia	181,035	2973	2530	443	Laos (555 km), Thailand (817 km), Vietnam (1158 km)
15	Honduras	112,090	2398	1575	823	Guatemala (244 km), El Salvador (391 km), Nicaragua (940 km)
16	Suriname	163,820	2293	1907	386	French Guiana (556 km), Brazil (515 km), Guyana (836 km)
17	Liberia	111,369	2246	1667	579	Sierra Leone (299 km), Guinea (590 km), Ivory Coast (778 km)
18	Benin	112,622	2244	2123	121	Niger (277 km), Burkina Faso (386 km), Togo (651 km), Nigeria (809 km)
19	Nicaragua	130,370	2163	1253	910	Costa Rica (313 km), Honduras (940 km)
20	Georgia	69,700	2124	1814	310	Armenia (219 km), Turkey (273 km), Azerbaijan (428 km), Russia (894 km)
21	Togo	56,785	1936	1880	56	Burkina Faso (131 km), Benin (651 km), Ghana (1098 km)
22	Bosnia and Herzegovina	51,197	1563	1543	20	Montenegro (242 km), Serbia (345 km), Croatia (956 km)
23	Sierra Leone	71,740	1495	1093	402	Liberia (299 km), Guinea (749 km)

(continued)

Table 2.5 (continued)

No	WSE	Area	Border length			WSE bordering countries and borders length
			Total	Land	Sea	
		km²	Km			
24	Guinea-Bissau	36,125	1112	762	350	Senegal (341 km), Guinea (421 km)
25	Albania	28,748	1059	697	362	Kosovo (112 km), Northern Macedonia (181 km), Montenegro (186 km), Greece (212 km)
26	Montenegro	13,812	973	680	293	Croatia (19 km), Kosovo (76 km), Albania (186 km), Serbia (157 km), Bosnia and Herzegovina (242 km)
27	Belize	22,966	928	542	386	Mexico (276 km), Guatemala (266 km)
28	Salvador	21,041	897	590	307	Guatemala (199 km), Honduras (391 km)
29	Djibouti	23,200	842	528	314	Somalia (61 km), Eritrea (125 km), Ethiopia (342 km)
30	The Gambia	11,300	829	749	80	Senegal (749 km)
31	Equatorial Guinea	28,051	824	528	296	Cameroon (183 km), Gabon (345 km)
32	Monaco	2	10	6	4	France (6 km)
The continental WSE with sea access in total		6,616,553	90,451	63,025	27,426	–

Source: Own compilation based on CIA The Factbook

Most of the island WSE have no land borders, except for that share islands with other countries. These include Brunei with Malaysia, on the island of Borneo (the third largest island in the world); Cyprus with the Turkish Republic of Northern Cyprus[2] on the island of Cyprus; Haiti with the Dominican Republic on the island of Hispaniola, Papua New Guinea

[2]The Turkish Republic of Northern Cyprus is only partially recognized internationally. Both the European Union and the United Nations do not recognize the republic, reffering to the area the Republic of Cyprus, which is under Turkish occupation.

with Indonesia on the island of New Guinea (the second largest island in the world), and East Timor with Indonesia on the island of Timor. However, land borders constitute only a small part of their total length (Table 2.6).

Borders are an essential part of states. They define the geographical location of their territories and their territory. In this way, they give a country the attribute of territoriality and sovereignty. They also play an important role in international perceptions. Despite the many changes in today's global economy, internationalization in the economic, political, and cultural spheres, which affect the opening of borders and reduce their role as a spatial barrier; the issue of borders continues to be significant. Only the functions of borders, both internal and external, have changed, although they remain an important element of today's global economy.

The elements discussed: the location of countries, neighborhoods with borders and territories occupied by countries, place them in the global space. All of them, albeit to different degrees, influence the growth and economic development of the WSE.

As part of the location analysis, the WSE were classified by continent (Table 2.7) and by access to the sea (Table 2.8). The lowest level of economic development was recorded by the WSE subgroup located in Africa, with a GDP per capita of US$ 1046 in 2019. (Table 2.7). One of the main reasons for this low average GDP per capita was the isolation of the countries in Africa, which were far from the markets of rich countries located on other continents. The growth of economic potential in many of these countries did not keep pace with the dynamics of population growth. An important role has been played not only by greater distances, but also by immediate neighbors. Geographic proximity strengthens partnerships between neighboring countries, which usually leads to trade integration. Meanwhile, the neighbors of the poorest WSE in Africa are countries with similar, very low levels of economic development, often even facing a food deficit. Examples include Niger (GDP of US$ 563 per capita) bordering Chad (GDP of US$ 814 per capita), GDP of Burundi (US$ 208 per capita) with Rwanda (GDP of US$ 901 per capita), Mali (GDP of US$ 792 per capita) with Guinea (GDP of US$ 921 per capita). In addition, these countries have often experienced conflicts that have spilled over into neighboring countries, negatively affecting their economies. One such example is the war in Liberia (1989–1996), which spilled over into neighboring Sierra Leone two years later. As a result, Sierra Leone's GDP fell dramatically over the next three years, from US$ 563 per capita to US$ 364 per capita between 1991 and 2002.

Table 2.6 Island WSE, bordering countries

No	WSE	Islands	Area	Border length			WSE bordering countries and borders length
				Total	Land	Sea	
		Quantity	km²	Km			
1	Micronesia	672	702	6112	824	6112	–
2	Papua New Guinea	1400	462,840	5976	376	5152	Indonesia (824 km)
3	Solomon Islands	900	28,896	5313	266	5313	–
4	Iceland	35	103,000	4970	253	4970	–
5	Madagascar		587,041	4828	156	4828	–
6	Bahamas	700	13,880	3542	0	3542	–
7	Vanuatu	83	12,189	2528	0	2528	–
8	Haiti	59	27,750	2147	0	1771	Dominican Republic (376 km)
9	Palau	208	459	1519	0	1519	–
10	Kiribati	54	811	1143	0	1143	–
11	Fiji	330	18,274	1129	0	1129	–
12	Jamaica	49	10,991	1022	0	1022	–
13	Cape Verde	24	4033	965	0	965	–
14	East Timor	3	14,874	959	0	706	Indonesia (253 km)
15	Cyprus	1	9251	804	0	648	Northern Cyprus (156 km)
16	Maldives	1192	298	644	0	644	–
17	Seychelles	115	455	491	0	491	–
18	Brunei	33	5765	427	0	161	Malaysia (266 km)
19	Tonga	169	747	419	0	419	–
20	Samoa	16	2831	403	0	403	–
21	Marshall Islands	58	181	370	0	370	–
22	Trinidad and Tobago	2	5128	362	0	362	–
23	Comoros	4	2235	340	0	340	–
24	Saint Thomas and Príncipe	2	964	209	0	209	–
25	Malta	24	316	197	0	197	–
26	Mauritius	5	2040	177	0	177	–
27	Saint Lucia	7000	616	158	0	158	–

(*continued*)

Table 2.6 (continued)

No	*WSE*	*Islands*	*Area*	*Border length*			*WSE bordering countries and borders length*
				Total	*Land*	*Sea*	
		Quantity	*km*^{2}	*Km*			
28	Antigua and Barbuda	56	443	153	0	153	–
29	Dominica	4	751	148	0	148	–
30	Saint Kitts and Nevis	8	261	135	0	135	–
31	Grenada	20	344	121	0	121	–
32	Barbados	5	430	97	0	97	–
33	Saint Vincent and the Grenadines	41	389	84	0	84	–
34	Nauru	1	21	30	0	30	–
35	Tuvalu	18	26	24	0	24	–
The island WSE in total		13,291	1,319,232	47,946	1875	46,071	

Source: Own compilation based on World Atlas, CIA The World Factbook

At times, however, the neighborhood has had positive economic effects, as evidenced by the geographic proximity of the WSE, such as Botswana (GDP of US$ 8093 per capita) and Namibia (GDP of US$ 5766 per capita), which border South Africa, and have higher levels of economic development. Despite their isolation from other continents and their rich markets, the close proximity of these countries allows them to achieve mutual economic benefits. It should be noted, however, that in addition to proximity, leadership and good governance have played a major role.

Another example of the positive impact of geographical proximity was the WSE located in Europe. This subgroup had the highest level of GDP of US$ 8558 per capita in 2019, an increase of more than two times compared to 2000 (Table 2.7). In particular, the WSE located in Western Europe have stronger economic ties, manifested in increased exchange of goods, services, and capital. For example, Andorra (GDP per capita of US$ 45,887) maintains a high level of economic development mainly due to its proximity to the highly developed economies of Spain and France; Liechtenstein (GDP per capita of US$ 177,698) with Switzerland and

Table 2.7 WSE by continents, population and GDP in 2000 and 2019

No	*WSE subgroups*	*Countries*	*Area*	*Population*		*GDP*		*GDP*	
				2000	*2019*	*2000*	*2019*	*2000*	*2019*
		quantity	*thousand km²*	*Thousand*		*$US million*		*$US per capita*	
1.	Africa	36	12,038	191,015	320,180	157,163	334,909	823	1046
2.	North America	15	348	31,291	40,045	86,315	129,818	2758	3242
3.	Europe	14	402	21,776	20,575	88,486	176,085	4063	8558
4.	Asia	14	3841	119,081	168,359	100,911	196,657	847	1168
5.	Australia and Oceania	12	527	7810	11,269	15,123	30,395	1936	2697
6.	South America	2	378	1217	1364	5407	9458	4443	6934
WSE group in total		93	17,536	372,192	561,792	453,405	877,322	1218	1562

Source: Own compilation based on CIA The World Factbook

Table 2.8 WSE by sea access, GDP and population

No	*WSE subgroups*	*Countries*	*Area*	*Population*		*GDP*		*GDP*	
				2000	*2019*	*2000*	*2019*	*2000*	*2019*
		Quantity	*thousand km²*	*Thousand*		*US$ million*		*US$ per capita*	
1.	Island	35	1318.0	42,581	62,448	134,998	216,086	3170	3460
2.	Continental with access to the sea	32	6616.4	163,203	239,856	197,426	377,350	1210	1573
3.	Landlocked	26	9598.2	166,408	259,487	120,981	283,887	727	1094
WSE group in total		93	17,536.6	372,192	561,792	453,405	877,322	1218	1562

Source: Own compilation based on CIA The World Factbook

Austria, Monaco (GDP per capita of US$ 209,241) with France, San Marino (GDP per capita of US$ 50,462) to Italy. Similarly, due to its geographic proximity especially to Scandinavia, Estonia became one of the richest post-socialist countries within a short period of time after seceding from the USSR, recording a GDP growth from US$ 896 per capita to US$ 20,854 per capita between 1990 and 2019.

The economic benefits of geographic proximity were also demonstrated by the WSE located in the North American region. The high GDP per capita in 2019 of Antigua and Barbuda (US$ 15,704 per capita), Barbados (US$ 16,100 per capita), and Saint Kitts and Nevis (US$ 17,295 per capita) was achieved largely due to their overseas proximity to the wealthy United States, to which many residents of the aforementioned island nations travel for work. In turn, the developed tourism industry of the WSE located in the Caribbean attracts large numbers of American tourists. The benefits also manifest themselves in trade; for example, the WSE, such as Trinidad and Tobago's oil and gas production, supplies most of its neighboring island nations. Profits from exports have contributed to Trinidad and Tobago's prosperity (GDP of US$ 5105 per capita in 2019).

In addition to the above factors, the location in relation to the sea or ocean is very important for the economic development of the WSE. An analysis showed that the island WSE had the highest level of economic development (Table 2.8). Moreover, this subgroup also had the highest 1.5-fold growth (from US$ 727 per capita to US$ 1094 per capita), as well as the 2.3-fold increase in GDP (from US$ 134 billion to US$ 216 billion) between 2000 and 2019. The continental WSE subgroup with access to the sea had slightly lower growth. In contrast, the landlocked WSE (Table 2.8) had the lowest level of economic development, depriving them of marine resources (including fisheries income), maritime transport and the development of other maritime-related services.

Coastal locations provide the WSE with access to marine products, both food resources (such as fish) and mineral resources; enables saltwater fishing and the development of maritime services, such as maritime transport, transit services, marine tourism, commodity trading, low-cost flagging and shipbuilding, hydroelectric and wind power generation. The WSE with sea access additionally benefit from their continental proximity to neighboring countries, especially if they border rich countries. However, many of them share the fate of their poor neighbors despite their advantageous coastal location. Examples include the Atlantic coastal The Gambia (GDP per capita of US$ 815), which borders with poor Guinea-Bissau

(GDP per capita of US$ 636), or Togo (GDP per capita of US$ 696) with Burkina Faso (GDP per capita of US$ 822). This problem also applies to the WSE that share an island with another country. One example is East Timor. The country was occupied by Indonesia for 3 decades. The big neighbor tried to take over the rest of the island, ruining Timor's entire economy in the process. The problem of proximity to another country can also affect the economies of the WSE that occupy entire islands, although this depends on the distance that separates them from the nearest continents. The greater the distance, the lesser the influence of the continent. This is evident in the case of the WSE such as Madagascar (GDP per capita of US$ 500), which is strongly influenced by mainland Mozambique; 1200 km away; Iceland (GDP per capita of US$ 51,332), which is influenced by the United Kingdom and Norway, 1300–1400 km away). On the other hand, the WSE such as Micronesia (GDP per capita of US$ 2700) and Kiribati (GDP per capita of US$ 1790) do not exhibit the characteristics of continental economies because they are too far away from Australia and New Zealand by about 4000 km. Instead, these two countries, 4000 km away from Australia, suffer from geographic isolationism. Their economic ties are weak, mainly due to high transportation costs.

In addition to location and neighborhood, some authors and researchers *consider the size of a country's land area as a determinant of its economic potential and international relations* (Rykiel, 2006). However, the WSE research does not support this theory (Table 2.9).

In 2019, the WSE subgroups of more than 1 million km^2 and less than 1000 km^2 had the lowest GDP (Table 2.9). However, the WSE with an area of more than 1 million km^2 showed the largest threefold increase between 2000 and 2019 (from US$ 22,515 million to US$ 63,651 million). As a consequence of its low GDP and small population, it had a very low GDP per capita (Table 2.9), but the highest growth (from US$ 631 per capita to US$ 955 per capita) compared to the other five subgroups (Table 2.9).

The lack of correlation between the size of a country's land area and its economic potential was also evident for the individual WSE. The largest country in terms of area, with more than 1 million km^2 ranked much lower in the WSE group (Table 2.10) and was overtaken by countries with much smaller areas.

Although the largest WSE of more than 1 million km^2, that is, Chad, Mali, Mauritania, Mongolia, and Niger, are territorially extensive, their areas are very inefficiently used and most of them are anecumenic. More

Table 2.9 WSE by occupied area versus changes in economic potential between 2000 and 2019

No	*WSE subgroups*	*Countries*	*Area*	*Population*		*GDP*		*GDP*	
				2000	*2019*	*2000*	*2019*	*2000*	*2019*
		Quantity	*thousand km²*	*thousand*		*US$ million*		*US$ per capita*	
1	over 1,000,000 km²	5	6386.0	35,661	66,666	22,515	63,651	631	955
2	500,000 km²–1,000,000 km²	9	5878.9	93,817	160,587	61,801	122,283	659	761
3	100,000 km²–500,000 km²	22	4395.5	163,493	230,953	154,341	306,994	944	1329
4	10,000 km²–100,000 km²	28	836.3	72,085	94,808	130,203	249,195	1806	2628
5	1,000 km²–10,000 km²	8	30.9	4875	5890	51,763	81,645	10,617	13,861
6	less than 1000 km²	21	8.9	2259	2885	32,779	53,552	14,511	18,560
WSE group in total		93	17,536.6	372,192	561,792	453,405	877,322	1218	1562

Source: Own compilation based on CIA The World Factbook

Table 2.10 WSE with land area over 1 million km²

No	*WSE*	*Position in the WSE group by GDP*	*GDP*		*Population*		*GDP*		*Land area*
			US$ million		*Thousand*		*US$ per capita*		*thousand km²*
		2019	*2000*	*2019*	*2000*	*2019*	*2000*	*2019*	
1	Mali	20	6075	15,562	10,946	19,658	555	792	1240.2
2	Mongolia	28	3837	14,037	2397	3225	1600	4353	1564.1
3	Niger	35	4863	13,127	11,331	23,310	429	563	1267.0
4	Chad	36	3862	12,976	8355	15,946	462	814	1284.0
5	Mauritania	48	3876	7947	2630	4525	1474	1756	1030.7
WSE with an area more than 1 million km²			22,515	63,651	35,661	66,666	631	955	6386.0

Source: Own compilation based on CIA The World Factbook

than 80% of Mauritania's territory is occupied by the uninhabited (except for oases) Sahara Desert. The same is true of Mali, 65% covered by the Sahara; Niger 80% and Chad 50%. In the case of Mongolia, on the other hand, more than 80% of its territory is occupied by depopulated mountain terrain and highland terrain, steppes, and the Gobi Desert. As a result, more than half of Mongolia's population (1.4 million out of 3.2 million) lives in the country's capital, Ulaanbaatar.

Bibliography

Bachvarov, M., & Suliborski, A. (2003). *Kompendium wiedzy geografii politycznej i geopolityce*. PWN.

Otok, S. (2012). *Geografia Polityczna*. PWN.

Rykiel, Z. (2006). *Podstawy Geografii Politycznej*. PWE.

CHAPTER 3

Natural Environment of the World's Smallest Economies

Nature (Latin: *natura*) encompasses the totality of both the organic and inorganic worlds that surround humans. It consists of two closely related but interdependent elements: animate and inanimate nature. The former includes biotic components, such as living organisms like plants, animals, fungi, bacteria. In contrast, inanimate nature provides the environment for these living organisms. This includes the Earth's atmosphere (air), lithosphere (soils, rocks, minerals), landforms, waters and climatic components that shape environmental conditions. The natural environment is one form of environment, alongside geographical and anthropogenic factors (Trzcinska, 2007), which includes natural elements such as the climate, the associated organic world and soil; water; and landforms. It refers to an environment that has not been altered by humans. With the development of civilization and socioeconomic development, the role of various elements of the natural environment in human life has changed and even diminished, although many forms of activity still depend heavily on nature. Examples include agriculture, which relies on soils, climatic conditions, and terrain; or the mining industry that depends on geological structure and the availability of mineral resources. Consequently, environmental resources continue to influence human activities while impacting the overall economy of countries. Favorable climatic conditions; location relative to land and ocean, which determines the degree of continentalism or

A. A. Tepeek, *Economic Development in the World's Smallest Economies*, https://doi.org/10.1007/978-3-031-63810-7_3

oceanicity; the organic world; soils; surface relief resulting from geological processes; and geological structure with mineral resources; accelerate economic growth. Conversely, unfavorable natural conditions, such as desert areas, high mountainous terrain hinder economic development. Many modern scientific studies indicate that among the elements of the natural environment, climate and a country's geographical location—along with access to rivers, seas, and oceans—are the most significant factors determining its wealth or poverty. These elemets distinguish nations and states from one another, much like humans beings share similarities regardless of their latitude. This perspective was already noted by Greek philosophers, including the father of geography, Herodotus of Halicarnassus, and the French philosopher Montesquieu. According to this theory, the natural elements of the environment of the WSE have been analyzed in detail, with particular attention to their economic suitability and use.

Bibliography

Trzcinska, B. (2007). In K. Kuchinski (Ed.), *Roznice i Podobienstwa. Zroznicowanie Przyrodnicze*. Geografia, Difin.

CHAPTER 4

Climatic and Vegetation Zonation of the World's Smallest Economies

The geographic location of the WSE is inextricably linked to the climate,[1] exerting a direct impact on both the climate zone and climate type. The location is determined by longitude and latitude, which in turn determine the angle of incidence of the sun's rays, approximately 90° at the equator and 0° at the poles. A lower angle of incidence is associated with a reduced solar energy input to the area. Therefore, the hottest climates are found in the equatorial WSE, such as Congo, Equatorial Guinea, Gabon, Kiribati, Maldives, Saint Thomas, and Príncipe, while the coldest climate is found Iceland, in the northernmost WSE and closest to the pole, Although varying amounts of solar heat at different latitudes significantly affect the formation of climate zones, ocean currents also play a crucial role. They modify temperature levels and precipitation in the coastal areas. For example, the cold Benguela Current, which flows along the southwest coast of Africa, cools and dries Namibia's west coast, where average air temperatures in the mid-20th century were 2–4° C higher than today (Radomski & Gasinsk, 2004). Another example is the Somali Current, which flows northward along the east coast of Africa during the summer as a cold branch of the North Equatorial Current. In winter, under the influence of the Asian monsoon, it reverses direction and flows south as a warm current.

[1] The word 'climate' comes from the Greek language, in which it refers to the angle of inclination of the sun.

A. A. Teperek, *Economic Development in the World's Smallest Economies*, https://doi.org/10.1007/978-3-031-63810-7_4

Together with the Equatorial Back Current, the Somali Current warms the coast of, Somalia, one of the WSE. Similarly, the warm Mozambique Current flows from north to south through the Mozambique Channel, warming Mozambique in spring and cooling in autumn. Normally, fall should be warmer than the spring under typical oceanic conditions.

In the analysis of the climate of the 93 WSE, the zonal classification of the global climate by the famous geographer and specialist in geomorphology and climatology Vincent Okolovich was used. There are five subgroups, each corresponding to one of the major climatic zones (Table 4.1): Equatorial, Tropical, Subtropical, Temperate, and Polar. Each climate zone is characterized by a different distribution and variation of temperatures throughout the year (annual and daily), as well as specific precipitation totals and their distribution by month. Each zone has several types of climate that are determined by astro-zonal factors. These include the location relative to the land and oceans, which determines the degree of continentalism or oceanicity of the climate, and altitude, which makes the air cooler (a decrease of 0.6°C per 100 meters). Accordingly, almost all climate zones (except the circumpolar) have mountain, humid, continental, transitional, monsoon types.

Most of the WSE (54 countries) are located in equatorial and subequatorial climate zones, but most of them have equatorial climates with hot, humid air masses forming at low atmospheric pressure, with annual precipitation exceeding 2000 mm (Table 4.1). The combined land area of the WSE with equatorial and subequatorial climates is more than 6.2 million km^2, or 35% of the WSE group, while it is home to almost half of the group's population (262 million in 2019), or 47% of the group's population. This subgroup consists mainly of small island states, primarily in the Caribbean (e.g., Barbados, Haiti, Jamaica, Saint Kitts and Nevis, Saint Lucia, and Trinidad and Tobago), and the Pacific (e.g., Kiribati, Nauru, Papua New Guinea, Samoa, Solomon Islands, Tonga, and Tuvalu). The remaining equatorial and subequatorial WSE are continental and located in Africa (e.g., Benin, Chad, Congo, Equatorial Guinea, Gabon, Guinea, Guinea-Bissau, Malawi, Mali, Mozambique, Somalia, South Sudan, and Zimbabwe) and Latin America (e.g., Belize, Guyana, Honduras, Nicaragua, and Suriname). Due to the vast area, some of the WSE are located in both equatorial and tropical climates. Countries such as Chad (1284 thousand km^2), Madagascar (587.4 thousand km^2), Mali (1240 thousand km^2), Mauritania (1030 thousand km^2), and Zimbabwe (390 thousand km^2) are located in two or three climate zones. Tropical climates are found in 18 of the WSE (Table 4.1),

Table 4.1 WSE by climate zones and types

Climate type	*Climate characteristics*	*WSE*
EQUATORIAL CLIMATE ZONE		
Humid subtropical equatorial	• Year-round temperatures above +25°C; • Small daily and annual temperature amplitudes • High year-round precipitation exceeding 2000 mm	Antigua and Barbuda, Bahamas (south), Barbados, Benin (south), Brunei, Central African Republic, Congo. Dominica, Equatorial Guinea, Fiji, Gabon, Grenada, Guinea, Guinea-Bissau, Guyana (north, east), Haiti, Honduras, Jamaica, Kiribati, Liberia, Madagascar (east), Maldives, Marshall Islands, Micronesia, Nicaragua, Papua New Guinea (center), Rwanda, Saint Kitts and Nevis, Saint Lucia, Saint Vincent and the Grenadines, Samoa, Saint Thomas and Principe, Seychelles, Suriname, Togo (south), Trinidad and Tobago, Tuvalu
Humid subequatorial	• Year-round temperatures above +20°C • Annual temperature fluctuations of up to 10°C • Zenithal rains with one or two rainy seasons • Annual precipitation of 1000–2000 mm	Belize (north), Burundi, Comoros, East Timor, El Salvador, Guinea, Guyana (Guyana highlands), Madagascar, Marshall Islands, Mozambique (central), Senegal (south), Sierra Leone, Solomon Islands, Tonga, Vanuatu
Dry subequatorial	• Year-round temperatures above +25°C • Annual temperature variations of 5–10°C • Zenithal rains with one or two rainy seasons and a prolonged dry season • Annual precipitation of 500–1000 mm	Belize (south), Benin (north and center), Burkina Faso, The Gambia, Madagascar (west), Malawi, Mali (south), Mauritania (south), Senegal (north), Somalia, South Sudan, Togo (north and center), Zimbabwe (north)

(*continued*)

Table 4.1 (continued)

Climate type	*Climate characteristics*	*WSE*
Equatorial monsoon	• Year-round temperatures above +20°C • Annual temperature fluctuations up to 10°C • Year-round rains and monsoon winds • Rainfall of 1500–2000 mm	Chad (south), Nauru, Palau, Papua New Guinea
TROPICAL CLIMATE ZONE		
Wet	• Temperatures of warmest months 25–30°C • Coolest months: 15–20°C • Year-round precipitation with predominance in summer • Annual precipitation of 1000–1500 mm	Bahamas (north), Eswatini, Lesotho, Madagascar (south), Mauritius
Continental dry and extremely dry	• Temperatures of warmest months more than 30°C • Temperatures of coolest months: 15°C • Annual temperature fluctuations of 15–20°C • Large daily temperature fluctuations • Annual precipitation in dry climates of 250–500 mm; in extremely dry climates, less than 250 mm and even less than 50 mm	Botswana, Cape Verde, Chad (Sahara), Djibouti, Eritrea (Arabian Desert, Nubian Desert), Mali (Sahara), Mauritania (Sahara), Namibia (Namib desert), Niger (Sahara), Yemen (Ar-Rab al-Khali Desert), Zimbabwe (south)
Tropical monsoon	• Temperatures of warmest months: 25–30°C • Temperatures of coolest months: 15–20°C • Precipitation mostly in summer • Rains and monsoon winds in summer blowing from sea to land and in winter from land to sea • Rainfall: 1000–2000 mm	Cambodia, Laos, Nepal (outside the mountains)

(*continued*)

Table 4.1 (continued)

Climate type	*Climate characteristics*	*WSE*
SUBTROPICAL CLIMATE ZONE		
Mediterranean	• Temperatures of warmest months: 25°C • Temperatures of coolest months: 5–10°C • Annual precipitation: 500–700 mm, mainly in the cool semester • Dry summers, but higher precipitation in the mountains	Albania, Bosnia and Herzegovina (west and south), Cyprus, Georgia, Malta, Monaco, Montenegro, North Macedonia, San Marino
Continental	• Temperatures of the warmest months: 25°C • Temperatures of the coolest months: 5–10°C • Annual precipitation: 350–600 mm	Albania (east), Andorra, Armenia
Continentally outstandingly dry	• Temperatures of warmest months: 20–30°C • Temperatures of coldest months: 10°C • Large daily temperature fluctuations • Annual precipitation: 250–50 mm	Afghanistan (Registan Desert), Tajikistan (south)
Subtropical monsoon	• Temperatures of warmest months: 20–25°C • Temperatures of coolest months: 0–15°C • Annual precipitation: 700–1000 mm	Bhutan (south)
TEMPERATE CLIMATE ZONE		
warm temperate climate zone		
Transitional	• Temperatures of warmest months: 17–19°C • Temperatures of coolest months: -1-4°C • Annual temperature fluctuation of about 23°C • Six seasons • Precipitation of about 550–600 mm year-round, with prevalence in summer semester	Liechtenstein

(*continued*)

Table 4.1 (continued)

Climate type	*Climate characteristics*	*WSE*
Continental and continental dry	• Temperatures of warmest months: 20°C • Temperatures of coolest months: 0–10°C • Annual temperature fluctuation: 23–30°C • Annual precipitation: 350–600 mm	Bosnia and Herzegovina (north and east), Kyrgyzstan (north), Moldova, Tajikistan (north)
Continental and continental extremely dry	• Temperatures of warmest months: 20–30°C • Temperatures of coolest months: 10°C • Large daily temperature fluctuations: 23–30°C • Annual precipitation: 250 mm, and even less than 50 mm	Mongolia (Gobi desert)
Temperate monsoon	• Temperatures of warmest months: 15–20°C • Temperatures of coolest months: -10°C • Year-round precipitation with prevalence in the summer half-year of 700–900 mm	North Korea (south)
Cool temperate climate zone		
Maritime	• Temperatures of warmest months: 15–20°C • Temperatures of coolest months: -10°C • Annual temperature fluctuations below 23°C; year-round precipitation with prevalence in the cool semester of 800–1000 mm	Iceland (south), Estonia (west)
Transitional	• Temperatures of warmest months: 10–12°C • Temperatures of coolest months: -10 to -12°C • Year-round precipitation with prevalence in the cool semester of 500–800 mm	Estonia (south)

(*continued*)

Table 4.1 (continued)

Climate type	*Climate characteristics*	*WSE*
Continental	• Temperatures of warmest months: 15–16°C • Temperatures of coldest months: reaching -40°C • Year-round precipitation: less than 250 mm	Mongolia
Temperate monsoon	• Temperatures of warmest months: 10–15°C • Temperatures of coolest months: -10°C • Year-round precipitation with prevalence in the summer half-year of 700–800 mm	North Korea (north)
POLAR CLIMATE ZONE		
Subpolar	• Temperatures of warmest months: up to 10°C • Temperatures of coolest months: -10 to -20°C • Polar night and day • Annual precipitation: less than 250 mm due to low evaporation	Iceland (north)

Source: Own compilation based on: (Trzcinska, 2007, pp. 22–26)

which cover an area of 8.1 million km^2, or almost half of the WSE group, and are home to 194 million people. Most of the tropical WSE have continental-type climates (e.g., Djibouti, Eritrea, Niger, and Yemen) with large 24-hour temperatures variations and low precipitation of less than 500 mm, and even less than 50 mm in deserts.

The remaining quarter of the WSE are located in the other three climate zones: subtropical, temperate, and polar (Table 4.1). The subtropical zone is found in most of them (14 countries), covers a land area of 1 million km^2 and was home to 65 million people in 2019. This climate zone is typical of the WSE located in the Mediterranean region (e.g., Albania, Bosnia and Herzegovina, Georgia, Malta, Monaco), where the warmest monthly temperatures reach 25°C and the coolest 15–20°C with precipitation of about 500 mm. On the other hand, the dry subtropics occurs only in a few countries (e.g., Afghanistan, Kyrgyzstan, Tajikistan).

Toward the cooler north of the temperate climate zone there are fewer of the WSE (6 countries), but their total land area is almost twice that of all 14 countries in the subtropical climate zone, although the temperate zone was home to two-thirds of their population (39 million in 2019). The temperate climate zone characterized by wider temperature ranges throughout the year and more pronounced seasonal changes than the subtropical climate, where such differences are often small. It is usually characterized by four distinct seasons, with summer being the warmest, fall being the transition season to winter, the colder season, and spring being the transition season from winter back to summer. The warm type of temperate climate zone is found in Liechtenstein, Moldova, etc., and the cool type in Estonia and southern Iceland. Both, warm and cold temperate climates are found in Mongolia (continental type) and North Korea (monsoon type).

Some features of a polar climate, with temperatures of the warmest month reaching 10°C and the coldest down to -20°C, and annual precipitation of less than 250 mm due to low evaporation, are found in the northern areas of Iceland.

Climatic zonation is characterized by differences in annual precipitation totals and distributions. The intensity of precipitation is influenced by a number of factors. These include atmospheric pressure and associated air circulation; distance from the sea and ocean (the greater the distance, the lesser the precipitation); altitude (the higher the altitude, the greater the precipitation, but only up to a certain level); surface topography (less precipitation on leeward slopes) and ocean currents. Warm currents bring abundant precipitation, while cold currents bring little precipitation, causing coastal areas to dry out. An example of this is the Atlantic coast of Namibia and the Namib Desert (Table 4.2), which was formed under the influence of the cold Bengal Current. A similar influence of the cold Canary Current on the western coasts of Senegal and Mauritania resulted in the formation of the Sahara Desert (Table 4.2), which extends from the Atlantic Ocean through the WSE: Mauritania, Mali, Niger, Chad, and Eritrea, to the Red Sea, with a total length of 5700 km (comparable to the distance between London and New York) and an area of about 9 million km^2 (slightly less than the area of the United States, which is 9.8 million km^2). The cold Canary Current flowing in from the Atlantic Ocean causes relatively low temperatures in the coastal zone, while the interior has very high temperature variations (influenced by the dry and extremely dry tropical climate) and very low rainfall (almost ten times less than in equatorial belt countries). In addition, its annual distribution,

Table 4.2 Deserts in the WSE

No	*WSE*	*Deserts*
1.	Afghanistan	Dasht-e Khash, Dasht-e Leili, Dasht-e Margo, Dasht-e Naomid, Ragistan
2.	Botswana	Kalahari
3.	Chad	Djurab, Tenere
4.	Djibouti	Danakil
5.	Eritrea	Danakil, Eastern, Sahara
6.	Iceland	Arctic
7.	Kyrgyzstan	Betpak-Dala, Muyunkum
8.	Mali	El Djouf, Tanezrouf
9.	Mauritania	Atlantic Coastal, El Djouf
10.	Mongolia	Gobi, Dzungaria, Khongoryn Els, Flaming Cliffs, Khongoryn Els
11.	Namibia	Kalahari, Namib
12.	Niger	Erg of Bilma, Talak, Tin-Toumma,Tanezrouf, Tenere
13.	Senegal	Ferlo, Lompoul
14.	Somalia	Danakil, Guban, Ogaden, Puntland
15.	Yemen	Arabian, Arabian Peninsula Coastal Fog, Empty Quarter, Ramlat al-Sab'atayn

Source: Own compilation

limited to a 3-month rainy season with violent tornadoes and downpours that wash away a thin layer of soil, greatly hinders plant vegetation and limits the territorial range of crops. Drought continues for another 9 months, contributing to famine. Limited agricultural production and lack of potable water force the population to migrate to countries where water is abundant. This has many side effects in their home countries, such as profound changes in the structure of societies, changes in the distribution of the population, and an increase in the extent of anecumene. In Mauritania for example, the annual drought is forcing the population to abandon its traditional nomadic lifestyle. History has shown that drought and the lack of sufficient drinking water for the growing population of the Saharan WSE have repeatedly contributed to civil unrest in countries such as Chad, Mauritania, and Niger, leading to conflicts and the collapse of governments. One reason for this unrest is rising unemployment, caused in part by the loss of jobs in traditional industries such as inland fishing and transportation due to the drying up of rivers, lakes and ponds.

It is not only the Saharan WSE that face the problem of drought, but other countries as well. Examples are Djibouti and Eritrea. The Danakil Desert (Table 4.2), which covers Djibouti and borders Eritrea, is one of the hottest areas on Earth. Average temperatures are around 27°C, with daytime temperatures reaching up to 50–60°C. In addition, it is the most seismically and volcanically active place in the world, as well as one of the lowest (-150 m below sea level). The problem of the arid climate also affects Yemen and especially the city of Aden, located on the coast of the Gulf of Aden. The lowest rainfall on the continent in the last 50 years was recorded there, with only 45.70 mm, which is less than recorded the Sahara.

In contrast, the WSE located in the equatorial belt is characterized by the highest rainfall intensity. The thermal convection that occurs there is responsible for the occurrence of zenithal rainfall. In countries such as Brunei, Central African Republic, Congo, Gabon, Guyana, Kiribati, Maldives, Marshall Islands, Saint Thomas and Príncipe and Suriname, annual precipitation ranges from 3000 to 7000 mm. On the island of Bioko, which is part of the WSE, Equatorial Guinea, the average annual rainfall reaches 10,000 mm, making it one of the wettest areas in the world. The highest precipitation is also recorded in the high mountains, such as the summit of the Pyrenees in Andorra, the Hindu Kush mountain range in Afghanistan, the Pamir in Tajikistan, the Western Tienshan in Kyrgyzstan, the Greater Caucasus in Georgia, the alpine Ratikon range in Liechtenstein, the Himalayas in Nepal, the Eastern Himalayas of Bhutan, the Cordillera of Honduras, the Dragon Mountains of Lesotho, and the Diamond Mountains of the Taebaek Range of North Korea. Precipitation there reaches 5000 mm. Similar levels of annual precipitation are found along sea and ocean coasts with hot or warm climates affected by warm monsoons. Abundant monsoon rainfall is found in the WSE, such as Cambodia, Laos, Nauru, Palau, Papua New Guinea, Solomon Islands, and Tuvalu.

The WSE have very different climatic conditions. They affect different aspects of life. Many human activities depend on the climate. This is particularly true of agriculture. Sunshine, temperature, and the associated growing season, along with frost, precipitation, and wind (speed and direction), affect the choice of crops. Some crops are only viable within certain ranges of thermal and precipitation conditions, which co-determine their distribution. The ranges of coffee, vanilla, wheat and rice vary significantly. In areas with different lengths of the growing season, maturation and production times also differ. Climate affects not only the structural variation of crops, but also their yields. Among all climatic zones, the most favorable conditions for crop development are found in the subtropical WSE, particularly the Mediterranean climate type as seen in Albania, Cyprus, Montenegro, Georgia; the warm temperate WSE found in Liechtenstein, Moldova, North Korea; and the tropical humid type WSE found in Eswatini, Madagascar (south), as well as the monsoon type found in Cambodia, and Laos. On the other hand, the most challenging conditions for cultivation occur in extreme climates—whether dry or cool. Examples include the Sahara Desert in the mainly tropical areas of Chad, Mali, Niger, or the Gobi Desert, which extends across the WSE of Mongolia in a warm temperate zone of the continental type. As a result, other areas of Mongolia, which fall in a cool temperate zone with a distinctly continental type of climate are also unsuitable for cultivation. Similarly, a cold circumpolar climate of the subpolar type is found in northern Iceland. The length of the growing season, which is too short in some extreme climates, does not allow for the cultivation of crops, which greatly limits the possibility of human settlement. An example is this is the uninhabited areas of the circumpolar zone, where the climate determines the anecumene. Climate affects not only the distribution of population, but also the diet. The diet of an Icelander living in a cool temperate climate is rich in animal protein. A Maltese eats mainly Mediterranean delicacies, that is, olives, fruits, and seafood. In contrast, the staple food of a Cambodian is rice, while a Fijian eats tropical fruits and fish. The climate dictates the way people dress, the use of certain forms of transportation, which are adapted to local conditions, determines the duration of sailing, and influences architecture. For example, in the WSE with higher rainfall (e.g., Nepal), building roofs tend to be sloped to allow snow to slide down them. In addition to agriculture, transportation (e.g., inland waterways) and construction, tourism is highly dependent on climatic conditions. Fiji, Jamaica, the Maldives, Mauritius, Saint Lucia, and the Seychelles, among others, have year-round hot tropical climate that attracts large number of tourists each year.

Climate plays a major role in the development of the WSE, both directly and indirectly. Favorable climatic conditions accelerate economic development processes, by promoting agricultural development, industrialization, urbanization, and tourism, while unfavorable conditions slow them down. Therefore, the WSE with less favorable climatic conditions have tried to find other sources of income to ensure their economic development. A prime example is Iceland (103,000 km^2; 360,000 inhabitants), which at the beginning of the twentieth century was one of the poorest regions in Western Europe. However, by harnessing hydropower, geothermal resources, and volcanic activity that had been a deadly threat for centuries,

Iceland has developed energy-intensive industries. These include aluminum remelting, where Iceland has become the 11th-largest producer in the world (850,000 tons in 2019). Cheap energy has also enabled the creation and expansion of data centers (including data transmission, virtual currency mining), which require large amounts of energy and round-the-clock cooling. Iceland's low air temperatures allow for natural cooling, so data centers don't need to use highly efficient and expensive cooling systems. In this way, Iceland has taken advantage of its challenging climate. At the same time, the widespread use of renewable energy, from geothermal and hydroelectric power plants (first in the world hydroelectric production per capita) has contributed to Iceland's tremendous economic growth. This can be seen by comparing Iceland's GDP per capita with the world's in 1970 and 2019. In 1970, Iceland's GDP per capita was US$ 15,694, while the world's was three times lower (US$ 5216 per capita). In 2019, this difference was even five times: Iceland's GDP was US$ 51,332 per capita and the world was US$ 11,059 per capita. Since then, Iceland's level of economic development has increased even more.

There is a strong correlation between climate and the ability of the biosphere to evolve. Climate largely determines the extent of the organic world, including vegetation cover. The distribution of natural vegetation is closely related to climatic zonation (Table 4.3). Although the plant communities found in areas inhabited by humans differ from the plant formations that originally existed there, they are still strongly dependent on climatic conditions.

When considering the vegetation formations of WSE, forests account for a significant portion of their area. In 2019, more than half of the countries analyzed had a forest cover of more than 34% of their total area (Fig. 4.1). The highest forest cover was found in the equatorial WSE, such as Suriname (97% of the total area), Guyana (94% of the total area), Micronesia (92% of the total area), Gabon (91% of the total area), Solomon Islands (90% of the total area), Palau (90% of the total area), and Equatorial Guinea (88% of the total area).

Looking at the last 30 years, a few of the WSE have seen an increase in the share of forest area in their total area (Fig. 4.1); between 1990 and 2019, Bhutan recorded from 53.7% to 71.4% of its area, Montenegro from 46.5% to 61.5% of its area, and Fiji from 51.4% to 62% of its area. The increase was mainly due to the restoration of forests through sustainable forest management, which contributes to solving the global crisis of climate change and biodiversity loss.

Table 4.3 WSE plant formations

Plant formation	*Plant formation feature*	*WSE*
Equatorial climate zone		
Equatorial forests	Evergreen, moist forests have a layered structure, reaching heights up to 40 to 50 m in height. Characteristic species include ebony, rubberwood, and mahogany, as well as lianas and epiphytes in the lower layers due to the lack of light.	Brunei (40% of area), Burundi, Cambodia (south and central; 40% of area), Central African Republic (south; Ubangi River region; lower course of the Kotto and Lobaye rivers), Comoros (15% of area), Congo (60% of area), Dominica, Guyana (85% of area), Equatorial Guinea (55% of area), Honduras (up to 600 meters above sea level), Jamaica (valleys), Marshall Islands, Papua New Guinea (lowlands), Rwanda (west; Karisimbi slopes, Wirunga Massif), Suriname (90% of area)
Mangrove forests	Evergreen coasts plant, flooded at high tide. The formation is adapted to living in a swampy environment.	Belize (on the Caribbean coast), Guinea (Atlantic coast), Guyana (Atlantic coast), Mozambique (Indian coast), Papua New Guinea (Pacific coast), Togo (Gulf of Guinea's coast)
Monsoon forests	Less dense than equatorial forests, they have a seasonal rhythm—blooming their leaves in the dry season.	Cambodia (north), Guyana (western part of the Guiana Highlands), East Timor, Madagascar (north)
Dry forests and thorny thickets	Dry thorny shrubs grow on weaker soils, entwined with clematis and shedding their leaves in the dry season. The are characteristic of the semiarid climates of the subequatorial areas.	Botswana, Madagascar (southwestern), Namibia
Savanna	Grassy formation with trees such as baobabs, acacias, and palms overgrows in areas of the subequatorial climate with a dry season during which the trees shed their leaves and the grass dries out. There are three types of savanna: high savanna, with grasses reaching 4 meters in height; low savanna, with grasses reaching 2 meters in height; desert savanna, with low grasses, thorny shrubs (in areas with a very long dry season).	Eswatini (east), Guinea, Guyana (western highlands of Guyana), Malawi (south), Mauritania (south), Namibia (north and central), Niger (south), Central African Republic (north), Rwanda (east), Senegal (north and south), South Sudan (south and east; White Nile basin), Togo, Zimbabwe (Zambezi River valley)

(*continued*)

Table 4.3 (continued)

Plant formation	*Plant formation feature*	*WSE*
Galleria forests	Similar to humid equatorial forests, but growing in river valleys.[a] (Beard, 1955; Labno, 2006)	Botswana (Chobe River), Burkina Faso (Arly National Park), Central African Republic (Ugangi River, Kotto River, Lobaye River), Congo (Congo River), Mozambique (Zambezi River), Senegal (Gambia River), Somalia (Juba River, Uebi Shebelle River), Togo (Oti River)
Tropical climate zone		
Desert and semidesert	Plant formations adapted to prolonged droughts, such as dryland plants and succulents—i.e., plants that accumulate water in their leaves (such as agave, aloe) or in their stem (cacti). Lush plans is found only in oases.	Botswana (southern Kalahari Basin), Chad (north and central part), Mauritania (north), Mali (north), Namibia (southern Kalahari Basin), Niger (north)
Subtropical climate zone		
Hardwood forests and thickets	Found in Mediterranean climates with dry and hot summers and cool and wet winters, these are characterized by needle-like leaves and thick bark. The main species include cork oak, cedar, pine, myrtle, pistachio.	Albania, Bosnia and Herzegovina, Cyprus, Malta, Montenegro
Subtropical forests	Lush, evergreen forest found in the subtropical or tropical humid zone, with shrubs and bamboos in the undergrowth.	Georgia (Kolkhida Plain, south), Nepal (up to 1200 meters above sea level), North Korea (south)
Temperate climate zone		
Steppe	Grassy-green formation typical of a warm, dry temperate climate with hot summers and cold winters. There are three types of steppe: meadow steppe with the dominance of broad-leaved grasses, spurge steppe with narrow-leaved grasses and wormwood steppe with the dominance of mugwort.	Moldova, Mongolia (eastern and central parts of the country), North Macedonia (south), Tajikistan

(continued)

Table 4.3 (continued)

Plant formation	*Plant formation feature*	*WSE*
Semidesert and cool desert	Plant formations found in extreme continental temperate and subtropical climates that store water in their leaves.	Armenia (semideserts in south), Georgia (semideserts in east), Kyrgyzstan (foothills of the Tienshan—semideserts), Mongolia (Gobi Desert, Great Lakes Basin), Tajikistan (up to 500 meters above sea level)
Deciduous forest	Forests that shed their leaves for the winter, growing in a warm temperate, maritime climate. The main tree species are beech, hornbeam, maple, and ash.	Bosnia and Herzegovina (below 60 meters above sea level), Estonia, Liechtenstein (lower areas), Moldova (south), North Korea (north), North Macedonia (west)
Taiga	Boreal forests, or pine forests, mostly growing on perpetually frozen ground, the thickness of which can exceed 500 m; often form in taiga areas. The main tree species are spruce, pine, larch, fir, tamarack, birch, and in the undergrowth are found blueberries, heather, mosses.	Estonia (north), Iceland (on the coast near Akureyri), Mongolia (north)
Circumpolar climate zone		
Tundra	Treeless formation with shrubs, mosses, and lichens found in subpolar climates. There are three types of tundra: arctic (with lichens and few mosses), bryophytic (with more mosses, lichens, and heath plants), and shrubby (with willow, dwarf birch, heath plants, mosses, and lichens).	Iceland
Ice desert	Polar area devoid of organic life.	Iceland (Jökulsárlón and Fjallsárlón ice lagoons, northern extremities touching the Arctic Circle)

Source: Own compilation based on: (Cox et al., 2016; Podbielkowski, 1997)

[a]The name comes from the galleries formed by the crowns of the trees. When rivers are narrow, the trees crowns on either side of the bank meet to form a shaded gallery

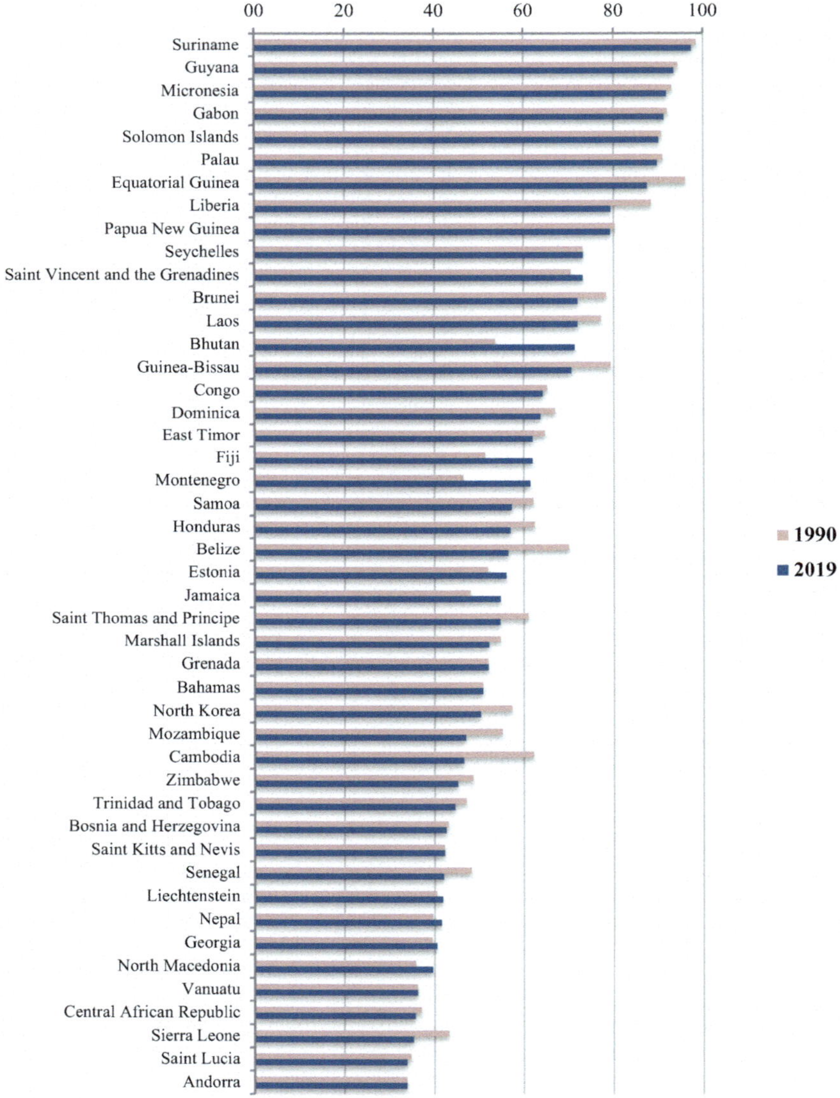

Fig. 4.1 WSE forest area in 1990 and 2019 (% of total area). (Source: Own compilation based on The World Bank)

However, forest cover has declined in most of the WSE. In countries such as Belize, Guinea-Bissau, Equatorial Guinea, Cambodia, Liberia, Mozambique, North Korea and Sierra Leone, forest cover declined by more than 7% between 1990 and 2019 (Fig. 4.1), equivalent to 149,000 km^2 of deforestation. For comparison, this is almost two-thirds the size of the United Kingdom (243,610 km^2). Deforestation was caused by the conversion of forest land to agricultural land, mainly for plantation crops and pasture, as well as for development and industrial areas (such as open pit mines). Forest cover was also reduced by fires.

Despite this, the WSE led the world in terms of forest cover. In the 2019 global ranking of the world's most forested countries, as many as 20 of the WSE were in the top 25 (Fig. 4.2). These were mainly the equatorial and subequatorial WSE with hot and humid climates, abundant rainfall and high sunshine with evergreen forest communities that are very species-rich (about 200 species per hectare).

Forests not only play an important role due to their ecological values, shaping bioclimatic conditions (e.g., providing oxygen in the process of photosynthesis, which cleans the atmosphere) and performing a protective function (including against floods and erosion, the progress of steppe processes), but also have a productive function. In the poorest WSE they provide wood that is used as construction material and fuel, while in the highly developed WSE, wood is mainly used for lumber, pulp, paper, and furniture. In addition to their productive function, forests also have a recreational function, improving people's quality of life and health.

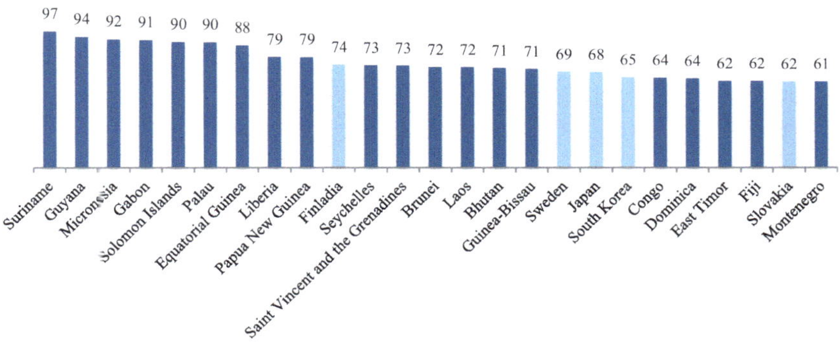

Fig. 4.2 Most forested WSE and global countries in 2019 (% of land area). (Source: Own compilation based on The World Bank)

Bibliography

Beard, J. S. (1955). A Note on Gallery Forests. *Ecology, 36*(2), 339–340.

Cox, C. B., Field, R., Ladle, R. J., & Moore, P. D. (2016). *Biogeography. An Ecological and Evolutionary Approach*. John Wiley & Sons Inc.

Labno, G. (2006). *Ecology, Encyclopedic Dictionary*. Europa Publishing House.

Podbielkowski, Z. (1997). *Szata Roslinna Ziemi, Wyd*. Kurpisz.

Radomski, A., & Gasinsk, M. (2004). *Elementy Oceanologii. Wprowadzenie do Srodowisk Morskich*. Wydawnictwo UJ.

Trzcinska, B. (2007). In K. Kuchinski (Ed.), *Roznice i Podobienstwa. Zroznicowanie Przyrodnicze*. Geografia, Difin.

CHAPTER 5

Soil Suitability for Agriculture in the World's Smallest Economies

Climatic conditions, and the associated natural vegetation influence the course of soil formation processes. The type of weathered soil, soil moisture, and the growing season of plants depend on the climate. Organic plant debris is the source of humus, accounting for 70–80% of soil organic matter. Thus, plant and climatic conditions determine the fertility of soils,[1] that is, their potential ability to provide plants with essential organic components, minerals, water, and soil air, which is richer in carbon dioxide than atmospheric air. Increasing fertility through fertilization and land reclamation enhances soil capacity. Thus, soil capacity is the result of fertility and agronomic treatments applied, which determines the productive value of the soil.

There are many classifications of soils. The strong influence of climatic zonation makes some of them (such as the Polish classification) based on climatic parameters, dividing soils into zonal and azonal. However, with a view to the economic use of soils, the international WRB (*World Reference Base*)[2] systematic, which is based on the utility of soils and their

[1] In addition to non-soil factors such as climate, vegetation, microorganisms, and topography soil fertility is determined by granulometric composition, mineralogy, organic matter content, sorption properties and chemical composition.

[2] The World Reference Base (WRB) is the international standard for soil classification systems endorsed by the International Union of Soil Sciences. FAO.

A. A. Teperek, *Economic Development in the World's Smallest Economies*, https://doi.org/10.1007/978-3-031-63810-7_5

agricultural suitability, was used to classify the WSE. On this basis, four subgroups were identified:

A. **Soils with high production potential**

a. Luvisol (high-activity clays) are found, among others, in Armenia, Burkina Faso (all of the country except river valleys), The Gambia (outside the Gambia River basin), Guinea (north, near the border with Senegal), Equatorial Guinea (continental), Cambodia (lowlands), Mali (south), Mozambique (Mozambique Highlands), Senegal (south), and Zimbabwe (north and central).
b. Cambisol (moderately developed) are found, among others, in Bosnia and Herzegovina (lowland areas), Burundi (on volcanic rocks), Cyprus, Eswatini (Low Weld), Georgia, North Korea (central part), Mongolia (north), and Rwanda (on volcanic rocks).
c. Chernozem (very dark and well-structured topsoil, secondary carbonates) are found, among others, in Armenia (in the mountains), Montenegro, Moldova (almost the entire area of the country), and Mongolia (in the steppe areas of the Eastern Mongolian Plain).

B. **Soils with medium and high, but conditional production potential**

a. Glyosol (groundwater-dominated) are found, among others, in Equatorial Guinea (coasts), Iceland (south and central parts), Congo (swampy areas of the Congo Basin), Mauritius, and Tajikistan (river valleys).
b. Fluvisol (containing alluvial deposits) are found, among others, in Belize (river basins of Belize, Hondo, Sibun), Botswana (Okawango River delta), Burkina Faso (Black Volta River delta, Kome), Cambodia (Mekong and Tonle Sap river valleys), Central African Republic (Ubangi and Ouham river valleys), Estonia (on islands), Eswatini (Umbeluzi and Usutu river valleys), Guyana (Essequibo River basin and delta), Malawi (Shire river valley), Mozambique (Zambezi river valley), Nepal (Tarai Phant plain), Nicaragua (Coco, San Juan river valleys), Suriname (Courantyne river basin), and Yemen (Wadi Hadramaut River basin).

c. Histosol (containing thick organic layers) are found, among others, in Benin (Atlantic coast), Brunei (Atlantic coast), Chad (around Lake Chad), East Timor (Timor Sea coast), Gabon (Atlantic coast), Guinea (Atlantic coast), Nauru (Lake Buada Lagoon coast), North Macedonia (Vardar River basins), Suriname (Atlantic coast), and Togo (Gulf of Guinea coast).
d. Planosol (stagnant water, abrupt textural difference) are found, among others, in Eswatini (Low Weld), Lesotho, and Niger (Air Highlands).
e. Andosol (containing allophones and humus complexes) are found, among others, in Mauritius, El Salvador (in mountain basins, river valleys, highlands), Samoa, Saint Thomas and Príncipe, Solomon Islands, Tonga, Vanuatu, and Zimbabwe (southern area in Limpopo and Lundi river basins).
f. Ferralsoil (dominance of kaolinite and oxides) are found, among others. in Barbados, the Bahamas, Bhutan (in the Lesser Himalayas), Cambodia (in lowland areas), Congo (southern Bateke Plateau area), East Timor (mountains), Georgia (the Kolkhida Plain), Haiti, Honduras, Jamaica, Madagascar, Malawi (Lilongwe Plain), Mozambique (Mozambique Plain), Saint Vincent and the Grenadines, Sierra Leone, (north), Suriname, and Togo.
g. Acrisol (low-activity clays) are found, among others, in Honduras (northern and northwestern parts of the country), Cambodia (at higher altitudes), Suriname.
h. Nitisol (low-activity clays) are found in Bosnia and Herzegovina (in karst areas), Cambodia (in the highlands), Guinea (all but the north and coasts), Guinea-Bissau (off the coasts), Laos (south), Malawi (on the southern plateaus), Montenegro, and Papua New Guinea.
i. Vertisol (high content or shrink–swell clays, alternating wet–dry conditions) are found, among others, in Barbados, Central African Republic (north), Haiti, Somalia (south), Trinidad and Tobago, and Togo (south).

C. Soils of very low fertility and agricultural suitability

a. Solonchak (high concentrations of soluble salts) are found, among others, in Afghanistan, and Mongolia.

b. Solonetz (containing a clay-enriched subsoil with high concentrations of exchangeable sodium) are found, among others, in Afghanistan (in the south of the country), Botswana (in the drainless depressions), and North Macedonia (the Sheep Field basin).
c. Arenosol (very sandy) are found, among others. in Botswana (all of the country except the Okavango River delta), Chad (except the Chad basin and areas around Lake Chad), Eritrea (coastal plain), Fiji (small islands), Kiribati, Maldives, Mali (northern part of the country), Marshall Islands, Mauritania (northern part of the country), Micronesia, Namibia (eastern part of the country), Niger (south), and Yemen.
d. Regosol (no significant profile development) are found, among others, in Afghanistan, Bhutan (in the Greater Himalayas), Eritrea (Eritrean Highlands), Mali (west), Mauritania (north), Mauritius (coast), Mongolia (mountains), Namibia (desert), Nepal (mountains), South Sudan, and Tajikistan (foothills and plains).
e. Podzol (subsoil accumulation of organic matter and oxides) are found, among others, in Montenegro, Estonia (almost the entire area), and North Macedonia (mountains).
f. Leptosol (thin or with many coarse fragments) are found, among others, in Afghanistan (in the Hindu Kush mountains), Albania (in the Dinaric mountains), Andorra (in the Pyrenees), Armenia (in the Little Caucasus mountains), Bhutan (in the Greater Himalayas), El Salvador (in the Cordillera), Eritrea (Eritrean highlands), Georgia (the higher regions of the Lesser and Greater Caucasus), Kyrgyzstan (in the Tienshan mountains), Liechtenstein (in the Alps), and Rwanda (the slopes of the Wirunga mountains).

D. **Soils completely unsuitable for agriculture**

a. Cryosol (permafrost-affected) are found, among others, in Iceland (north, Vatnajökull glacier), and Mongolia (western and central Khentej mountain range).

The typology of the soils allowed formulating some conclusions. The most common soils in the WSE are those *with medium and high, but conditional production potential*, that is, excessively wet, equatorial and heavy clay soils (including Glysol, Fluvisol, Histosol, Planosol, Andosol, Ferralsoil, Acrisol, Nitisol, Vertisol) and those *with very low fertility and suitability for agriculture* (including Solonchak, Solonetz, Arenosol, Regosol, Podzol, Leptosol). The presence of this type of soil is mainly due to the location of most WSE in an equatorial climate zone, with unique flora and fauna that contribute to the formation of soil humus, as well as the location in a dry tropical climate zone, with dry vegetation and poor quality decomposed organic matter. The poor soil quality of most of the WSE was also related to the rocky terrain, as most of them have a mountainous or upland surface.

Although, the importance of soils declines with the economic development of countries, and cropping patterns and yields are more determined by the level of agricultural culture, the natural production of soils and their agricultural suitability still play an overriding role for most of the WSE. It should be noted that more than half of the countries analyzed represent a very low level of economic development (GDP of less than US$ 2500 per capita in 2019). A large part of the population of these underdeveloped and very underdeveloped WSE relies on low-productivity agriculture to meet only their own food needs. In addition to climate and agricultural policies, soil plays a key role in food production.

Soil is the primary resource for land use. At the same time, soil—that is, its type and fertility—is the main determinant of land use. There are three categories of land use: agricultural land, forest land and other land and wasteland (man-made, e.g., communication, service, recreational areas, and natural, e.g., swamps, deserts). Most agricultural land (more than 70% of the total land area in 2019) had the following WSE: Burundi, Comoros, Djibouti, El Salvador, Eritrea, Lesotho, Madagascar, Moldova, Mongolia, Rwanda and Somalia (Fig. 5.1). In contrast, less agricultural land (less than 7% of the total land area in 2019) was held by the forested WSE located in the equatorial zone, such as Belize, Brunei, Guyana, Monaco, Papua New Guinea, Seychelles, Solomon Islands and Suriname, and the highly industrialized and urbanized WSE, such as Cyprus, Monaco, and San Marino (Fig. 5.1). By comparison, the global average share of agricultural land in total land area was 36.5%.

The distribution of agricultural land in the WSE is a function of two key elements population pressure and the degree of suitability of soil conditions for agriculture. Agricultural land includes: arable land (i.e., land under intermittent crops such as cereals, intermittent meadows for mowing or grazing, land under market or kitchen gardens, and temporarily

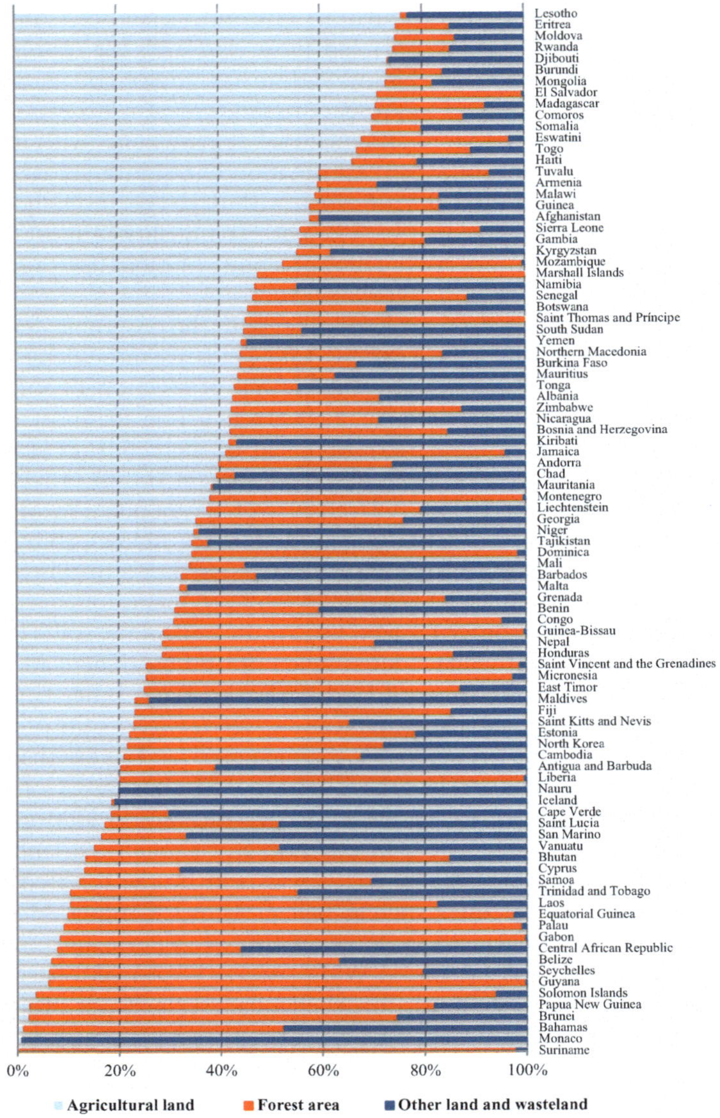

Fig. 5.1 WSE land use structure in 2019. (%) (Source: Own compilation based on CIA The Factbook)

fallow land); permanent crops (i.e., land under crops that do not require annual replanting, such as orchards, fruit bushes, vineyards, plantations) and permanent pastures and meadows (i.e., natural or artificial meadows and thickets that can be used for grazing livestock).

Arable land is concentrated in areas with the most fertile soils (Table 5.1). In the WSE group, the largest share of arable land was found in Moldova (55.1% of the total area), which is covered by more than three-fourths fertile black soils, namely very dark and well-structured black soils with a high humus content. There is also a large proportion of arable land in Rwanda (47% of the total area), covered by Cambisols; Comoros (46.7% of the total area), which is covered by Andosols containing humus complexes; Togo (45.2% of the total area) is covered by Nitisols and Vertisols; The Gambia (41% of the total area) is covered by high-activity clays Luvisols; Burundi (38.9% of the total area) is covered by Cambisols and Veritisols; Haiti (38.5% of the total area) is covered by Ferralsoils and Veritisols; Mauritius (38.4% of the total area) is covered by Ferralsoils, Glyosols, and Andosols.

In contrast, the lowest share of arable land in total land area (less than 4%) characterizes the heavily forested WSE (e.g., Bhutan, Brunei, Congo, Guyana, Papua New Guinea, Solomon Islands, Suriname), the highly urbanized WSE (e.g., Andorra, Monaco), and the WSE with unfavorable soil conditions for agriculture (e.g., Botswana, Chad, Djibouti, Iceland, Mauritania, Mongolia, Namibia, Somalia, Tuvalu, Yemen). These countries, whose soils were not used for arable farming, have a high percentage of permanent grasslands and meadows (Table 5.1). In Djibouti, Eritrea, Mongolia, and Somalia, for example, pastures and grasslands account for more than 68% of the total area. They are dominated by nomadic pastoralism practiced by nomads, involving extensive grazing of cattle, sheep, camels, and moving with herds from place to place in search of food, water, firewood, or pasture.

For the WSE group as a whole, agricultural land accounted for 36% of its total area, of which 12% was arable land. In comparison, these shares for the world were 36.5% and 11%, respectively, so the group had similar shares. The average group's share of arable land was associated with medium to low soil fertility in most of the WSE. To improve their quality, many of the WSE use various agrochemical and agrotechnical treatments. Agrochemical treatments include mineral and organic fertilization,

Table 5.1 WSE agriculture area structure in 2019 (%)

WSE	*Arable land*	*Permanent crops*	*Permanent pastures and meadows*	*Agricultural land as a percentage of total land area*	*WSE*	*Arable land*	*Permanent crops*	*Permanent pastures and meadows*	*Agricultural land as a percentage of total land area*
	% of the total land area					*% of the total land area*			
Moldova	55.1	9.1	10.7	74.9	Dominica	8.0	24.0	2.7	34.7
Rwanda	47.0	10.1	17.4	74.5	Marshall Islands	7.8	31.2	11.7	50.7
Comoros	46.7	29.6	8.1	84.4	Eritrea	6.8	0.0	68.3	75.1
Togo	45.2	3.8	18.4	67.4	Kyrgyzstan	6.7	0.4	48.3	55.4
The Gambia	41.0	0.5	14.6	56.1	Mozambique	6.4	0.3	49.6	56.3
Burundi	38.9	15.6	18.8	73.3	Laos	6.2	0.7	3.7	10.6
Haiti	38.5	10.2	17.7	66.4	Tajikistan	6.1	0.9	27.7	34.7
Mauritius	38.4	2.0	3.4	43.8	Madagascar	6.0	1.0	64.1	71.1
Malawi	38.2	1.4	19.6	59.2	Georgia	5.8	1.8	27.9	35.5
Salvador	33.1	10.9	30.7	74.7	Mali	5.6	0.1	28.4	34.1
Malta	28.4	3.9	0.0	32.3	Liberia	5.2	2.1	20.8	28.1
Barbados	25.6	2.3	4.7	32.6	Saint Lucia	4.9	11.5	1.0	17.4
Sierra Leone	23.4	2.3	30.5	56.2	East Timor	4.9	10.1	10.1	25.1
Benin	22.9	3.5	4.9	31.3	Trinidad and Tobago	4.9	4.3	1.4	10.6
Cambodia	22.7	0.9	8.5	32.1	South Sudan	4.4	4.7	11.3	56.4
Albania	22.3	3.0	17.4	42.7	Equatorial Guinea	4.3	2.1	3.7	10.1
Tonga	22.2	15.3	5.6	43.1	Chad	3.9	0.0	35.7	39.6

Burkina Faso	22.0	37.0	21.9	80.9	Belize	3.3	1.4	2.2	6.9
Bosnia and Herzegovina	19.7	2.0	20.5	42.2	Central African Republic	2.9	0.1	5.1	8.1
North Korea	19.5	1.9	0.4	21.8	Samoa	2.8	7.8	1.8	12.4
Saint Kitts and Nevis	19.2	0.4	3.5	23.1	Bhutan	2.6	0.3	10.7	13.6
Liechtenstein	18.8	0.0	18.8	37.6	Kiribati	2.5	39.5	0.0	42.0
Senegal	17.4	0.3	29.1	46.8	Micronesia	2.3	19.7	3.5	25.5
San Marino	16.7	0.0	0.0	16.7	Yemen	2.2	0.6	41.7	44.5
Northern Macedonia	16.4	1.4	26.5	44.3	Palau	2.2	4.3	4.3	10.8
Armenia	15.8	1.9	42.0	59.7	Seychelles	2.2	4.3	0.0	6.5
Nepal	15.1	1.1	12.5	28.7	Guyana	2.1	0.1	6.2	8.4
Estonia	14.9	0.1	7.2	22.2	Somalia	1.8	0.0	68.5	70.3
Montenegro	12.9	1.2	24.1	38.2	Andorra	1.7	0.0	38.3	40.0
Saint Vincent and the Grenadines	12.8	7.7	5.1	25.6	Congo	1.6	0.2	29.3	31.1
Nicaragua	12.5	2.5	27.2	42.2	Vanuatu	1.6	10.3	3.4	15.3
Niger	12.3	0.1	22.7	35.1	Gabon	1.2	0.6	17.2	19.0

(*continued*)

Table 5.1 (continued)

WSE	*Arable land*	*Permanent crops*	*Permanent pastures and meadows*	*Agricultural land as a percentage of total land area*	*WSE*	*Arable land*	*Permanent crops*	*Permanent pastures and meadows*	*Agricultural land as a percentage of total land area*
	% of the total land area					*% of the total land area*			
Afghanistan	11.8	0.3	46.0	58.1	Iceland	1.2	0.0	17.5	18.7
Guinea	11.8	2.8	43.5	58.1	Namibia	1.0	0.0	46.2	47.2
Cape Verde	11.7	0.7	6.2	18.6	Bahamas	0.8	0.4	0.2	1.4
Jamaica	11.1	9.2	21.1	41.4	Brunei	0.8	1.1	0.6	2.5
Zimbabwe	10.1	0.3	31.3	41.7	Papua New Guinea	0.7	1.5	0.4	2.6
Lesotho	10.1	0.1	65.9	76.1	Solomon Islands	0.7	2.9	0.3	3.9
Maldives	10.0	10.0	3.3	23.3	Botswana	0.6	0.0	45.2	45.8
Cyprus	9.8	3.2	0.4	13.4	Mauritania	0.4	0.0	38.1	38.5
Eswatini	9.8	0.8	57.7	68.3	Mongolia	0.4	0.0	72.6	73.0
Honduras	9.1	4.0	15.7	28.8	Suriname	0.4	0.0	0.1	0.5
Saint Thomas and Príncipe	9.1	40.6	1.0	50.7	Djibouti	0.1	0.0	73.3	73.4
Antigua and Barbuda	9.0	2.3	9.0	20.3	Monaco	0.0	1.0	0.0	1.0
Fiji	9.0	4.7	9.6	23.3	Nauru	0.0	20.0	0.0	20.0
Grenada	8.8	20.6	2.9	32.3	Tuvalu	0.0	60.0	0.0	60.0
Guinea-Bissau	8.2	6.9	29.7	44.8					

Source: Own compilation based on CIA The Factbook; The World Bank

application of pesticides, and agrotechnical treatments include scarification, mechanical destruction of weeds and land reclamation by draining or irrigating the land, among others. In terms of irrigation, Afghanistan is a leader among the WSE. As much as 32,000 km^2 of the country is irrigated (5% of the total area). This compares to one-fifth of the irrigated area in the entire European Union (154,500 km^2 of land in the EU is irrigated). North Korea ranks second in the WSE group (14,600 km^2, or 12% of its total area), closely followed by Nepal (13,300 km^2, or 9% of its total area). In both Nepal and North Korea, irrigated land accounts for a much larger percentage of the total area than in Afghanistan. Irrigation and other treatments used in these countries not only contribute to permanently maintaining the favorable genetic characteristics of the soil, but also help to improve these characteristics.

Soil conditions determine the structure of agricultural production in the WSE. Some crops, such as sugar beets, require developed soil types, so Moldova, rich in very fertile Chernozem soils, has led the way in the production of this crop. The same is true for sunflower, which requires good soil and sunshine. Rice's soil requirements are not so exacting, but the best yields are obtained on clay soils with low permeability, such those found in Cambodia and Laos, in the humid monsoon climate zone. Coffee, on the other hand, requires highly permeable, airy and firm soils, which is why it is grown in the fertile tropical soils of Honduras and Nicaragua. In addition, tobacco yields best on Luvisol soils with favorable physical and chemical properties, such as those found in northern and central Zimbabwe. As a result, Zimbabwe is one of the world's leading tobacco producers.

Soils, in addition to their productive function of creating space for plants to take root, which influences the agricultural production (size, quality, and structure) of the WSE, also have other important economic functions. They are land for urbanized areas of the WSE, as well as land for the construction of transportation and recreational infrastructure. They are areas of industrialization and exploration of natural resources used in industry and construction, such as clay, sand. They have hygienic and sanitary functions, as the inhabitants of the WSE store pollutants and wastes containing nutrients elements and hazardous substances in them. It is worth mentioning that in addition to economic functions, soils also have ecological functions (including retention, filtration). As an integral component of all ecosystems and an element of animate nature, they have the ability to produce biomass, in which the processes of decomposition and synthesis of mineral and organic compounds take place. By fulfilling social functions, soils are a kind of archive of human settlement in a given area, which gives them both informative and historical value. Thus, this biologically active surface that is the soil performs a very important and multifaceted role in the functioning of countries, while affecting disparities in their socioeconomic development.

CHAPTER 6

Geomorphic Features of the World's Smallest Economies

Terrain, along with climate and soil conditions, are the main natural factor that determine the level of economic development of a country. It is the result of geological processes that took place over 500 million years.[1] These processes included both endogenous processes (i.e., rock-forming movements, land-forming processes, volcanic processes, earthquakes) that caused the uplift and differentiation of the land, and exogenous processes that occurred as a result of external forces such as wind, temperature, glaciers, ice sheets, seas (i.e., weathering, erosion, mass movements, accumulation) that contributed to the flattening of their surfaces. As a result of the aforementioned internal and external processes, as well as human activities, new surface landforms have been created, and existing ones have been destroyed. Consequently, the relief of the Earth's surface and that of the WSE is diverse, manifested in the variety of elevation forms including the macrostructures of mountains, highlands, and lowlands. These three categories of elevation were used to divide the WSE into subgroups for detailed analysis. The aim was to determine the extent to which the surface topography influences the economic development of the WSE.

[1] Although the age of the Earth is about 4.6 billion years, it includes: the Cenozoic (11,700–145 million years), Mesozoic (145–299 million years), Paleozoic (299–541 million years), and Precambrian (541–4.6 billion years) eras. Most of the mountains were formed in the Paleozoic.

A. A. Teperek, *Economic Development in the World's Smallest Economies*, https://doi.org/10.1007/978-3-031-63810-7_6

The first subgroup identified was the mountain WSE (Table 6.1), which included 21 countries with an average altitude of more than 100 meters above sea level and covered by mountain ranges in more than 60% of the countries surveyed. Their origin is related to the theory of tectonics and the movement of lithospheric plates, which can involve, sliding apart (spreading zone), colliding (subduction zone) or parallel vertical or horizontal movement, resulting in the formation of mountains over millions of years.

Mountain ranges with the highest peaks over 7000 meters are found in Afghanistan, Bhutan, Kyrgyzstan, Nepal, and Tajikistan. Middle mountain ranges are found in Armenia, Georgia, Mongolia, Rwanda, among others, while lower mountain ranges with the highest peaks below 2500 meters are found in Dominica, Comoros, Solomon Islands and Saint Thomas and Príncipe (Table 6.1).

The lowest point for almost half of the WSE is sea level, defined by the Atlantic, Indian or Pacific Oceans. However, there are countries in the WSE group, such as Andorra, Lesotho and Rwanda, whose lowest points reach much higher elevations. In Andorra it is the Gran Valira River (840 m), in Lesotho—the Orange and Makhaleng Rivers (1380 m) and in Rwanda—the Ruzizi River (950 m).

The highland WSE subgroup, with an average altitude of 300–1000 meters above sea level is the most numerous (43 countries). They are located on all continents, with almost half of them situated in Africa (Table 6.2). Although, some of the highland WSE have mountains that reach several thousand meters (e.g., El Salvador with Cerro El Pital—2730 meters above sea level, Papua New Guinea with the highest peak of Mount Wilhelm at 4509 meters above sea level, Yemen with Jabal An-Nabi Shu'ayb—3666 meters above sea level), they are not classified because the mountain WSE subgroup, since mountains cover less than 50% of their land area.

The relief of many of the highland WSE is in the form of plateaus, or plains bordered by steep slopes (e.g., the Central African Republic with Mont Ngaoui, Jamaica with its highest peak Blue Mountain Peak, the Congo with Mount Nabemba, Madagascar with Maromokotro, Mali with Hombori,and Zimbabwe with Mount Nyangani).

In some countries, basins, or depressions with flat or hilly bottoms extend into the highlands (e.g., the Kalahari Basin in Botswana, the Chad Basin in Chad, the Danakil Basin in Eritrea, the Niger Basin in Niger). Two countries have depressions: Djibouti with Lake Assal at 155 meters below sea level and Eritrea with Lake Kulul—75 meters below sea level (Table 6.2). However, the vast majority of the countries studied (28 countries) have sea level as their lowest point.

Table 6.1 Mountain WSE surface topography

No	*WSE*	*Average altitude*	*Surface relief*	*Highest altitude*		*Lowest altitude*	
		m MSL		*Name*	*m MSL*	*name*	*m MSL*
1.	Afghanistan	1885	Afghanistan is located in the heart of Asia's southern mountain belt. Its area is 80% covered by mountains, among which more than 50% are mountains exceeding 2000 meters. The eastern part occupied by the Hindu Kush Mountains, while the central part is covered by the central Afghan highlands. To the north of them, the mountains and highlands transition into the highland plains of the Amu-Darya basin (region of Afghan Turkestan). In the south there are deserts: Registan (sandy) and Dasht-e Margo (gravel). There are no lowlands, except for the low-lying Sistan Basin.The four major river systems are the Amu Darya (Oxus) in the north, flowing into the Aral Sea; the Harirūd and Morghāb in the west; the Helmand in the southwest; and the Kabul in the east, flowing into the Indus.	Noshak	7492	Amu Darya River	258
2.	Andorra	1996	Most of the country is roughed and mountainous, with little flat surface, situated in a single drainage basin, but its main stream, the Riu Valira, has two distinct branches and six open basins.	Coma Pedrosa	2942	Gran Valira River	840
3.	Armenia	1792	Located in Transcaucasia on the border of Europe and Asia, Armenia has more than 90% of its area covered by mountains. The topography includes the high Armenian Plateau and three major mountain ranges, the Lesser Caucasus Mountains in the north, the Vardenis Range in central Armenia, and the Zangezur Range in the southeast. There are many extinct volcanoes (including Mount Aragats) as well as lava uplands and lava fields (the Aragac lava fields cover an area of about 9000 km^2), along with fold ranges crisscrossed by sinkholes. Frequent earthquakes indicate that the process of uplifting the mountains is not yet complete.	Mount Aragats	4090	River Debed	400

(*continued*)

Table 6.1 (continued)

No	*WSE*	*Average altitude*	*Surface relief*	*Highest altitude*		*Lowest altitude*	
		m MSL		*Name*	*m MSL*	*name*	*m MSL*
4.	Bhutan	2220	This is one of the highest regions on Earth, located in the eastern part of the Himalayas, and is covered with high altitude mountains and irregular terrain that vary in elevation by several thousand feet within a short distance. The mountains are a series of parallel ranges with a north–south alignment. A small part of the area is occupied by steep hills separated by narrow valleys. Numerous rivers flow between the ranges, most of which drain south to the Brahmaputra River in India.	Gangkar Puensum	7570	Drangme Chhu River	97
5.	Burundi	1504	Most of the area is occupied by plateaus crisscrossed by mountain ranges, especially in the west, which run from north to south and extend into Rwanda. From the mountains to the east, the terrain descends gradually toward the southeast and the southern border. The main rivers Kanyaru and Kagera, the southernmost sources of the Nile, separate the country from Rwanda. The main lakes are Tanganyika, Cohoha, and Rweru.	Heha Mountain	2684	Lake Tanganyika	772
6.	Comoros	1180	Mountainous and volcanic in origin, the islands have with their highest peak, Kartala, which is as an active volcano, located near the southern tip of Grande Comore Island. In the center of Grande Comore is a desert lava field. To the north, a series of volcanic peaks rise from the plateau. Anjouan Island, located to the southeast, features steep hills, while Mohéli, to the west of Anjouan, has wide and fertile valleys.	Mount Karthala on the Great Chamber	2360	Indian Ocean	0

7.	Dominica	1447	A rugged island covered with many peaks, ridges, and ravines. It has several volcanic mountains above 1200 meters, featuring peaks in the form of volcanic cones with lava craters and small lakes of boiling water (Boiling Lake near Roseau—the second largest thermally active lake in the world). The coastal edge of the island is a thin strip bounded by mountain slopes that extend directly down to the shore.	Morne Diablotins	1447	Caribbean Sea	0
8.	Georgia	1432	More than 54% of the area is covered by mountains with the Greater Caucasus to the north and the Lesser Caucasus to the south. These two mountain systems are separated by a latitudinal belt of tectonic mid-mountain depressions that constitute the watershed between the Black Sea and the Caspian Sea drainage basins. The western part of the tectonic depression is occupied by the Kolkhida Plain, the eastern part of which includes a series of flat basins that are located in the valley of the Kura River (1514 km). The Black Sea coast in the central part is flat, low and marshy, while in the northern part it is rocky.	Mt'a Shkhara	5193	Black Sea	0
9.	Kyrgyzstan	2988	More than 90% of the area is occupied by the mighty, seismically active Tien-Shan mountains and their associated valleys and basins (including Lake Issyk-kul—the second largest mountain lake in the world). The western part of the country is occupied by the basins (the Fergana Valley). Just over 5% of Kyrgyzstan's land is irrigated.	Yengish Chokusu	7439	Kara Darya River	435
10.	Lesotho	2161	Country's entire area is at an altitude of more than 1000 meters, as the only country in the world. More than 80% of its area is occupied by volcanic mountains, crisscrossed by deep valleys. Along the southeastern border runs the Drakensberg mountain range. South Africa's longest river, the Orange, flows out of the northwestern Maloti Mountains. Toward the west, the landscape changes from mountainous to highland.	Thabana Ntlenyana	3482	The confluence of the Orange and Makhaleng rivers	1400

(*continued*)

Table 6.1 (continued)

No	*WSE*	*Average altitude*	*Surface relief*	*Highest altitude*		*Lowest altitude*	
		m MSL		*Name*	*m MSL*	*name*	*m MSL*
11.	Liechtenstein	1115	Area is divided into a narrow plain that borders the right bank of the Rhine (drained and converted to agricultural land in the 1930s), which occupies 60% of the western part of the country, and an upland-mountainous region (the Rhaetian Alps) extending into the eastern and central parts.	Grauspitz	2599	River Rhine	430
12.	Mongolia	1528	More than 80% of the area is occupied by a vast plateau, except for a mountainous section in the extreme west dominated by the Altay Mountains, the Hentiyn, along the border with Russia, and the Hangayn, in west-central Mongolia. The mountain ranges are separated by large tectonic basins (including the Great Lakes Depression) filled with lakes (including Lake Uvs). To the east stretches the Mongolian Plateau, and to the south are the vast expanses of the rocky Gobi Desert.	Khuiten Peak	4374	Hoh Nuur Lake	518
13.	Montenegro	1086	Coast area is covered by a narrow strip of lowland with beaches and bays (including the Bay of Kotor—the world's southernmost fjord). The lowland region is formed by the Zeta Plain and the Zeta River Valley region with Lake Scutari. The southwestern coastline is highly elevated (the Rumija, the Sutorman, the Orjen, and the Lovcen mountains). In the northwest, there are mountain ranges (the Durmitor) rich in forests, and mountain lakes. The Piva, Tara, Moraca, and Cehotina rivers have carved deep canyons (the Tara Canyon—the deepest canyon in Europe at 1300 meters).	Bad Kolata	2534	Adriatic Sea	0

14.	Namibia	1141	Most of the area is largely occupied by an elevated, waterless plateau descending toward a narrow coastal plain with sandy wastelands and tall, reddish dunes. The coastal strip includes the Namib Desert, and the eastern region is part of the Kalahari Desert. The borders are formed by the four permanent rivers: the Kunene and Okavango in the north, the Zambezi in the northeast and the Orange in the south.	Konigstein	2573	Atlantic Ocean	0
15.	Nepal	3265	More than 80% of the area is occupied by mountain ranges (Mahabharat, Churia, and the Himalayan), stretching across the northern part of the country from east to west and featuring 90 peaks exceeding 7000 meters. The southern area, forming the northern end of the Indo-Gangetic Plain, is occupied by the alluvial plain.	Mount Everest	8849	Mukhiyapatti Musharniya	59
16.	Cape Verde	1415	Islands of volcanic origin with a rocky, cliff-like coastline, surrounded by numerous rings of coral reefs. The surface of the islands is subject to intense wind erosion, making their relief particularly varied. There is an active volcano on Fogo island.	Pico do Fogo	2829	Atlantic Ocean	0
17.	Rwanda	1598	Its area is 95% part of the Great East African Plateau, descending from west to east. The water systems of the Nile and Congo rivers pass in a north–south direction, (the Nile drains about 80% of the country and the rest comes from the Congo via the Rusizi River). There are many lakes are there (including Lake Kivu—one of the 20 deepest lakes in the world). The central and western area is dominated by mountains (part of the Albertine Rift), running north to south along the western border. The highest peak is in the Virunga volcano chain The eastern border consists of savanna, plains, and swamps.	Volcan Karisimbi	4507	Ruzizi River	950

(*continued*)

Table 6.1 (continued)

No	*WSE*	*Average altitude*	*Surface relief*	*Highest altitude*		*Lowest altitude*	
		m MSL		*Name*	*m MSL*	*name*	*m MSL*
18.	Tajikistan	3186	More than half of the area lies above 3000 meters, and only 7% of the area is below 1000 meters. The eastern part is occupied by the latitude-aligned Pamir ranges. In the central part the Alai Mountains are located. In the southwest, the terrain descends into extensive valleys (the Kafirnigan and Vakhsh valleys), which are also found in the western part (the Fergana Valley). In the south, the Panj River separates southern Tajikistan from northern Afghanistan. The country is located in a seismically active area, where earthquakes often occur.	Ismoili Somoni	7495	Syr River Darya	300
19.	East Timor	1482	Most of the area is occupied by mountains (Gunung Tata Mai Lau) with many gorges and waterfalls. Lowlands are limited only to the coastal zone. The island belongs to a seismically active zone.	Mount Ramelau on the island of Timor	2963	Timor Sea	0
20.	Solomon Islands	1166	Area is dominated by volcanic forested mountain ranges crisscrossed by precipitous, narrow valleys. The highest peak is on Guadalcanal, an island that also contains the country's most extensive alluvial plains. Extensive coral reefs and lagoons surround the coasts of the islands, some of which are coral atolls.	Mount Popomanaseu on the island of Guadalcanal	2335	Pacific Ocean	0
21.	Saint Thomas and Prince	1122	The area consists of the two main islands of Saint Thomas and Príncipe and six small offshore islands that are uplifted, extinct volcanic cones, making the islands mountainous.	Pico de Sao Tome on the island of Saint Thomas	2024	Atlantic Ocean	0

Source: Own compilation based on: CIA The World Factbook; (Frydrych et al., 2016)

Table 6.2 Highland WSE surface topography

No	*WSE*	*Average altitude*	*Surface relief*	*Highest altitude*		*Lowest altitude*	
		m MSL		*Name*	*m MSL*	*Name*	*m MSL*
1.	Albania	708	Over 70% of the area is occupied by hills and mountains, which form a southern continuation of the Dinaric system, descending abruptly onto the plains and then onto a coastal lowland. The most important rivers (the Drin, the Buna, the Mat, the Shkumbin, the Seman, and the Vijose) flow into the Adriatic. Albania shares Lake Scutari (Skadarsko Jezero) with Serbia and Montenegro, Lake Ohrid (Ohridsko Jezero) with Macedonia, and Lake Prespe (Prespansko Jezero) with Macedonia and Greece.	Korab	2764	Adriatic Sea	0
2.	Bosnia and Herzegovina	500	Most of the area is occupied by hills, mountains, and valleys, with over 50% forested. The country is divided into three regions: high plains and plateaus along the northern border (including the valley of the Sava River), low mountains in the center, and the higher Dinaric Alps, which cover the rest of the area.	Maglic	2386	Adriatic Sea	5
3.	Botswana	993	Most of the area is occupied by a vast plateau, which divides the country into two regions. The eastern part consists of hilly bush country and grassland (veld). In the northwest are the Tsodilo Hills. To the west lie the Okavango Swamps and the Kalahari Desert, along with the southeastern highlands (including the Damara, and the Nama). The sources of year-round surface water are the Chobe River in the north, the Limpopo River (1600 km) in the southeast, and the Okavango River in the northwest, which forms the swampy delta Lake Ngami and Lake Xau.	Otse Hill	1491	Confluence of the Limpopo and Shashe Rivers	513

(*continued*)

Table 6.2 (continued)

No	*WSE*	*Average altitude*	*Surface relief*	*Highest altitude*		*Lowest altitude*	
		m MSL		*Name*	*m MSL*	*Name*	*m MSL*
4.	Brunei	478	Most of the area covers uplands and lowlands, with the Tomabo Mountains in the southeastern part of the country.	Bukit Pagon	1850	South China Sea	0
5.	Central African Republic	635	Most of the country is occupied by the Azande Plateau, which in the northeast passes into mountain ranges (Bongo Massif, Yade Massif). The highland area gradually descends in a northerly direction and passes into the Lake Chad Basin and in a southerly direction into the Congo Basin. The watershed between the Lake Chad Basin and the Congo Basin runs through the highlands.	Mont Ngaoui	1410	Ubangi River	335
6.	Chad	543	Most of the country is occupied by the vast Chad Basin, bounded by highlands (including Wadai) and mountains (including Tibesti). To the west is the only large body of water—Lake Chad, which is shrinking due to the expansion of the Sahara. It is fed by only two rivers: the Chari and the Logone. Extending to the west, the Bodele Basin sinkhole and adjacent areas are covered with sand dunes (mobile in the eastern part).	Emi Koussi	3445	Djourab	160
7.	Congo	430	Most of the area is occupied by a plateau (500–1000 m), forming bands of hills that define the western edge of the Congo River valley, which, along with its largest tributary, the Ubangi, marks the southern boundary. To the northeast stretch the flat and swampy plains of the Congo Basin, while to the west the plateau descends to a 60-kilometer strip of lowland coastline that forms the maritime boundary.	Mount Nabemba	1020	Atlantic Ocean	0

8.	Djibouti	430	The Afar tectonic depression divides the country into an upland southern part and a mountainous northern part. Between the two is the salt lake Asaal, which is the lowest point in Africa (-155 meters).	Mousa Ali	2028	Lake Assal	-155
9.	Eritrea	853	Most of the area is covered by mountains and highlands, with only a narrow strip of desert coastal plain stretching along the coastal of the Red Sea. Parallel to it rises the Danakil Mountains, and to the west is the Danakil Basin, a tectonic sinkhole that is an extension of the East African Rift, along with the Eritrean Highlands (part of the Abyssinian Highlands). Eritrea also includes the Dahlak Archipelago.	Emba Soira	3018	Kulul Lake	-75
10.	Eswatini	305	Along the eastern border are the Lebombo Mountains at an altitude of around 600 meters. The mountains are interrupted by the canyons of three rivers: the Ngwavuma, the Great Usutu and the Mbuluzi. The western border, with an average altitude of 1200 meters above sea level (MSL), lies on the edge of an escarpment.	Emlembe	1862	Maputo River	21
11.	Equatorial Guinea	577	The country's continental area consists of a highland-mountainous region with isolated peaks of volcanic origin (an extension of the Crystal Mountains) and a belt of coastal lowlands. The volcanic island of Bioko, located on the continental shelf (160 km from the mainland), is where the capital, Malabo, is situated. It is characterized by undulating coastlines with three volcanoes in the central part, including one active volcano, Santa Isabel.	Pico Basile on Bioko Island	3008	Atlantic Ocean	0
12.	Fiji	662	Of the 322 islands, the two largest, covering 87% of the area (Viti Levu and Vanua Levusa), are volcanic. The low mountains of the large islands slope gently toward the coast. The area of most low-lying atolls does not exceed 1 km^2.	Tomanivi on the island of Viti Levu	1324	Pacific Ocean	0

(*continued*)

Table 6.2 (continued)

No	*WSE*	*Average altitude*	*Surface relief*	*Highest altitude*		*Lowest altitude*	
		m MSL		*Name*	*m MSL*	*Name*	*m MSL*
13.	Gabon	377	Most of the area includes a plateau and mountains. The plateau covers the north, east, and most of the south, and it is divided into distinct blocks, such as the Crystal Mountains and the Chaillu Massif. These blocks transit into the coastal lowlands toward the coast. The northern coastline is deeply indented with bays, estuaries, and deltas as far south as the mouth of the Ogooué River. Further south, the coast becomes more precipitous. Virtually the entire territory is contained in the basin of the Ogooué River (1100 km).	Mount Bengoue	1070	Atlantic Ocean	0
14.	Grenada	420	Low mountains in the central part feature lakes, such as Lake Antoine and Grand Etang Lake, with the highest peak, Mount St. Catherine, rising to 840 m. Other major mountains include Mount Granby and South East Mountain, from which several small rivers with waterfalls flow into the sea. The coastline contains several bays.	Mount Saint Catherine	840	Caribbean Sea	0
15.	Guinea	472	The area divided into four geographic regions: a narrow plain, a coastal belt and the rocky Kaloum Peninsula, where the country's capital is located (Lower Guinea); the pastoral Fouta Djallon Plateau in the central part (Middle Guinea); the northern savannah (Upper Guinea); and a southeastern rainforest region (Forest Guinea). The Niger River, Gambia River, and Senegal River are among the 22 West African rivers that have their origins in Guinea.	Mont Nimba	1752	Atlantic Ocean	0

16.	Haiti	470	Most of the country is covered by hills and mountains. Three principal mountain ranges stretch across the country: one runs east and west along the southern peninsula, while the others extend northwest between the mountains stretch the plains: the Plaine du Nord extending in the northeast, the Artibonite and Cul-de-Sac plains reaching west to the Gulf of Gonave. The gulf lies between a long southern peninsula and a shorter northern one formed by the irregular coastline.	Pic la Selle	2680	Caribbean Sea	0
17.	Honduras	684	Much of the area is occupied by the Cordillera, which is cut by river valleys and tectonic collapses into numerous volcanic massifs and mountain ranges (including Sierra de Agalta, Sierra de Opalaca). Along the Caribbean Sea stretches a narrow strip of lowlands dotted with coastal lagoons (including the Caratasca Lagoon on the Mosquito Coast). The Pacific coast is formed by the encroaching Gulf of Fonseca, characterized by its peninsulas and bays.	Cerro Las Minas	2870	Caribbean Sea	0
18.	Iceland	557	Area is formed by a young post-glacial island, eroded from the Mid-Atlantic Ridge, and crossed by three rifts, where numerous volcanoes have formed (Hekla, Laki, Askja, Hvannadalshnukur), making the country one of the most volcanically active areas on Earth. The north part of the island has valleys with steep slopes, while the central part is occupied by a high, partially glaciated plateau surrounded by mountains. Glaciers occupy more than one-tenth of the country's area (the largest is Vatnajokull, with an area of 8300 km^2). In the southwest, there are hot springs—geysers.	Hvannadalshnukur	2110	Atlantic Ocean	0
19.	Jamaica	340	Most of the area is occupied by a limestone plateau with karst formations developed especially in the west. Mountains rise in the southwest (Don Figuerero, Santa Cruz, and May Day), while the highest mountains range (the Blue Mountains) lies in the eastern part Lowland areas are limited to coastal regions.	Blue Mountain Peak	2256	Caribbean Sea	0

(continued)

Table 6.2 (continued)

No	*WSE*	*Average altitude*	*Surface relief*	*Highest altitude*		*Lowest altitude*	
		m MSL		*Name*	*m MSL*	*Name*	*m MSL*
20.	Laos	710	More than 90% of the country's land area is rugged and mountainous, especially in the north and the Annam range. Mountains reach heights of up to 2700 meters. The plateaus in the northeast (Tran Ninh), reach 1370 meters, while those in the south (Bolovens) reach up to 1070 m. In the south and west, along the Mekong River and its tributaries, are alluvial plains, the most extensive of which is Vientiane. Almost the entire area of Laos is drained by the Mekong River (1805 km) and its tributaries, which is almost dry during the low-water phase but rises more than 6 meters during the monsoon season.	Phu Bia	2817	Mekong River	70
21.	Madagascar	442	About two-thirds of the area, once part of African precontinent Gondwana, is occupied by a plateau with extensive crystalline highlands and mountains (including Tsaratanana and Ankaratra) featuring extinct volcanoes. The plateau, rising sharply from the narrow plain of the east coast and descends to the strip of sedimentary rocks along the west coast. On the eastern edge, the high plateau is cut by deep gorges and waterfalls, descending steeply toward a narrow coastal plain. The west, it slopes gently toward the plain, intersected by the Betsiboka and Mangoky Rivers, with numerous lagoons stretching from Foulpointe to Farafangana, featuring coral reefs.	Maromokotro	2876	Indian Ocean	0
22.	Malawi	779	The area is a crystalline plateau, reaching heights of more than 3000 meters (at Mulanje). The eastern part of the country, including Lake Niasa, which occupies one-fifth of the country's area, lies in the depression of the Great Rift Valley, where the valley floor drops to depths of up to 200 m.	Mount Flanje	3002	River Shire	37

23.	Mali	343	Most of the country is occupied by plateaus sloping toward the Niger Valley, descending toward the west and northwest, with few mountainous areas. The highest-altitude regions are in the northeast (Adrar des Iforas) and in the southeastern part of the country, on the edge of the Niger Basin. Untapped desert and semi-desert areas extend to the north and northeast.	Hombori Tondo	1155	Senegal River	23
24.	Mozambique	345	Almost half of the area is occupied by coastal lowlands, rising toward the west to a plateau 150 to 610 meters, and along the western border to a higher plateau, reaching 910 meters, with mountains nearing a height of 2440 meters. The highest mountains are in Zambézia Province (Namuli) and in Manica Province (Binga) on the Zimbabwean border. The most important rivers are the Zambezi (flowing southeast across the center of Mozambique into the Indian Ocean), the Limpopo in the south, the Save (Sabi) in the center, and the Lugenda in the north. The most important lakes are the Lake Malawi (Lake Niassa) and Lake Cahora Bassa.	Monte Binga	2436	Indian Ocean	0
25.	Mauritius	414	Islands of volcanic origin and are surrounded by coral reefs. The wide coastal plains gradually turn into highlands with huge volcanic cones.	Piton de la Petite Riviere Noire	828	Indian Ocean	0
26.	Niger	474	Over 80% of its area lies in the Sahara Desert. In the north-central region is the volcanic Air Massif, reaching a height of 1900 meters. Massifs along the Libyan border average about 800 meters. The southern plateau is at an elevation of 300–500 meters. The Niger River flows for about 563 km through southwestern Niger. To the north of the Niger are many ancient stream channels that flow periodically during wet weather. A portion of Lake Chad is situated in the southeast.	Mount Idoukal-n-Taghes	2022	Niger River	200

(*continued*)

Table 6.2 (continued)

No	*WSE*	*Average altitude*	*Surface relief*	*Highest altitude*		*Lowest altitude*	
		m MSL		*Name*	*m MSL*	*Name*	*m MSL*
27.	Nicaragua	304	Along the west coast stretches a belt of coastal plains. To the north lies a range with 25 volcanic cones, 11 of which are active (including Momotombo and Viejo). Behind it stretches a tectonic rift with lakes (Nicaragua and Managua). To the northeast extend the Cordillera ranges (C. Dariense, C. Isabelia and Montaa de Huapi). The mountains diminish eastward passing into the flat, lagoon-laden Mosquito Coast.	Mogoton	2085	Pacific Ocean	0
28.	North Korea	600	Highlands and mountains account for 80% of the area, with most of the peninsula's 2000 meters mountains located in North Korea. To the north and northeast stretch The Hamgyong Range, in the north-central—the Rangrim Mountains, and along North Korea's border with China runs the Kangnam Range. In the south stretches South Korea's Kumgangsan, or Diamond Mountain in the Thaebaek Range. The plains do not cover a large area. The most extensive are on the west coast (the Pyongyang and Chaeryong) and on the east coast—very small, because the eastern mountains drop abruptly to the sea. The Yalu River is the longest river in North Korea (790 kilometers) and flows southwest to the Yellow Sea. The second, Tumen River, flows east to the Sea of Japan.	Paektu-san	2744	Sea of Japan	0
29.	Northern Macedonia	741	Most of the area is occupied by young mountains of the Alpine system (including Shar Plnina and Yakupitsa) with high seismic activity. They are crisscrossed by valleys of the Vardar's tributaries and numerous catchment basins (including Skopskaya and Sheep Field).	Golem Korab	2764	Vardar River	50

30.	Papua New Guinea	667	Over fourt-fifths of the area lies on the world's second largest island, New Guinea. The central part of the country is occupied by numerous mountain ranges (including the Bismarck Mountains and Owen Stanley Mountains). To the south and north, along the coast, stretch alluvial plains with river deltas. The islands, which comprise the country, are of volcanic origin, varying in size from the Trobriand Islands in the southeast to the vast and mountainous (including New Britain and New Ireland).	Mount Wilhelm	4509	Pacific Ocean	0
31.	Saint Kitts and Nevis	578	Dormant volcano, Mt. Liamuiga, is located in the northwest, where it drops striaght to the sea as cliffs to the south and west. On the southern arm of the island lies the Great Salt Pond. The island of Nevis could be considered to be one large dormant volcano.	Mount Liamuiga on the island of St. Kitts	1156	Caribbean Sea	0
32.	Saint Lucia	432	Area shaped by volcanic activity. There are highlands in the north and mountains in the central part. In the southwest, the active Qualibou volcano rises above the coast.	Mount Gimie	950	Caribbean Sea	0
33.	Saint Vincent and the Grenadines	304	Volcanic formation islands, with an active volcano on Saint Vincent that has a crater. Coastal, low-lying areas have wide beaches and shallow bays. Lowland areas are limited to the coastal zone, with wide beaches and shallow bays. Smaller islands are surrounded by coral reefs.	La Soufriere	1234	Caribbean Sea	0
34.	Salvador	442	Most of the area is covered by mountains and highland plains. It is divided into three general regions: the lowland narrow strip of the Pacific coast, the central plateau, cut from east to west by two mountain ranges (Sierra Madre and Cadena Costera), and the northern lowlands, formed by the wide Lempa River valley, bounded by a high mountain range.	Cerro El Pital	2730	Pacific Ocean	0
35.	Samoa	929	Archipelago of 16 islands, stretching more than 600 km, surrounded by coral reefs. The largest islands (Savai'I, Upolu, Apolima, and Manono) are volcanic.	Mauga Silisili on the island of Savai'i	1857	Pacific Ocean	0

(*continued*)

Table 6.2 (continued)

No	*WSE*	*Average altitude*	*Surface relief*	*Highest altitude*		*Lowest altitude*	
		m MSL		*Name*	*m MSL*	*Name*	*m MSL*
36.	San Marino	433	Most of the area is a hilly plateau belonging to the southeastern Tuscan Apennines (Monte Titano), which slopes steeply northeastward toward the alluvial coastal plain.	Monte Titano	755	Ausa River	55
37.	Seychelles	453	Larger islands, of volcanic origin, are upland-mountainous with flat coastlines, while the smaller coral islands have a flat surface, rising only a few meters above sea level.	Morne Seychellois on the island of Mahe	905	Indian Ocean	0
38.	Somalia	410	Northern region is mountainous (the Migiurtina and the Ogo), with plateaus reaching up to 2100 meters. South and west up to the Shabeelle River lies a plateau region (the Mudug Plain). The region between the Yuba and the Shabeelle rivers is lowland.	Mount Shimbiris	2450	Indian Ocean	0
39.	South Sudan	867	Most of the area consists of vast plains and plateaus, drained by the Nile River and its tributaries. The Nile flows from north to south, crossing the country in the central part, where there is a clay plain, the middle of which is occupied by the swampy Sudd region. From this region the Nile is called the White. In the southern part, there is the vast expanse of the White Nile basin.	Kinyeti	3187	White Nile River	381
40.	Tonga	517	Archipelago comprises approximately 170 islands, which are divided into the Tongatapu, Ha'apai, and Vava'u island groups, of which 36 are inhabited. The first two groups are coral islands, while the third consists of volcanic, with active volcanoes still present.	Kao Island	1033	Pacific Ocean	0
41.	Vanuatu	398	Volcanic islands feature a varied landscape, as they form the peaks of and underwater oceanic ridge. Three active volcanoes are located within the country.	Mount Tabwemasana on Espiritu Santo	1877	Pacific Ocean	0

42.	Yemen	999	Most of the area is covered by mountains and plateaus, which form part of the desert landscape. In the north lies one of the largest deserts in the world, the Empty Quarter (The Rub' al Khali), while in the northwest is the Ramlat Dahm desert, in the center Ramlan al-Sab' atayn desert. The southern and western areas of the country are covered by mountains. In the central southeastern region are the Mahra mountains (Jabal Mahra, rising to an elevation of to 1300 meters). The mountains in the west descend toward the coastal plains of the Tihamah, which stretch along the shores of the Red Sea.	Jabal An-Nabi Shu'ayb	3666	Arabian Sea	0
43.	Zimbabwe	961	Most of Zimbabwe is a plateau, with over 75% of it lying between 600 and 1500 meters, and almost all of it over 300 meters. This central ridge is known as the highveld, culminates in the northeast in the Inyanga mountains. It also forms the country's watershed, with streams flowing southeast to the Limpopo and Sabi rivers and northwest into the Zambezi. On either side of the highveld is the middleveld, a plateau ranging from about 600 to 1200 meters. Below 610 meters are the lowlands, plains located in the basins of the Zambezi and the Limpopo.	Mount Nyangani	2592	Confluence of Runde and Save	162

Source: Own compilation based on: CIA The World Factbook; (Frydrych et al., 2016; (Szaflarski, 1977)

Countries where the hypsometric limit does not exceed 300 meters above sea level were considered as a subgroup of the lowland WSE (Table 6.3). There are 29 such countries, located mainly on the west coast of Africa (e.g., Benin, Burkina Faso, The Gambia, Guinea-Bissau, Liberia, Mauritania, Senegal, Sierra Leone, Togo) and on the American continent (e.g., Antigua and Barbuda, Bahamas, Barbados, Belize, Guyana, Suriname, Trinidad and Tobago). Some have a flat surface, with little relief (e.g., Bahamas, The Gambia, Kiribati, Maldives, Nauru, Tuvalu, Marshall Islands). Many countries, although mostly low-lying, have mountain ranges with peaks over 1000 meters above sea level (e.g., Belize with Doyles Delight at 1124 meters, Cyprus with Mount Olympus at 1951 meters, Guyana with Mount Roraima at 2775 meters, Liberia at Mount Wuteve 1447 meters, Cambodia with Phnom Aural—1810 meters, Sierra Leone with Mount Bintimani at 1948 meters, Suriname with Juliana Top at 1230 meters). The lowest point for almost all of the lowland WSE is sea level. The exceptions are Burkina Faso (with -200 meters below sea level) and Mauritania (with -5 meters below sea level), with areas below sea level (Table 6.3).

The WSE are characterized by a diversity of landforms. Almost all types of relief can be found in their areas, developed as a result of centuries of geomorphological processes. Unfortunately, the richness of these landforms often hinders the development of transportation, construction, industry, and, especially agriculture, which is highly dependent on the relief. The most favorable area for agriculture and cultivation are the lowland WSE, but this does not apply to flat land surfaces, as water stagnation forms on such areas. Slightly undulating terrain with a slight slope facilitates the movement of water, reducing water stagnation, and improving agricultural mechanization and transportation. On the other hand, too steep slopes (more than 25 degrees) in the highland WSE or the mountain WSE promote too rapid water runoff and erosion, and make mechanization of fieldwork difficult or impossible. Such land is used for agriculture, but only after labor-intensive prior leveling of the land, ensuring appropriate microclimatic and agro-biological conditions. The angle of slope is associated with the cultivation of certain types of crops. However, mountainous areas are used for nomadic pastoralism (transhumance), which includes grazing animals (especially sheep) in the warm season and grazing them lower down for the winter. In addition to agriculture, transportation is a sector of the economy that is highly dependent on the terrain. Although less so than in the past, the development of

Table 6.3 Lowland WSE surface topography

No	*WSE*	*Average altitude*	*Surface relief*	*Highest altitude*		*Lowest altitude*	
		m MSL		*Name*	*m MSL*	*name*	*m*
1.	Antigua and Barbuda	202	Volcanic Antigua is characterized by lowland and hilly terrain, whereas coral Barbuda is predominently lowland and forested.	Boggy Peak on the island of Antigua	402	Caribbean Sea	0
2.	Bahamas	32	More than 700 flat islands of the Bahamas are part of a coral and limestone shelf. The islands' coasts, devoid of rivers due to the extensive development of karst phenomena, are lagoonal and surrounded by coral reefs.	Mount Alvernia on Cat Island	63	Atlantic Ocean	0
3.	Barbados	170	Island of coral origin, partially covered with volcanic ash, is almost completely surrounded by coral reefs. The terrain rises from the coastal plains to the hills in the central part of the country.	Hillaby Mountain	336	Atlantic Ocean	0
4.	Belize	173	Land is mostly level, interrupted only by the Manatee Hills. To the south the land rises sharply toward a mountainous interior (the Maya and the Cockscomb mountains) from a flat and swampy coastline that is indented by many lagoons. The coastal waters are sheltered by a line of reefs, beyond which there are numerous islands and cays (Ambergris Cay, the Turneffe Islands, Columbus Reef, and Glover Reef).	Doyle's Delight	1124	Caribbean Sea	0
5.	Benin	273	Area stretches in a narrow strip from the coast of the Gulf of Guinea northward along the Oueme River. The southern areas are sandy coastal lowlands, dotted with numerous lagoons. Toward the north, the terrain rises, gradually turning into highlands (the Atakora Mountains—an extension of the Togo Mountains). To the northeast, the highlands drop steeply toward the Niger River.	Mont Sokbaro	658	Atlantic Ocean	0

(*continued*)

Table 6.3 (continued)

No	*WSE*	*Average altitude*	*Surface relief*	*Highest altitude*		*Lowest altitude*	
		m MSL		*Name*	*m MSL*	*name*	*m*
6.	Burkina Faso	297	Most of athe rea is covered by a vast lateritic plateau in the West African savanna. The land is slightly inclined toward the south and cut by valleys formed by the three principal rivers, the Black, White, and Red Voltas, and their main tributary, the Sourou.	Tena Kourou	749	River Black Volta	200
7.	Cambodia	126	More than 75% of the area is covered by a vast alluvial, well-watered plains. In the central part of the country is the Great Lake, and the Mekong River, which flows down from Laos to the southern border with Vietnam. Between the Tonle Sap and the Gulf of Thailand lie the range of the Cardamom Mountains and the Elephant Range. To the north are the Dangrek Mountains, and to the east the Chlong Highlands.	Phnom Aural	1810	Gulf of Thailand	0
8.	Cyprus	91	Most of the area is occupied by two mountain systems. The Troodos Massif, in the southwest, spreads towards the northwestern, northern, and southern coasts. In the north, a geologically older range, the Kyrenia Mountains, extend along the coast. Between these major formations lies a plain, the Mesaoria, extending from Famagusta Bay on the east to Morphou Bay in the west. There are few lakes or rivers, with the exceptions of rocky channels that carry away torrents.	Olympus Mountain	1951	Mediterranean Sea	0

9.	Estonia	61	Located in the East European Plain, it is mostly lowland lying below 50 meters with a hilly region in the southeast. Only 10% of the area rises above 90 meters in elevation. Along the coast are numerous islands (1500), the largest of which are Saaremaa & Muhu islands, which account for 9% of the country's area. The country also contains more than 1000 natural and artificial lakes (the largest being Lake Peipus, along the border with Russia).	Suur Munamagi	318	Baltic Sea	0
10.	The Gambia	34	Gambia River plays a dominant role in the landscape of the elongated country (480 km long and 25–40 km wide), flowing in a vast valley. The land on either side of the river is generally open savanna with wooded areas along the drainage channels, low hills (up to 80 meters) and a sandy plateau.	No name	64	Atlantic Ocean	0
11.	Guyana	207	The area is divided into three main natural regions: a low-lying coastal plain, a region comprising almost five-sixths of country's area of heavily forested, hilly land, which contains most of the mineral wealth; and in the south and west, a region of mountains (The Guiana Shield with the Guiana Highlands with Pakaraima Mountains and waterfalls such as Angel Falls, Kaieteur Falls and Cuquenan Falls). There are several large rivers, including the Essequibo Demerara, and Berbice.	Mount Roraima	2775	Atlantic Ocean	0
12.	Guinea-Bissau	70	Most of Guinea-Bissau is occupied by a lowland, dissected by the meandering rivers Geba, Corubal, Mansoa, and Cacheu, flowing into the ocean. The southeastern slice of the country is upland (the western end of the Futa Jalon massif). In the northeast there is a central plateau. Where the plateau stretches to the eastern frontier, it is called the Planalto de Gabú.	No name (east of the country)	300	Atlantic Ocean	0

(*continued*)

Table 6.3 (continued)

No	*WSE*	*Average altitude*	*Surface relief*	*Highest altitude*		*Lowest altitude*	
		m MSL		*Name*	*m MSL*	*name*	*m*
13.	Kiribati	2	Archipelago of flat islands (up to 2–3 meters), surrounded by coral reefs, scattered across a vast area spanning four hemispheres. Due to the prominent low-lying nature of most of the islands, they face the risk of flooding as a result of rising ocean levels.	No name on Banaba Island	81	Pacific Ocean	0
14.	Liberia	243	The area is divided into three distinct belts lying parallel to the coast: the low coastal belt with tidal creeks, shallow lagoons, and mangrove marshes, which rises to rolling hills up to 150 meters high, and the third belt, covering most of Liberia, with low mountains and plateaus (including the Nimba Mountains and the Wologizi Mountains).	Mount Wuteve	1447	Atlantic Ocean	0
15.	Maldives	2	Includes about 1200 coral islands having the character of atolls, of which 202 are inhabited. The archipelago has a meridional orientation (about 800 km long). Due to the prominent low-lying nature of most of the islands, they are in danger of flooding as a result of rising ocean levels.	Mount Villingi on the island of Villingi	5	Indian Ocean	0
16.	Malta	127	It covers the Maltese archipelago, which includeş the three main inhabited islands of Malta, Gozo, and Comino. They are the tips of a limestone massif, stretching south from Sicily, dissected by deep bays, rocky coves, and valleys. The coastline of the islands is varied and the coasts are steep with well-developed cliffs. The landscape is varied with surface and underground karst formations.	Ta'Dmejrek on the island of Malta	253	Mediterranean	0

17.	Marshall Islands	2	It is composed of more than 1200 islands and islets in two parallel chains of coral flat atolls—the Ratak, or Sunrise, to the east, and the Ralik, or Sunset, to the west.	No name on Liklep Island	10	Pacific Ocean	0
18.	Mauritania	276	Mostly flat area is divided into three regions: a strip along the Senegal River valley in the south; in the north, a broad east–west range characterized by extensive sand plains and fixed dunes; and the large northern Sahara region, moving southward by several kilometers each year and characterized by shifting sand dunes, rocky outcrops, and mountain plateaus (including the Adrar).	Kediet ej Jill	915	Sebkhet de Ndrhamcha	-5
19.	Micronesia	2	607 islands span 2900 kilometers and constitute the four states that include large, mountainous islands of volcanic origin and coral atolls: Kosrae is largely mountainous, Pohnpei contains a large volcanic island, Truk contains 14 mountainous islands of volcanic origin, and Yap contains four large high islands. The remaining islands are mostly coral atolls.	Nanlaud on Pohnpei	782	Pacific Ocean	0
20.	Moldova	139	More than 75% of the country's land area does not exceed an elevation of 200 meters and consists mostly of a hilly plain, which is crisscrossed by deep valleys with numerous rivers and streams. The terrain descends gradually toward the south. The Codri Hills run through the center of the country. The Dniester, along the eastern border, is the longest river with a total length of 1400 km.	Balanesti Hill	430	Dniester River	2
21.	Monaco	81	It occupies a narrow strip of high-cliff coastline on the Mediterranean Sea with a small rocky peninsula. The seashore has been largely transformed by humans.	Chemin des Revoires on Mount Agel	162	Mediterranean	0
22.	Nauru	36	Lone phosphate-rock island fringed by a wide coral reef. A relatively fertile belt surrounds the island. From this belt, a coral cliff rises to a central plateau about 60 m above mean sea level (MSL). At the southeastern end of the plateau is the permanent Buada Lagoon.	Command Ridge	71	Pacific Ocean	0

(continued)

Table 6.3 (continued)

No	*WSE*	*Average altitude*	*Surface relief*	*Highest altitude*		*Lowest altitude*	
		m MSL		*Name*	*m MSL*	*name*	*m*
23.	Palau	121	More than 200 islands include four types of formation: volcanic (Babelthuap, Koror, Arakabesan, Malakal, and several small northern islands), high limestone (including the Rock Islands), low platform (including Peleliu and Angaur), and coral atoll (Kayangel atoll). The Palau group (except Angaur Island and the Kayangel atoll) is barricaded by reef.	Mount Ngerchelchuus on the island of Babeldaob	242	Pacific Ocean	0
24.	Senegal	69	Landscape is predominantly flat alluvial plains. Much of the northwest (known as the Ferlo) is semi-desert (including Cap Vert dunes, Saint-Louis), but the center and most of the south, except for the forest of Casamance, are open savanna country. In the southeast there are higher-lying areas (including the Tamgué foothills). The country is drained by the Gambia, Casamance, Senegal and Salum rivers, which flow latitudinally and drain into the ocean.	No name	648	Atlantic Ocean	0
25.	Sierra Leone	279	A wide swampy coastal plain stretches along the coast. In the extreme west, the peninsulas are mostly mountainous. Farther east, a coastal plain extends inland. Stretches of wooded hill country lead east and northeast to a plateau region (the Loma Mountains).	Mount Bintimani	1948	Atlantic Ocean	0
26.	Suriname	246	Area is covered by coastal plains, further south, there are dense rainforests interspersed with grassy savannas and higher ground, including mountains (two mountain ranges: the Bakhuis and the Van Asch Van Wijck Mountains). From the southern highlands several rivers (including the Maroni and the Courantyne) flow to the Atlantic Ocean.	Juliana Top	1230	Atlantic Ocean	0

27.	Togo	236	Southern part of the country is occupied by an alluvial coastal plain, covered with coconut trees and separated from the mainland by lagoons and lakes. In the center, there is a chain of hills (the Togo Mountains), stretching roughly southwest and northeast (the Atakora Mountains).	Mont Agou	986	Atlantic Ocean	0
28.	Trinidad and Tobago	83	Area is occupied by three ranges of hills that cross the island through the northern, central, and southern parts. The highest is the Northern Range (a continuation of the mountains of the Paria Peninsula of Venezuela) which is the most extensive. The hills in the Central Range are lower. In between are flatlands, dissected by small streams. Along the east, south, and west coasts are swamp areas, including the world's largest natural asphalt peat bog, Pitch Lake). Tobago is a volcanic island with a central core of hill rising to over 550 meters, filling most of the island and reacheing the sea in many places.	El Cerro del Aripo on the island of Trinidad	940	Caribbean Sea	0
29.	Tuvalu	2	It consists of low-lying coral atolls less than 5 meters high, largely the result of human activity. On five islands the reefs are surrounded by lagoons, while on the others they are just pinnacles rising abruptly from the ocean floor. The low-lying nature of most of the islands means that they are in danger of flooding as a result of rising ocean levels.	Niulakita Island	5	Pacific Ocean	0

Source: Own compilation based on: CIA The World Factbook; (Frydrych et al., 2016; Szaflarski, 1977)

transportation is still determined by natural factors and includes vertical landforms, which influence its nature, forms, density and the means of transportation used. The terrain has the greatest impact on land transportation (i.e., railroads, automobiles, and transmission systems such as pipelines, gas lines, conveyor belts, and electric power lines), much less on water (inland and maritime shipping) and air (aviation). An attempt was made to estimate how much of an impact this has on the WSE on the basis of the rail and road density indexes, assuming that the WSE with the lowest indicators have the greatest constraints due to difficult terrain. This is because the terrain is one of the main factors, along with a lack of capital, in the underdevelopment of the land transport network in most of the WSE.

In 2019, the WSE group had 2.4 km of railways per 1000 km^2. By comparison, the global average was more than four times higher at 10.2 km per 1000 km^2. Road transport showed a similar difference. The WSE group had 90 km of roads per 1000 km^2 (Table 6.4), while the rest of the world had almost five times as much, or 432 km per 1000 km^2. The group's rail and road network length was also very low as a percentage of the world's rail and road network length, at 2.8% (38,400 km of rail) and 2.4% (1,574,100 km of road), respectively. These percentages were very low, especially considering that the WSE group's share of the land area was as high as 12.3% and its share of the world's population was as high as 7.3%. Such a high percentage of the population would indicate that the share of roads and railroads should be at a similar level, since residents use roads and railroads as their daily means of transportation. The low share of both indicators confirms the underdevelopment of land transport networks in most of the countries analyzed due in part to unfavorable terrain.[2]

The mountainous and upland terrain of most of the WSE makes the construction of roads and railways not only difficult but often impossible. It is much easier to build land transport infrastructure in the lowlands, taking advantage of natural permeabe elements (e.g., gently sloping river valleys, mountain passes, low catchment areas), than to build expensive bridges or tunnels in highland and mountainous areas. Many of the 93 analyzed countries cannot afford such exorbitant costs due to their low level of economic development, as the GDP of most of them did not exceed US$ 2500 per capita in 2019. As a result, the density of the rail

[2] Other factors include low levels of economic development, large forests, as well as deserts within the occupied area.

Table 6.4 WSE road length in 2019

No	*WSE*	*Road length*		*No*	*WSE*	*Road length*	
		km per 1000 km²	*Km*			*km per 1000 km²*	*km*
1.	Monaco	38,500	77	48.	Togo	207	11,734
2.	Marshall Islands	11,204	2028	49.	Lesotho	196	5940
3.	Malta	7133	2254	50.	Bahamas	194	2700
4.	San Marino	4787	292	51.	Nepal	190	27,990
5.	Barbados	3944	1700	52.	Fiji	188	3440
6.	Liechtenstein	3938	630	53.	Nicaragua	183	23897
7.	Grenada	3276	1127	54.	Guinea	180	44,301
8.	Antigua and Barbuda	2647	1170	55.	Rwanda	178	4700
9.	Cyprus	2151	19,901	56.	Kyrgyzstan	170	34,000
10.	Saint Vincent and the Grenadines	2131	829	57.	Laos	167	39,586
11.	Dominica	2013	1512	58.	Sierra Leone	163	11,700
12.	Jamaica	2013	22,121	59.	Haiti	154	4266
13.	Santa Lucia	1952	1210	60.	Yemen	154	71,300
14.	Trinidad and Tobago	1870	9592	61.	Belize	143	3281
15.	Saint Kitts and Nevis	1467	383	62.	South Sudan	140	90,200
16.	Nauru	1429	30	63.	Benin	139	16,000
17.	Saint Thomas and Príncipe	1349	1300	64.	Albania	137	3945
18.	Estonia	1292	58,412	65.	Eritrea	136	16,000
19.	Mauritius	1190	2428	66.	Honduras	131	14,742
20.	Seychelles	1164	526	67.	Malawi	130	15,452
21.	Tonga	910	680	68.	Djibouti	125	2893
22.	Kiribati	826	670	69.	Iceland	125	12,898

(*continued*)

Table 6.4 (continued)

No	*WSE*	*Road length*		*No*	*WSE*	*Road length*	
		km per 1000 km²	*Km*			*km per 1000 km²*	*km*
23.	Andorra	684	320	70.	Guinea-Bissau	122	4400
24.	Micronesia	570	400	71.	Mali	112	139,107
25.	Montenegro	562	7762	72.	Equatorial Guinea	103	2880
26.	Northern Macedonia	552	14,182	73.	Liberia	95	10,600
27.	Brunei	516	2976	74.	Vanuatu	88	1070
28.	Comoros	473	880	75.	Senegal	85	16,665
29	Bosnia and Herzegovina	448	22,926	76.	Mongolia	72	113,200
30.	Burundi	443	12,322	77.	Congo	68	23,324
31.	Salvador	428	9012	78.	Namibia	59	48,875
32.	Samoa	405	1150	79.	Burkina Faso	56	15,304
33.	East Timor	405	6040	80.	Botswana	55	31,747
34.	Cape Verde	335	1350	81.	Afghanistan	54	34,903
35.	Bhutan	318	12,205	82.	Madagascar	54	31,640
36.	Maldives	310	93	83.	Gabon	53	14,300
37.	Tuvalu	308	8	84.	Solomon Islands	48	1390
38.	Georgia	291	20,295	85.	Mozambique	39	31,083
39.	Moldova	276	9352	86.	Central African Republic	39	24,000

40.	Palau	272	125	87.	Chad	31	40,000
41.	The Gambia	264	2977	88.	Suriname	26	4304
42.	Cambodia	261	47,263	89.	Somalia	24	15,000
43.	Armenia	259	7700	90.	Papua New Guinea	20	9349
44.	Zimbabwe	249	97,267	91.	Guyana	19	3995
45.	Eswatini	219	3769	92.	Niger	15	18,949
46.	North Korea	212	25,554	93.	Mauritania	12	12,253
47.	Tajikistan	210	30,000				
	WSE group in total					90	1,574,103
	World					432	64,285,009

Source: Own compilation based on: CIA The World Factbook

network in the poor WSE, such as Afghanistan, Lesotho, Nepal, and Niger, was less than 0.5 km per 1000 km^2. Almost one-fourth of the WSE had no rail transport at all (including Bhutan, Burundi, Chad, East Timor, Haiti, Papua New Guinea, and Rwanda). The mountainous terrain, with an average altitude of more than 1000 meters above sea level, makes the construction of transport infrastructure difficult and significantly more expensive. This also applies to the road network (Table 6.4), which in many of the highland-mountain countries analyzed has a very low road network density rates, not exceeding 75 km per 1000 km^2 (e.g., Afghanistan 54 km per 1000 km^2, Botswana 55 km per 1000 km^2, Mongolia 72 km per 1000 km^2, Namibia 59 km per 1000 km^2, Papua New Guinea 20 km per 1000 km^2, and Solomon Islands 48 km per 1000 km^2).

In summary, the terrain of most of the WSE is unfavorable for their economies, especially for the transportation, agriculture, and mining sectors. The areas of more than two-thirds of the WSE are dominated by mountains (21 countries) and highlands (43 countries), whose slopes are not conducive to the construction of transport routes (including tunnels, bridges), resulting in difficulties and huge costs. Most countries are unable to afford these costs, and only a few wealthy of the mountain WSE, such as Liechtenstein (GDP US$ 177,698 per capita; with a road length of 3938 km per 1000 km^2) can afford to build roads on hills, high bridges, or tunnels in the rocks. It is not only the mountains that pose a problem for the development of land transport infrastructure. An additional obstacle or constraint is the desert, which extends over tens or hundreds of thousands of kilometers in some of the WSE (e.g., in Chad, Mali, Mauritania, and Niger) or the abundant equatorial forests that cover more than 90% of the area of several countries studied (e.g., in Gabon, Guyana, Solomon Islands, and Suriname). As a result, these countries have very low ratios of railroad and roads in relation to their area, amounting to only 31 km per 1000 km^2 in Chad, 53 km per 1000 km^2 in Gabon, 19 km per 1000 km^2 in Guyana, 12 km per 1000 km^2 in Mauritania, 15 km per 1000 km^2 in Niger, 26 km per 1000 km^2 in Suriname, 48 km per 1000 km^2 in Solomon Islands in 2019 (Table 6.4).

The mountainous and highland terrain of most of the WSE is also an obstacle to agricultural development. Poorly fertile or rocky land is not conducive to crop production. Therefore, the WSE such as Bhutan, Eritrea, Kyrgyzstan, Lesotho, Mongolia, Nepal, Tajikistan, and Yemen were characterized by greater emphasis on livestock, rather than crops which is associated with a particular type of economy.

It has also been observed that mountainous terrain can prevents the development of the mining industry. The hard ground makes it difficult to access the mineral resources that lie underground, rendering their exploitation very expensive and often unprofitable or impossible. An example is Papua New Guinea and the untapped valuable gold and silver deposits in its mountain ranges. However, many of the WSE with favorable terrain and resource-rich geology have benefited greatly from their extraction. Examples include Brunei (oil and natural gas), Gabon (oil and natural gas), Equatorial Guinea (oil and gas), Jamaica (bauxite), Liberia (iron), Congo (diamonds), Mauritania (iron), Mozambique (coal), Nauru (phosphorites), Suriname (bauxite), and Trinidad and Tobago (oil and gas).

It should be added that some of the WSE have taken advantage of their upland mountainous terrain and water resources to develop hydropower power. The development was led by the WSE such as Albania, Nepal, Tajikistan, Namibia, Mozambique, and Kyrgyzstan (Fig. 6.1), where hydropower accounted for more than 80% of the energy balance.

Some of the WSE, such as Andorra, Bhutan, Georgia, Kyrgyzstan, Liechtenstein, Lesotho, Namibia, Nepal, Tajikistan, and Saint Thomas and Príncipe, have turned their mountainous terrain into a tourist asset, generating income from the tourism sector. Of particular note is Nepal, famous for its high mountain tourism, which charges fees to climb the 326 peaks in its territory (the cost of a permit to climb Earth's highest peak, Mt. Everest, was US$ 11,000, and the total cost of the expedition, excluding the cost of a guide, was US$ 35,000) (Apollo, 2017).

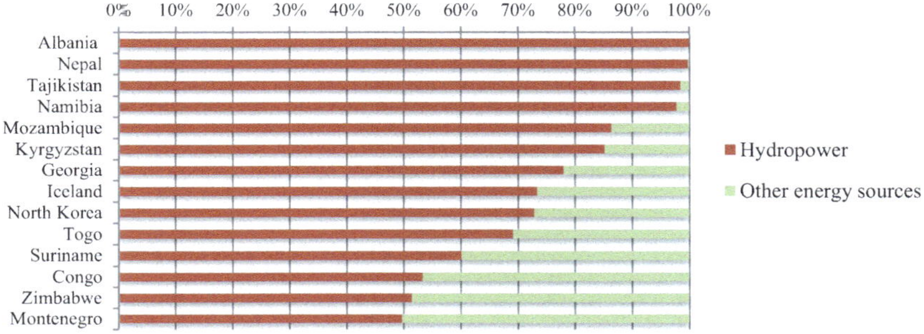

Fig. 6.1 WSE with the highest proportion of hydropower generation in 2019 energy balance (%). (Source: Own compilation based on The World Bank)

An analysis of the WSE's relief shows that it has a major impact on various sectors of their economies. It determines agriculture (including the distribution and structure of crops), opportunities for the development of industry, transportation and construction, as well as the formation of areas of population concentration and determines the urbanization processes of the WSE. Thus, the terrain of the WSE largely determines their development opportunities. Its natural role should not be forgotten either. The relief is one of the most important components of the natural environment, which, together with the geological structure, influences the hydrological, soil, and plant relationships of the countries under study.

Bibliography

Apollo, M. (2017). The True Accessibility of Mountaineering: The Case of the High Himalaya. *Journal of Outdoor Recreation and Tourism, 17.*

Frydrych, M., Kobojek, S., & Rdzany, Z. (2016). *Geografia Swiata*. SBM.

Szaflarski, J. (1977). In J. Szaflarski (Ed.), *Slownik Geografii Swiata*. Wiedza Powszechna.

CHAPTER 7

Utilization of Water Resources in the World's Smallest Economies

The Earth's total water resources in the form of oceans, seas, rivers, lakes, glaciers and ice caps amount to 1385 million km^3, of which up to 97% is saltwater (seas and oceans). The remaining 3% of water is freshwater (Simmons, 1979), two-thirds of which is trapped in glaciers, permanent snow cover, and permafrost (Table 7.1). The remaining one-third of freshwater is stored in groundwater, surface water, the atmosphere, and in the cells of living organisms (Gleik, 1996).

The main difference between saltwater and freshwater is their chemical composition. While freshwater is dominated by carbonates (80%), seawater is dominated by chlorides (89%), especially sodium chloride, which gives it a salty taste. The salinity of surface waters in the open ocean varies, on average, from 32‰ to 38 ‰[1] (compared to the salinity of freshwater, which is around 1‰) and this variation depends on latitude, evaporation intensity, the amount of precipitation, freshwater supplied by rivers, and distance from the ocean. The highest salinity of seawaters in the world is found in the Red Sea (46‰), where three of the WSE are located: Djibouti, Eritrea, and Yemen. This high salinity is due to its tropical location, high evaporation, low rainfall, negligible freshwater input from rivers (there are no rivers in Djibouti and Yemen), and limited water exchange due to its

[1] Changes in salinity up to a depth of 400 meters are caused by latitude and evaporation, while below 400 meters, the salinity level of seawater remains at 34‰.

A. A. Teperek, *Economic Development in the World's Smallest Economies*, https://doi.org/10.1007/978-3-031-63810-7_7

Table 7.1 Earth's water resources

Water source	*Share fresh water*	*Global distribution of water resources*
	%	
Oceans, seas	–	96.5
Ice caps, glaciers, eternal snows	68.7	1.74
Permafrost	0.82	0.022
Groundwater	30.1	1.7
Water retention in soil	0.05	0.001
Surface water:		
Lakes	0.26	0.013
Swamps	0.03	0.0008
Rivers	0.006	0.0002
Water in atmosphere	0.04	0.001
Water in stored in cells	0.003	0.0001
Total	100	100

Source: Own compilation based on: (Gleik, 1996)

narrow connection with the Indian Ocean. In contrast, the lowest salinity of marine waters is found in the inland seas and those connected to the ocean by narrow straits. An example is the Baltic Sea, where one of the WSE, Estonia, is located. Low evaporation (especially in winter), a large influx of freshwater from rivers, melting snow and precipitation, and poor oceanic water exchange result in an average salinity of 7‰ in the Baltic Sea. The salinity of seawater is of great importance because it affects the density of water in the ocean, and therefore the movement of ocean currents and marine life (e.g., consumption of water with an elevated salt concentration is very harmful to whales).

Both saltwater and freshwater play a major role in the lives of humans and the surrounding nature, as they are the basic elements that shape the environment and sustain life on Earth. Water participates in the process of photosynthesis, which, among other things, produces organic compounds that serve as a source of energy for all organisms and oxygen for the atmosphere, and also participates in geochemical processes. It influences the climate (including ocean currents) and serves as a habitat for many living organisms, water protects them from overheating and cooling by storing heat. At the same time, water is a component of living organisms, such as plants, animals, and humans (it makes up 75% of the human body mass and 70% of the brain and muscles) and must be constantly replenished. It determines the life and health of man; it affects both his mental and physical regeneration of strength. Man also uses it for activities such as personal hygiene and food preparation. Water bodies have been used for transportation for thousands of years. Huge amounts of water are consumed in various production processes such as industry, agriculture, hydropower, among others. As a result, both human activities and the socioeconomic activities of entire countries depend on water. The multifaceted functions of saltwater and freshwater resources, as well as the world's growing population, mean that the demand for both saltwater and freshwater is increasing year after year.

The area of saline ocean waters on Earth is 361 million km^2, or two-thirds of the Earth's surface. It consists of the World Ocean, which, according to the International Hydrographic Organization's classification (in effect since 2000), is divided into the Pacific, Atlantic, Indian and Arctic and the Southern Oceans. These five oceans also include smaller water areas such as seas, bays, canals, lagoons, and straits. Of the 93 WSE, 67 are coastal countries, both continental with access to the sea (32 countries) and island nations (35 countries). The length of their coastlines varies (Fig. 7.1), ranging from 4 km (Monaco) to 6112 km (Micronesia), with island countries having the longest coastline. Of the 19 WSE with coastlines longer than 1000 km, 12 are island states (e.g., Bahamas, Fiji, Haiti, Iceland, Jamaica, Kiribati, Madagascar, Micronesia, Palau, Papua New Guinea, Solomon Islands, and Vanuatu). In contrast, the countries with the shortest coastlines have small land areas of less than 800 km^2.

The total length of the WSE maritime border is 73,497 km (Fig. 7.2), which is about one-third of the length of all land and maritime borders of the group (225,113 km). This means that the group's coastal development index is 4 9, indicating a high level of coastal development. For comparison, North American continent has the same ratio and ranks first among other continents.

Some countries border the ocean directly (37 countries), while others have indirect access—through seas that are part of the oceans. The largest number of countries are located on the Atlantic Ocean or its adjacent seas (39 countries). They include Cape Verde, Congo, Equatorial Guinea, The Gambia, Guyana, Guinea, Guinea-Bissau, Honduras, Jamaica, Liberia, Mauritania, Nicaragua, Senegal, Sierra Leone, and Suriname. Among the seas, the largest number of the WSE is in the Caribbean Sea (13 countries), including Grenada, Haiti, Honduras, Jamaica, Nicaragua, Saint Kitts and Nevis, Saint Lucia, Saint Vincent, and the Grenadines.

The seas in which the WSE are located (20 countries), namely Adriatic, Arabian, Baltic, Bismarck, Black, Red, Fiji, Greenland, Japanese, Ionian,

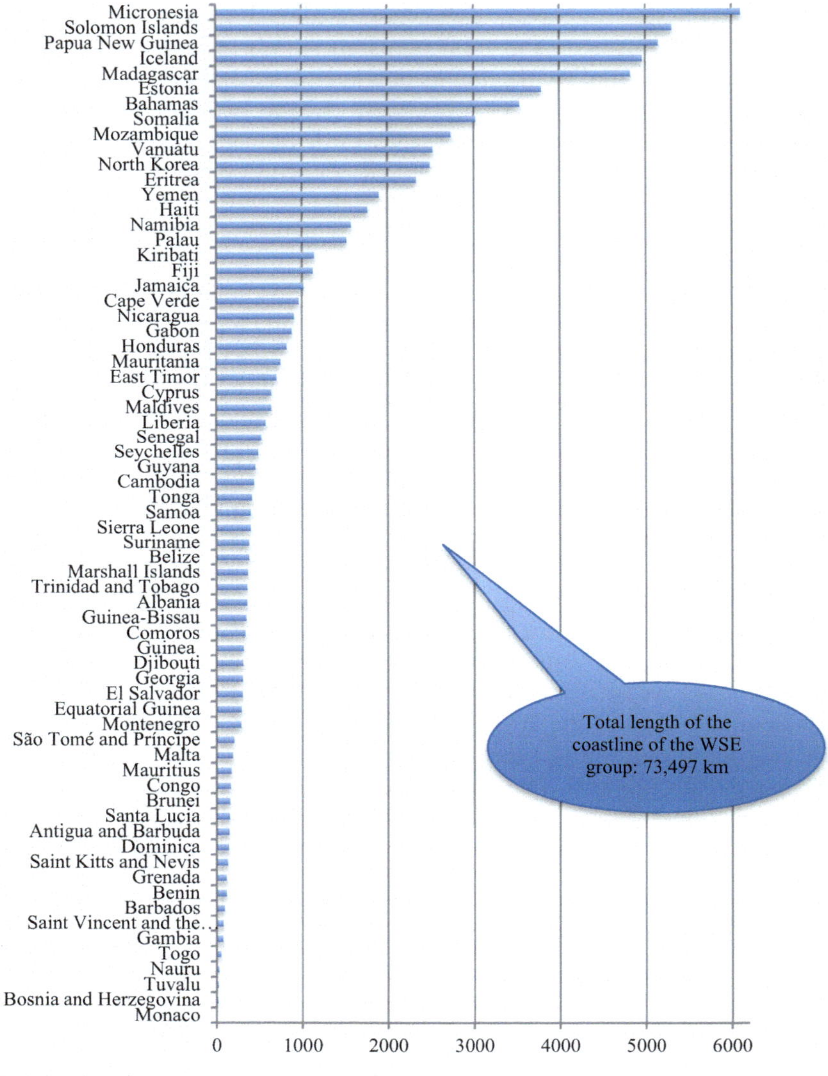

Fig. 7.1 WSE maritime borders length (km). (Source: Own compilation based on CIA The World Factbook)

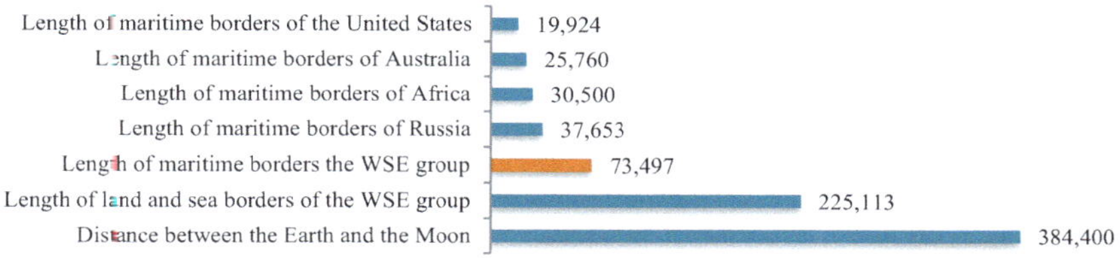

Fig. 7.2 Comparison of the WSE group's maritime border with other borders (km). (Source: Own compilation based on CIA The World Factbook)

Caribbean, Coral, Laccadive, Norwegian, South China, Solomon, Sargasso, Mediterranean, Timor, and Yellow Seas (Table 7.2) are of various types. Some are open, which are connected to the ocean, such as the Arabian Sea, in which Yemen lies, or the Greenland Sea, which borders the coast of Iceland. Others are coastal seas, separated from the ocean by chains of islands or peninsulas, such as the Adriatic Sea (Bosnia and Herzegovina), the Sea of Japan (North Korea), the South China Sea (Brunei, Cambodia), and still others are seas between islands, such as the Solomon Sea (Papua New Guinea, Solomon Islands) and the Bismarck Sea (Papua New Guinea). On the other hand, the Mediterranean Sea, which includes Cyprus, Malta, and Monaco, is an inland sea connected to the ocean by straits.

Although, in a physical sense the sea and ocean form a single entity, from a legal point of view they are divided into zones: *internal marine waters*, the *territorial sea*, the maritime *exclusive economic zone* and the remainder of the All-Ocean or *open sea*, accessible to all countries both coastal and inland (Goralczyk, 1957).

Internal maritime waters extend from the landward shore of the coastal state and include bays, estuaries, harbor waters, flowing waters (Goralczyk, 1964). Immediately adjacent to *internal waters is a* strip of *territorial sea*, up to 12 miles wide. According to the provisions of the Convention on the Legal Status of Maritime Areas (1982), the waters of both zones are within the territory of coastal states and are subject to their exclusive sovereignty. Accordingly, the passage of vessels (e.g., commercial, fishing, sport, tourist, ships, border guards) in the strip of both internal waters and territorial sea does not require international legal permission.

Table 7.2 WSE geographical location in relation to seas and oceans

Ocean	*Ocean area*	*Average depth*	*WSE*	*Seas*	*WSE*
	million km	*m*			
Pacific Ocean	155.5	4100	East Timor, El Salvador, Honduras, Kiribati, Marshall Islands Micronesia, Nauru, Nicaragua, Palau, Samoa, Tonga, Tuvalu	Bismarck Sea	Papua New Guinea
				Fiji Sea	Fiji
				Sea of Japan	North Korea
				Coral Sea	Papua New Guinea, Solomon Islands, Vanuatu
				South China Sea	Brunei, Cambodia
				Sea of Solomon	Papua New Guinea, Solomon Islands
				Yellow Sea	North Korea
Atlantic Ocean	76.7	3339	Benin, Cape Verde, Congo, Equatorial Guinea, Gabon, The Gambia, Guinea, Guinea-Bissau, Guyana, Liberia, Mauritania, Namibia, Saint Thomas and Principe, Senegal, Sierra Leone, Suriname	Adriatic Sea	Albania, Bosnia and Herzegovina, Montenegro
				Baltic Sea	Estonia
				Black Sea	Georgia
				Ionian Sea	Albania
				Caribbean Sea	Antigua and Barbuda, Barbados, Belize, Dominica, Grenada, Haiti, Honduras, Jamaica, Nicaragua, Saint Kitts and Nevis, Saint Lucia, Saint Vincent and the Grenadines, Trinidad and Tobago
				Norwegian Sea	Iceland
				Saragasso Sea	Bahamas
				Mediterranean Sea	Cyprus, Malta, Monaco

(*continued*)

Table 7.2 (continued)

Ocean	*Ocean area*	*Average depth*	*WSE*	*Seas*	*WSE*
	million km	*m*			
Indian Ocean	68.5	3890	Comoros, Madagascar, Maldives, Mauritius, Mozambique, Seychelles, Somalia, Yemen	Arabian Sea Red Sea Lakkadiv Sea Timor Sea	Maldives, Yemen Djibouti, Eritrea, Yemen Maldives East Timor
Arctic Ocean	15.5	1201	Iceland	Greenland Sea	Iceland

Source: Own compilation based on The World Bank

Beyond the territorial sea, the maritime *Exclusive Economic Zone*[2] (EEZ) extends up to 200 nautical miles (370 km), from the coastal baseline. While the *internal marine waters* and *the territorial sea* are an integral part of the coastal States, which have sovereignty over their waters, airspace, seabed, and subsoil, they do not have sovereignty over the area of the maritime *Exclusive Economic Zone* (EEZ). They do, however, have special authority to explore and exploit the living and nonliving marine resources of the seabed, its subsoil and adjacent waters. They have sovereign rights over the exploitation of natural resources and jurisdiction over the construction and use of artificial islands, installations and structures, the scientific exploration of the sea, and the protection and preservation of the marine environment.

Of the 93 WSE, all the coastal WSE (67 countries), that is, the continental WSE with access to the sea (32 countries) and the island WSE (35 countries) have access to a maritime *Exclusive Economic Zone* (EEZ). Their area varies considerably (Table 7.3), ranging from 50 km^2 (Bosnia and Herzegovina) to 3.4 million km^2 (Kiribati). The largest areas of maritime Exclusive Economic Zones belong to the island WSE, that is, Fiji, Kiribati,

[2] The Exclusive Economic Zone is also regulated in the 1982 Convention on the Law of the Sea, signed in Montego Bay, Jamaica (Part V, Articles 55–75).

Table 7.3 WSE maritime Exclusive Economic Zone (km^2)

No	*WSE*	*Maritime EEZ*	*Coastline length*	*Land area*
		km²	*km*	*km²*
1.	Kiribati	3,441,810	1143	811
2.	Micronesia	2,996,419	6112	702
3.	Papua New Guinea	2,402,288	5152	462,840
4.	Marshall Islands	1,990,530	370	181
5.	Solomon Islands	1,589,477	5313	28,896
6.	Seychelles	1,336,559	491	452
7.	Mauritius	1,284,997	177	2040
8.	Fiji	1,282,978	1129	18,272
9.	Madagascar	1,225,259	4828	587,041
10.	Maldives	923,322	644	300
11.	Somalia	825,052	3025	637,657
12.	Cape Verde	800,561	965	4033
13.	Iceland	751,345	4970	103,000
14.	Tuvalu	749,790	24	26
15.	Vanuatu	663,251	2528	12,189
16.	Tonga	659,558	419	747
17.	Bahamas	654,715	3542	13,940
18.	Palau	603,978	1519	459
19.	Mozambique	578,989	2740	799,380
20.	Namibia	564,748	1572	825,615
21.	Yemen	552,669	1906	527,970
22.	North Korea	475,469	2495	120,540
23.	Nauru	308,480	30	21
24.	Equatorial Guinea	303,509	296	28,051
25.	Jamaica	258,137	1022	10,991
26.	Liberia	249,734	579	111,369
27.	Honduras	249,542	823	112,494
28.	Sierra Leone	215,611	402	71,740
29	Gabon	202,790	885	267,668
30	Barbados	186,898	97	431
31	Mauritania	165,338	754	1,030,700
32	Comoros	163,752	340	1862
33	Senegal	158,861	531	196,722
34	Guyana	137,765	459	214,969
35	Saint Thomas and Príncipe	131,397	209	1001
36	Samoa	127,950	403	2842
37	Suriname	127,772	386	163,820
38	Haiti	126,760	1771	27,750

(*continued*)

Table 7.3 (continued)

No	*WSE*	*Maritime EEZ*	*Coastline length*	*Land area*
		km²	*km*	*km²*
39	Nicaragua	123,881	910	130,370
40	Guinea-Bissau	123,725	350	36,125
41	Antigua and Barbuda	110,089	153	442
42	Cyprus	98,707	648	9251
43	Salvador	90,962	307	21,041
44	Eritrea	77,728	2334	117,600
45	Trinidad and Tobago	74,199	362	5130
46	East Timor	70,326	706	14,919
47	Cambodia	62,515	443	181,035
48	Guinea	59,426	320	245,857
49	Malta	54,823	197	316
50	Estonia	36,992	3794	45,228
51	Saint Vincent and the Grenadines	36,302	84	389
52	Belize	35,351	386	22,966
53	Benin	33,221	121	114,763
54	Congo	31,017	169	342,000
55	Dominica	28,985	148	751
56	Grenada	27,426	121	344
57	The Gambia	23,112	80	11,295
58	Georgia	21,946	310	69,700
59	Saint Lucia	15,617	158	620
60	Albania	13,691	362	28,748
61	Togo	12,045	56	56,785
62	Brunei	10,090	161	5765
63	Saint Kitts and Nevis	9974	135	261
64	Montenegro	7745	293	13,812
65	Djibouti	7459	314	23,200
66	Monaco	288	4	2
67	Bosnia and Herzegovina	50	20	51,209
WSE group in total		30,765,752	73,497	7,939,446

Source: Own compilation based on The World Bank

Madagascar, Maldives, Marshall Islands, Mauritius, Micronesia, Papua New Guinea, Seychelles, and Solomon Islands (more than 900 thousand km²). The land area of some of them is large, while others is very small, reflecting the lack of correlation between the land area occupied and the maritime exclusive economic zone belonging to the country (Table 7.3). Countries with small areas, such as the Marshall Islands (181 km²), the

Maldives (300 km^2), Micronesia (702 km^2), Kiribati (811 km^2) have the maritime *Exclusive Economic Zone* larger than their land territory by more than 5300 times (Marshall Islands), 1400 times (Maldives), almost 500 times (Micronesia) that are more than 3000 times (Kiribati). This also applies to coastlines. Some countries with the largest maritime zones have very short maritime borders such as Mauritius (177 km), and Seychelles (491 km). Accordingly, there is also no connection between the land area and the length of the maritime borders as well as the area of the maritime EEZ. However, location does have an impact. In general, the more geographically isolated the WSE are, the larger their maritime zone. On the other hand, the WSE located on continents tend to have access to smaller maritime exclusive economic zone, as can be observed in the case of Albania, Belize, Benin, Bosnia and Herzegovina, Congo, The Gambia, Georgia, Monaco, Montenegro, and Togo (Table 7.3).

The total area of the maritime EEZ of the 67 WSE is 30.7 million km^2, or almost four times their land area (7.9 million km^2). This vast maritime territory, whose waters and seabed contain many valuable natural resources, serves an important economic function for many of the coastal WSE, which prioritize fishing and exploitation of the deposits at the bottom of their maritime EEZ. The landlocked WSE (e.g., Afghanistan, Armenia, Botswana, Laos, Moldova, Mongolia) have more limited rights, but nevertheless, the aforementioned United Nations Convention on the Law of the Sea (1982) guarantees them priority in purchasing fishing licenses in the water areas of coastal countries. They also enjoy the right of free transit through the maritime territory of coastal states, which means that their vessels are treated in seaports on an equal footing with those of coastal states, and transit itself is not subject to customs duties.

Maritime transport plays a major role in the economies of the WSE, and is one of the most intensively developing sectors related to the economic use of the seas and oceans. It is estimated in 2019, it handled more than 80% of global trade in goods, as it is the cheapest available and most common mode of transport (Kuchinski, 2007). In addition, it is characterized by its extensive global coverage of oceans and seas (two-thirds of the Earth's surface is covered by oceans) and relatively easy accessibility to ports around the world. Maritime transport has an advantage over air and land transport due to its large carrying capacity and volume, which cannot be achieved by similarly sized unit loads.

The greatest intensity of global maritime traffic occurs in the Northern Hemisphere. This includes the regions of the North Atlantic between Western Europe and the eastern coasts of the United States and Canada, and the North Pacific between Japan and the United States. In addition, the Strait of Malacca (between Malaysia and Indonesia), the Suez Canal, and the Panama Canal in the northern hemisphere are characterized by a high level of maritime traffic, mainly due to their strategic locations. Canal shipping brings benefits not only in terms of shorter routes and savings—such as in the case of the Suez Canal, reduces transit time up to 60% and freight costs—also benefits the countries that manage the canals and generate revenue from shipping services. One such example is the African WSE of Djibouti, located on the Red Sea in the northeastern Horn of Africa. The Port of Djibouti handles maritime traffic for both Djibouti and the entire region, generating huge revenues for the national budget. These revenues come from port services and transit fees on goods exported mainly from Ethiopia. Lacking direct access to the sea, Ethiopia's trade with the rest of the world is conducted through the port of Djibouti, which is connected by rail to Ethiopia's capital Addis Ababa (Domanski et al., 1999). Thus, tiny Djibouti (23,000 km^2) has become a leading shipping player in the African region thanks to its strategic location at the crossroads of one of the world's busiest shipping routes, as well as its long coastline (314 km).

In contrast to the Northern Hemisphere, the WSE in the Southern Hemisphere, with generally lower shipping intensity, benefits less from shipping. This is due to the much smaller land area of the Southern Hemisphere, as well as the smaller populations and weaker economic ties of the countries there. Apart from highly developed but sparsely populated Australia and a few developing countries, most of the countries along the Indian Ocean route are underdeveloped (e.g., East Timor, Madagascar, and Mozambique) and participate less in international trade of goods.

Associated with seaborne trade of goods are container ports, which play a key role in maritime transport through loading and unloading. In 2019, China by far dominated the global ranking of the world's 50 busiest ports, generating more than one-third of the world's total container terminal throughput. The ports of the WSE did not make the global top rank. The highest position was held by Malta (73rd) with the port of Marsaxlokk handling 2.7 million TEUs, followed by Jamaica with the Kingston port with a throughput of 1.8 million TEU.

Ports typically include container terminals, which are facilities for transshipment from various modes of transportation for onward shipment. In terms of container throughput, the WSE ranked much higher in the world (Table 7.4). Malta was ranked 42nd with a throughput of 2712 thousand TEUs (for comparison, the throughput of China, ranked first in the world,

Table 7.4 WSE with the largest container throughput in 2019 (Twenty-foot Equivalent Unit, TEU)

World position	*WSE*	*Container Throughput*
		TEU[a]
42	Malta	2,712,800
47	Jamaica	1,873,399
54	Togo	1,503,169
56	Bahamas	1,473,169
69	Djibouti	932,000
75	Cambodia	779,205
80	Mauritius	570,817
81	Senegal	562,875
82	Congo	557,875
83	Yemen	531,097
84	Benin	510,896

Source: Own compilation based on The World Bank

TEU (*Twenty-foot Equivalent* Unit) is a unit of capacity used for ports and ships, equal to the volume of a 20 × 8 × 8.5-foot container, or 6.10 × 2.44 × 2.59 meters, or approximately 39 meters[3]

was 242,030 thousand TEUs). Malta was followed by Jamaica, Togo, Bahamas, Djibouti (just ahead of Denmark and Norway, ranked 71st and 72nd in the world, respectively).

The accelerated processes of globalization at the turn of the twentieth and twenty-first centuries were accompanied not only by an increase in international trade in goods, but also by technological developments, including the shipbuilding industry. New innovations required new designs and equipment. Outdated oil-carrying tankers and bulk carriers transporting coal and metal ores were being replaced by much faster and safer smaller ships, such as OBO (Oil-Bulk-Ore), COB (Container-Oil-Bulk), Ro-Ro (passenger-cargo ships adapted to carry cars, among other things), as well as chemical carriers, container gas carriers, and reefer ships (Furmaga & Wojcicki, 1993). The intensity of interstate economic ties has contributed to an increase in the deadweight tonnage of the world maritime fleet. In 2020, it amounted to 1972 million DWT, more than twice as much as in 2006 (959 million DWT) and more than three times as much as in 1980 (680 million DWT). In 2020, more than 95% of the world's maritime fleet was controlled by only 35 countries in the world, among which were the 2 WSE: Monaco and Cyprus. Monaco generated 2.14% of the world's tonnage, ranking 13th in the world, while Cyprus

Table 7.5 Deadweight tonnage of the WSE ships compared to global leading countries

Global position	*The world's leading countries*	*Ships*	*Ships deadweight*	*Share of global carrying capacity*
		No	*million DWT*	*%*
1	Panama	7886	328,950	16
2	Liberia	3716	274,786	13
3	Marshall Islands	3683	261,806	13
4	Hong Kong, China	2694	201,361	10
5	Singapore	3420	140,333	7
6	Malta	2207	115,879	6
7	China	6192	100,086	5
8	Bahamas	1381	77,869	4
9	Greece	1294	68,632	3
10	Japan	5041	40,323	2
11	Cyprus	1065	34,533	2
12	Indonesia	10,137	25,574	1
	WSE group in total:	12,052	764,873	38
	World:	98,140	2,061,944	100

Source: Own compilation based on UNCTAD, Maritime Transport Services and Infrastructure Supply, Review of Maritime Transport 2020

generated 0.57%, ranking 28th in the world. Monaco's merchant fleet consisted of 473 vessels with a carrying capacity of 43.8 million DWT. Although these were Monaco-controlled vessels, they all sailed under foreign flags. The Cypriot merchant fleet, on the other hand, consisted of 306 vessels with a total tonnage of 11.6 million DWT, but only part of them (6.6 million DWT) sailed under foreign flags. While only two WSE hold significant positions in generating global tonnage of the world's maritime fleet, many others offered their flags. The top 'flag of convenience' (FOC) were Liberia (2nd globally), the Marshall Islands (3rd), Malta (6th), the Bahamas (8th) and Cyprus (11th). The number of registered vessels in these five countries totaled 12,052, representing almost 12.3% of the world's registered vessels (98,140). Their total tonnage amounted to 764.8 billion DWT (Table 7.5), which represented more than one-third of the world's tonnage in 2020. The WSE offering flags of convenience allows foreign owners and shipowners to register ships in their territory, offering favorable financial terms (including low taxes, fees, no accounting and financial reporting requirements) that make the overall maintenance of a ship many times cheaper than registering it in its home country. There are also other advantages, such as low social requirements and technical conditions of the vessel thanks to very liberal safety regulations. The registration process itself is also much less formal.

In addition to Liberia, Marshall Islands, Malta, Bahamas, and Cyprus, less popular WSE were Antigua and Barbuda, Barbados, Belize, Cambodia, Comoros, Equatorial Guinea, Georgia, Honduras, Jamaica, Mauritius, Mongolia, North Korea, Saint Vincent and the Grenadines, Saint Thomas and Principe, Tonga, and Vanuatu. It is worth noting that the share of vessels registered by these countries in 2019 was much higher for foreign vessels than for local vessels (Fig. 7.3), with the exception of Equatorial Guinea, North Korea, and Tonga.

Maritime transport includes not only the international cargo exchange, but also the international passenger transportation. Although, transoceanic passenger transport began to decline in the twentieth century in favor of faster air transport, tourist travel by ferries, yachts, ships in the form of cruises began to play an increasingly important role (Mika, 2007). This is evidenced by the almost fourfold increase in the number of cruise ship passengers worldwide between 2000 and 2019 between 2000 and 2019 from 7.2 million to 27.7 million. The most popular destinations were the WSE located in the Caribbean. Port Nassau (3.5 million passengers) and Port Out Islands (2.5 million), located in the Bahamas, were the most visited ports in 2018. They ranked fifth and eighth in the world in terms of traffic intensity and cruise ship passenger inflows (Table 7.6).

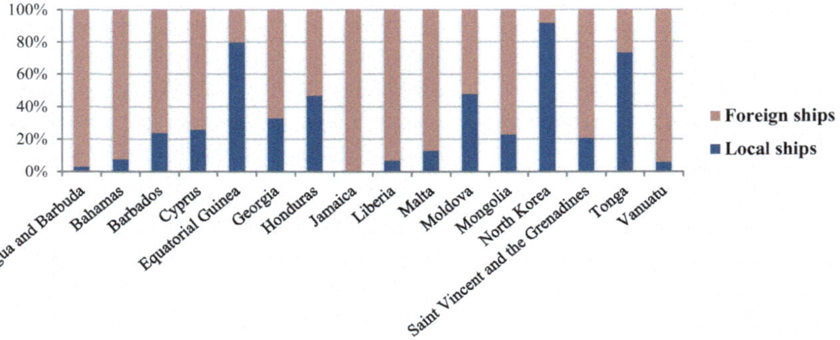

Fig. 7.3 Foreign and local ships registered in the sample WSE (%). (Source: Own compilation based on UNCTAD, Maritime Transport Services and Infrastructure Supply, Review of Maritime Transport 2020)

Table 7.5 Largest cruise ports in the WSE in 2018

Global position	*Cruise port*	*WSE*	*Passengers*
Rank	*Name*	*Name*	*Quantity*
5	Port of Nassau	Bahamas	3,521,178
8	Port of Out Islands	Bahamas	2,549,803
15	Port of Jamaica	Jamaica	1,655,565
26	Port of Roatan	Honduras	1,037,645
33	Port of Basseterre	Saint Kitts and Nevis	951,021
43	Port of Barbados	Barbados	818,752
45	Port of Valetta	Malta	778,596
58	Port of Kotor	Montenegro	598,672
95	Port of Monaco	Monaco	168,017
	Largest 9 ports in the WSE group		3,315,058
	Ports of the world in total		26,504,600

Source: Own compilation based on Cruise Industry News, Annual Report 2021

The next places in the ranking of the 50 most popular cruise ports in the world were occupied by the ports of the WSE: the Port of Jamaica in Jamaica (15th), Port of Roatan in Honduras (26th), the Port of Basseterre in Saint Kitts and Nevis (33rd), Port of Barbados in Barbados (43rd) and Port of Valetta in Malta (45th). Together, these seven ports welcomed more than 42% of the world's cruise ship passengers (11.3 million in 2018), the vast majority of whom went to the Caribbean. The world's largest passenger ships, including Symphony of the Seas, Harmony of the Seas, Allure of the Seas, and Oasis of the Seas, all 362 meters long and 66 meters wide, operated by Royal Caribbean International, sailed between these ports. Ocean and sea cruises have become an increasingly popular form of tourism, combining a stay on the seas and oceans with visits to coastal countries. Ships provide tourists with permanent and comfortable accommodations and during the day tourists can enjoy other attractions offered by the ships or spend time sightseeing. This growing branch of the tourism industry brings many benefits not only to cruise passengers, who are tourists, but also to the WSE, where the cruise ships arrive, and to the home countries of the cruise companies.

The exploitation of the oceans and seas plays an important role in the economies of the WSE, especially in the coastal economies (67 countries). The waters of the oceans and seas are a source of food for the population, serve an important transportation function, and contribute to the development of tourism in coastal regions (e.g., Bahamas, Belize, Cyprus, Fiji,

The Gambia, Jamaica, Malta, Maldives, Mauritius, Palau, Saint Kitts and Nevis, Saint Lucia). Ocean waters are also a source of mineral resources that are slowly being depleted on land. Many WSE exploit mineral resources from shelf waters, and profits from their export are often the main source of income for their economies. For example, as much as 86% of Brunei's exports in 2019 were oil and gas, 80% of which came from shelf deposits in the South China Sea. Similarly, in Equatorial Guinea, oil and gas, are accounting for 90% of total exports, are extracted from the shelf waters of Bioko Island, in Equatorial Guinea, located in the Atlantic Ocean. Another example is Trinidad and Tobago, which exports oil (61% of exports in 2019) from the Gulf of Paria in the Caribbean Sea, and in the case of East Timor (74% of exports), from underwater deposits in the Timor Sea. In addition to oil and natural gas, other resources have been extracted from the oceanic shelf waters. Examples include phosphates (Nauru), and diamonds (Namibia).

Maritime areas have a very important economic function for the WSE with access to the sea. Their original inhabitants engaged in fishing and shellfish gathering along the coast. Over time, the local fisheries of the coastal WSE evolved into deep-sea and oceanic fisheries, and sea travel evolved into transoceanic commercial shipping. Over time, shipping, port services and shipbuilding developed. In turn, the growing demand for mineral resources became a motivation for scientists to explore the seabed and ocean floor. This scientific research activity was initiated to serve the development of marine mining and exploitation of the riches deposited on the seabed. The oceans and seas provide employment for the inhabitants of the coastal WSE and contribute to their economic growth. However, the economic use of marine areas by humans is only one of the benefits. Seas and oceans also play a fundamental role in shaping the environment and life on Earth.

Ocean and seawater heated by solar energy, accumulate huge amounts of heat. As a result of this heat's evaporation and condensation at low temperatures, clouds are formed. Precipitation forms in them. Precipitation in the form of rain, snow, hail and snowmelt flows into the oceans and seas and onto the land, where it enters marine and inland reservoirs in proportions of 80% and 20%, respectively. Some of the infiltrating water seeps into the ground, forming groundwater, while the near-surface portion flows down to, feed surface waters, oceans and seas. This process inititates a water cycle, where water transforms into vapor due to solar energy and gravitational force. This cycle illustrates the continuous movement of water between the atmosphere, hydrosphere, and lithosphere and the

Earth's biosphere, both seawater and freshwater. Freshwater accumulates in among other places, inland waters, which consist of groundwater and surface water. Because they contain dtinking water inland waters play an enormous role in human life. They are essential to life on Earth and the survival of not only humans, but also many species of plants and animals.

While *surface water* is not found in all areas of the Earth, groundwater is found beneath every surface of the Earth except frozen ground. Therefore, all the WSE have groundwater, with the exception of the permafrost in Iceland. However, the depth at which groundwater is found varies, as does its availability. The depth to which groundwater, and especially its first aquifer, can be found depends on three basic factors: climate (the amount of precipitation); the configuration and permeability of the bedrock encountered by water as it travels underground under the influence of gravity; and the presence of surface water. The latter is much more limited. Some of the WSE do not even have surface water, such as the smallest WSE in terms of area Monaco (2 km^2), located on the Mediterranean Sea. Due to its lack of surface water and difficult access to deep groundwater, Monaco has to import water from France, a few kilometers away.

From the perspective of the WSE group, permanent surface waters make up a small percentage of its land area (17,536,000 km^2), accounting for just 0.66%, or just 116,000 km^2. This includes lakes (about 86%), swamps (11%), and a small percentage of rivers, ponds, streams, and canals (3%). The WSE such as the Maldives, Malta, Monaco, and San Marino have no lakes, while the Bahamas, Comoros, Djibouti, Kiribati, Maldives, Malta, Monaco, Nauru, Tonga, Tuvalu, Marshall Islands, and Yemen have no rivers. In contrast, the largest surface water areas are found in Malawi (23,700 km^2), Mongolia (13,900 km^2), Mozambique (11,300 km^2), and Nicaragua (9500 km^2). These four countries account for half of the surface waters of the entire WSE group (Fig. 7.4). Other countries with significant surface water areas include: Kyrgyzstan (7200 km^2), Papua New Guinea (3500 km^2), Cambodia (3400 km^2), Zimbabwe (3400 km^2), Madagascar (2600 km^2), Gabon (2300 km^2), Congo (2200 km^2), and Estonia (2100 km^2).

The areas of these 12 countries (Fig. 7.4) accumulate 73% of the surface waters of the entire WSE group, which is mainly contained in lakes and rivers (Table 7.7). However, the areas of freshwater reservoirs in these countries are a small fraction of their land area (Table 7.7), ranging from 1.11% (Congo) to 20.61% (Malawi).

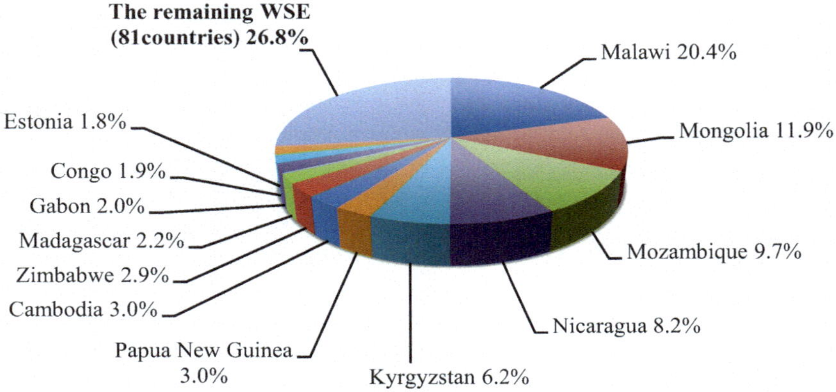

Fig. 7.4 WSE permanent surface water as a share of the group in 2019 (%). (Source: Own compilation based on OECD, Stat, Surface water 2015 and The World Bank)

Table 7.7 Largest lakes and longest rivers in the WSE in 2019

Group position	*WSE*	*Surface water*			
		Area	*Share of land*	*Largest lakes*	*Longest rivers*
		km²	*%*		
1	Malawi	23,774	20.61	Malawi (29,600 km²) Chilwa (1750 km²)	Shire (402 km)
2	Mongolia	13,895	1.17	Uvs (3350 km²) Hovsgol (2770 km²) Buyr (610 km²) Hyargas (1407 km²) Har Us (1760 km²)	Dzawchan (808 km) Tula (704 km) Kobdo (593 km)
3	Mozambique	11,332	2.31	Malawi (29,600 km²) Cahora Bassa (2739 km²) Chilwa (1750 km²)	Zambezi (2574 km) Ruvuma (800 km) Lurio (620 km)
4	Nicaragua	9562	8.54	Nicaragua, Cocibolca (8264 km²) Managua (1016 km²)	Segovia (480 km) San Juan (195)
5	Kyrgyzstan	7217	3.94	Aralskie (13,500 km²) Issyk-Kool (6236 km²)	Naryn (616 km) Talas (254 km) Chu (214 km)

(*continued*)

Table 7.7 (continued)

Group position	*WSE*	*Surface water*			
		Area	*Share of land*	*Largest lakes*	*Longest rivers*
		km²	*%*		
6	Papua New Guinea	3559	1.88	Murray (647 km²) Chambri (216 km²)	Sepik (1126 km) Fly (1120 km) Ramu (720 km)
7	Cambodia	3470	13.19	Tonie Sap (30,000 km²)	Mekong (4880 km) Sangke (250 km)
8	Zimbabwe	3403	1.16	Kariba (5400 km²) Mutirikwi (90 km²)	Zambezi (2574 km) Limpopo (1750 km)
9	Madagascar	2625	1.53	Alaotra (900 km²) Tsimanampetsotsa (39 km²) Itasy (35 km²)	Mongoro (300 km) Mandrare (270 km) Maningory (260 km)
10	Gabon	2315	1.13	Tail	Ogowe (1200 km) Nyanga (600 km) Komo (230 km)
11	Congo	2164	1.11	Tumba (500 km²)	Congo (4700 km) Ubangi (1300 km) Kouilou (725 km)
12	Estonia	2159	5.16	Peipus (3555 km²) Vortsjarv (271 km²)	Vohandu (162 km) Parnu (144 km)

Note: The total areas of lakes and lengths of rivers have been given.

Source: Own compilation based on World Lake Database, International Lake Environment Committee Foundation and OECD, Stat, Surface water, Permanent water 2015

Lakes and rivers, like seas and oceans, play a very important role both naturally and economically. They increase surface water retention, stabilize groundwater level, thus improving local water conditions and contributing to the humidification of the local climate. Their economic use in the WSE is extensive. They are used for irrigation of agricultural land, as well as a raw material for the development of many industries (including energy, textile, chemical, and metallurgical), as receptors for domestic and industrial wastewater, as transportation routes for people and goods, or as a tourist attraction for recreation and water sports (such as sailing). Lakes and rivers influenced the development of settlements and determined the attractiveness of settlements, which usually became ports, for example, Port Chipoka on Lake Malawi in Malawi, Port Boma on the Congo River in Congo, Port Parnu on the Parnu River in Estonia, Port Phnom Penh on the Mekong River in Cambodia, Port Granada on Lake Nicaragua in Nicaragua.

Water consumption (quantity and use) varies according to the level of economic development of the WSE and their geographical location. In highly developed WSE, such as Cyprus, Estonia, Iceland, and Malta, industry is an important consumer of water and households are the largest consumers. On the other hand, in developing countries such as Albania, Armenia, Belize, Dominica, El Salvador, Georgia, and Namibia, a lot of water is used for agricultural purposes. In contrast, the consumption is lowest in the poorest of the WSE. This is due to rapid population growth and water scarcity, resulting from low rainfall and the lack of large reservoirs. Difficult access to drinking water forces women and children to walk an average of 6 km a day and carry 20 liters of drinking water.[3] The lack of water causes many diseases and increases mortality. According to the WHO, about 6000 children die every day from diseases related to lack of water or drinking contaminated water. These figures mean that one child dies every 15 seconds.

In 2019, drinking water resources in the tropical WSE, such as Djibouti, Mauritania, Niger, Somalia, ranged from 93 m^3 per person (Mauritania) to 411 m^3 per person (Somalia). Slightly higher but still low rates, ranging from 558 m^3 per person to 999 m^3 per person, were recorded in other African WSE, such as Benin, Burkina Faso, Burundi, Cape Verde, Chad, Eritrea, Malawi, Niger, Rwanda, and Zimbabwe (Fig. 7.5). However, the Maldives had the smallest resources of the entire studied group of 93 countries, with only 60 m^3 per person. It did not have enough freshwater to meet the needs of its growing local population (from 279,000 to 530,000 between 2000 and 2019) and, most importantly, tourists arriving every year (from 0.5 million to 1.8 million arrivals between 2000 and 2019). Since there is no surface water on the Maldivian islands, freshwater is obtained by desalinating seawater, as well as from rainwater that collects on the roofs of houses. Houses, once thatched with palm leaves, are now covered with corrugated metal sheets to collect rainwater. Tourist resorts are also equipped with expensive seawater desalination systems. It is worth noting that the Maldives is the only country in the world where Coca-Cola

[3] In 2019, more than 1.2 billion people around the world had limited access to water, and 200 million of the world's population were without water.

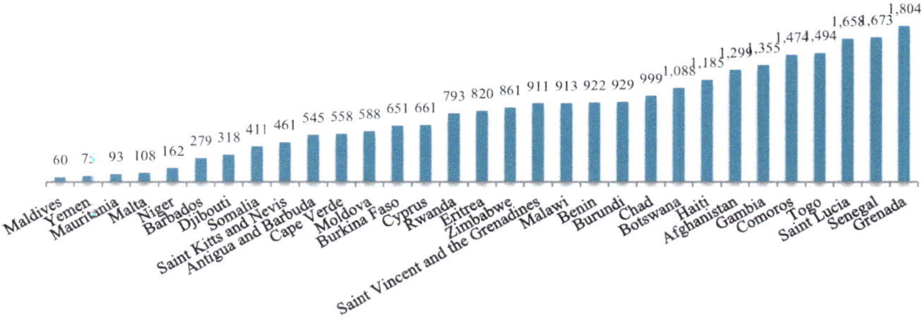

Fig. 7.5 WSE with the least drinking water resources in 2019 (m³ per person). (Source: Own compilation based on The World Bank)

is made from salt water, desalinated at a local factory operating since the 1980s on Thulusdhoo Island.

The people of Malta also face a shortage of drinking water (108 m³ per person). Malta, with the exception of a few periodic rivers, has no permanent surface water. This is due to the seasonality of precipitation, which falls mostly in the winter. Additionally, the rocky ground causes water to flow through cracks deep below the surface. The situation is similar in Cyprus, whose average water availability, although more than six times higher than Malta's (661 m³ per person), is still relatively low compared to the world average (5732 m³ per person), and even more so compared to the water-rich WSE, such as Iceland 495,049 m³ per person, Guyana 310,880 m³ per person, Suriname 173,532 m³ per person, Bhutan 104,618 m³ per person, Papua New Guinea 94,927 m³ per person, and Gabon 79,426 m³ per person. This leads to the conclusion that the largest amounts of potable water are available in the equatorial WSE, which benefit from abundant zenithal rains, and in the WSE located in climates with permafrost near glaciers and in snow-covered mountains terrain. These particular countries have also not experienced significant losses of drinking water. Between 1990 and 2019, the decline in Iceland was from 651,199 m³ per person to 495,049 m³ per person, in Guyana from 321,936 m³ per person to 310,880 m³ per person, and in Suriname from 235,346 m³ per person to 173,532 m³ per person. Meanwhile, other of the WSE showed declines of up to more than double. This is due to climate change, melting glaciers, rising sea levels, and irrational management of freshwater. Reduced availability of drinking water, deterioration of water quality and increased consumption due to rapid population growth have led to growing number of the WSE using desalinated seawater, which is extracted through a complex and energy-intensive, and costly technological process. This trend is expected to intensify as the population of the WSE continues to grow, nearly doubling over the past three decades, from 299 million to 561 million between 1990 and 2019. As a result, demand for both fresh- and seawater will continue to rise.

Freshwater and marine reservoirs are suppliers not only of beverages, but also of food. Both freshwater, and saltwater fish are the bases in the diet of many people living in the WSE. In 2019, Maldivians consumed the most fish, at 139 kg per person. Second in the world and among the WSE group were Icelanders at 88.3 kg per person, followed by residents of Kiribati—72.4 kg per person (3rd place in the world), the Seychelles—57.4 kg per person (5th place in the world), and Antigua and Barbuda—54.6 kg per person (8th place in the world). Thus, the largest amount of fish in the world was consumed by the inhabitants of the island WSE, due to easy availability. The population's awareness of the nutritional value of fish (i.e., valuable protein, fats, mineral salts, and vitamins), especially in economically developed WSE, also played a large role.

Oceanic and marine fisheries played a dominant role in catches of the WSE, accounting for more than 90% of the fish caught, while freshwater fisheries accounted for less than 10%. In 2018, total saltwater and freshwater catches amounted to 9,795,000 tons of fish, a 33% increase compared to 2000, which is camparable to a similar 32% increase worldwide. Between 2000 and 2018, the WSE group's fish production accounted for a stable share of global catches, ranging from 4.8% to 4.9%. On the other hand, this share was very low, if we consider only the area of the maritime Exclusive Economic Zone to which the WSE have access. This group has almost 1/4 of the area of the maritime EEZ of all countries in the world (30.7 million km^2), which contains a substantial share of the world's fish stocks. Thus, such a low share of global catches indicates the very limited use of marine resource potential by the coastal WSE.

Among the 93 WSE, Iceland was the largest producer of fish (1297 thousand tons), and its catch accounted for more than 13.2% of the total group's catch (Fig. 7.6) and 0.64% of global catch. Iceland's fisheries are mainly concentrated in areas of the North Atlantic, where the waters of the warm North Atlantic Current, aided by the warm Irminger Current, mix with those of the cold East Greenland Current. The waters there are well oxygenated and contain a lot of plankton.

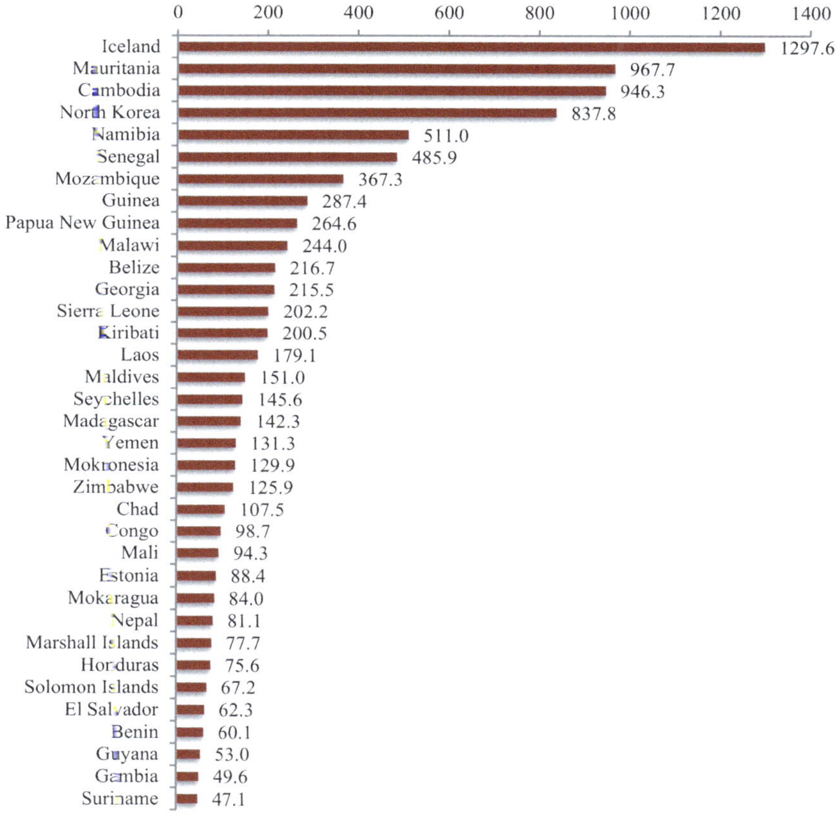

Fig. 7.6 Largest saltwater fish producers in the WSE group in 2018 (thousands of tons). (Source: Own compilation based on World Food and Agriculture—Statistical Yearbook 2020)

Second in terms of fish production was Mauritania (967,000 tons), whose fertile ocean fishery is the result of the phenomenon of upwelling, that is, cold, well-oxygenated and nutrient-rich deep ocean waters rising to the surface and then being replaced by warm waters flowing down from the coast. A similar phenomenon occurs in the monsoon zone of Southeast Asia, where the direction of ocean currents are variable. For example, near the coasts of Cambodia, which ranked third in the WSE group in terms of fish production (9.6% of the WSE group's production) and North Korea—fourth in the WSE group in terms of fish production (8.5% of the WSE group's production). The fifth place in fish production (5.2% of the WSE group) was occupied by Namibia, whose shelf waters are abundant in fish thanks to the cold Bengal Current that flows around southwest Africa. Together, these five countries—Iceland, Mauritania, Cambodia, North Korea, and Namibia—accounted for almost half of the fish production (saltwater and freshwater) in the WSE group.

Surprisingly, the smallest catches were recorded by the island WSE that had access to some of the largest areas of maritime EEZ, namely Nauru with a zone of 308,000 km^2, Palau 603,000 km^2, and Tonga 659,000 km^2. In contrast, their fish production in 2018 did not exceed 1300 tons. In the case of Nauru, the lack of developed fisheries can be explained by the economy's focus on industrial sector—phosphate mining, which brings most revenue to the state, while in Palau, the lack of incentive to develop fisheries is linked to the strong development of tourism, which generates over 46% of Palau's GDP. In the case of Tonga, neither industry, agriculture, nor tourism services generated income to the economy. Its industrial development was limited by the lack of mineral resources, and tourism—by the dispersion of Tonga's 170 islands over an area of 260,000 km^2, comparable to the area of New Zealand. The lack of indigenous agricultural and industrial production forced the inhabitants of the Kingdom of Tonga to emigrate en masse for work. As a result, Tonga ranked first in the world in terms of the remittance as a share in GDP, amounting to 37% in 2019. Thus, the main source of income for the Tonga's population was money transfers from Tongans working abroad, while its maritime territories with the potential of its waters were almost untapped.

To compare the freshwater and saltwater fish catches of the WSE, a per capita indicator was used. In 2018, Iceland ranked first among the WSE (5th in the world), with 3679 kg of fish per Icelander (Fig. 7.7). In second place, with a rate of more than half as high, was Kiribati (1731 kg per person) and in third place was the Seychelles (1505 kg per person). All three countries saw an almost threefold increase between 2000 and 2018.

The next leading positions were held by the Pacific WSE (Fig. 7.7), that is, the Marshall Islands (1330 kg per person), Micronesia (1153 kg per person), and Tuvalu (1106 kg per person). These, in turn, increased their catches by more than six times between 2000 and 2018. The WSE with the highest per capita fish catches had small populations, ranging from 11,000 (Tuvalu) to 352,000 (Iceland). In addition, they all had huge

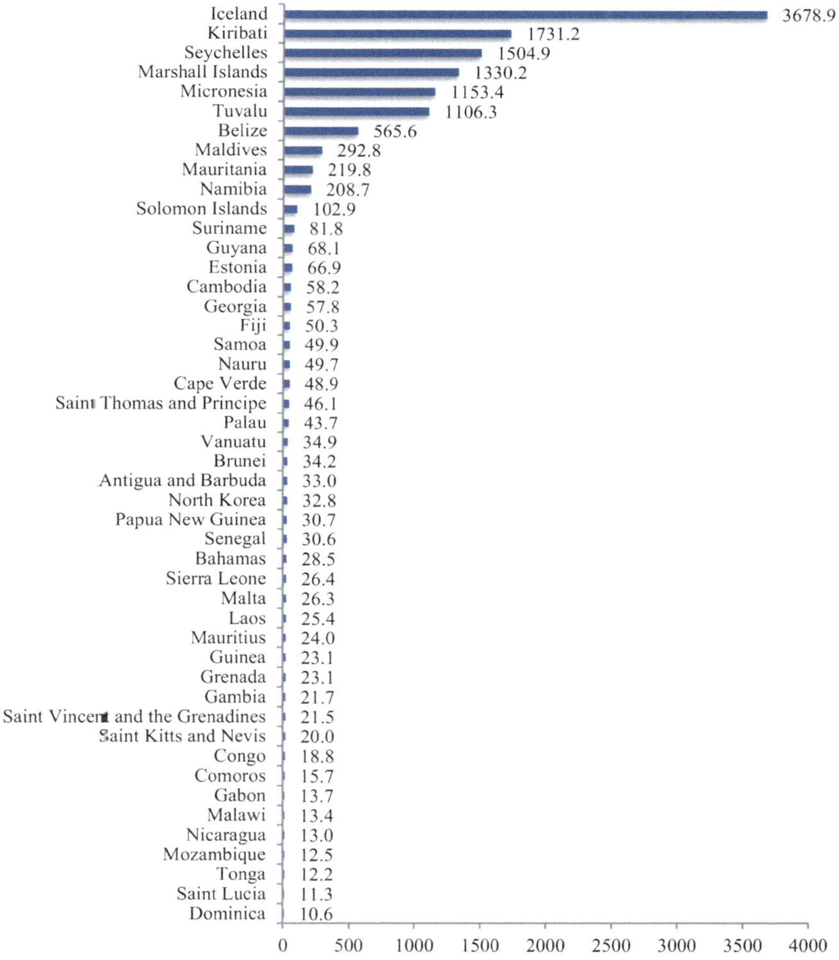

Fig. 7.7 WSE saltwater and freshwater fish producers with over 10 kg per person in 2018 (kg). (Source: Own compilation based on The World Bank)

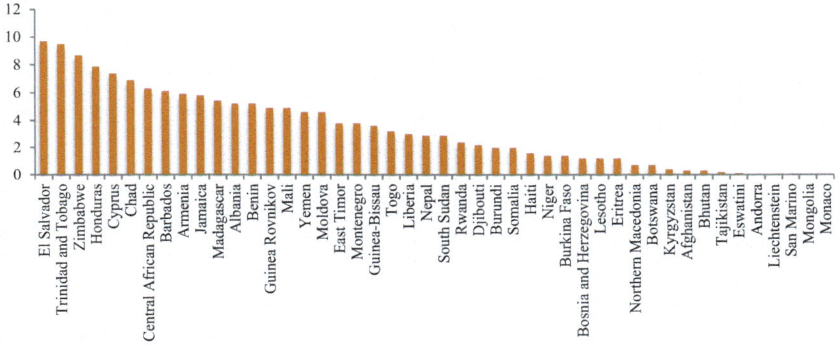

Fig. 7.8 WSE saltwater and freshwater producers with less than 10 kg per person in 2018 (kg). (Source: Own compilation based on The World Bank)

areas of marine EEZ, ranging from 0.7 million km^2 (Tuvalu) to 3.4 km^2 (Kiribati). Access to them conditioned their fishing.

The WSE producing less than 10 kg per person (46 countries) (Fig. 7.8) are primarily landlocked nations (e.g., Armenia, Bhutan, Burundi, Central African Republic, Eswatini, Lesotho, Moldova, Nepal, Rwanda, Zimbabwe). Most of them occupy mainly regions with hot tropical climate, with surface water reservoirs that dry out during periods of drought (e.g., Chad, Djibouti, Eritrea, Mali, Niger, Somalia, Yemen) and subtropical or temperate continental dry climates (e.g., Afghanistan, Kyrgyzstan, Mongolia, Tajikistan). Among them, are also mineral-rich WSE whose economic policy objective is mining (e.g., Botswana, Equatorial Guinea, Liberia, Mongolia, South Sudan, Trinidad and Tobago) or service industries (e.g., Andorra, Liechtenstein, Monaco, San Marino) rather than fishing.

While almost all the WSE have access to freshwater inland reservoirs, only the 67 WSE have access to seas and oceans. These are the ones that derive the greatest economic benefits from their water resources. Aside from a few WSE that do not capitalize on the potential of their marine waters (i.e., The Gambia, Guinea-Bissau, Somalia, Tonga, Yemen), others are effectively exploiting it by developing various industries such as offshore mining (e.g., Brunei, East Timor, Namibia, Trinidad and Tobago), shipbuilding, cosmetics, pharmaceutical, as well as services like cruise tourism (e.g., Bahamas, Barbados, Saint Kitts and Nevis, Saint Lucia), transportation, port services (e.g., Cyprus, Djibouti, Jamaica, Malta), flags of convenience (e.g., Liberia, Malta, Marshall Islands), and especially fishing (e.g., Cambodia, Iceland, Kiribati, Maldives, Mauritania).

The hydrosphere of the other 36 landlocked WSE is much poorer and therefore more limited in terms of economic use of their water resources. Nevertheless, using the potential of their rivers and lakes, these countries are developing freshwater fisheries (e.g., Laos, Malawi), tourism (e.g., Botswana, Laos, Rwanda, Zimbabwe), fuel and energy, chemical, metallurgical industries (e.g., Kyrgyzstan, Tajikistan), as well as agriculture requiring field irrigation (e.g., Laos). Unfortunately, the hot tropical WSE with a negative water balance (e.g., Chad, Mali, Niger, South Sudan) are in the worst situation. Lack of access to the sea and permanent rivers and lakes deprives them of the possibility of economic use of their water resources, and, above all, limits access to drinking water.

The interaction between the environment and the economy has always taken place, with the strength of environmental elements being much greater in the past, as they determined the ways and pace at which economies developed. However, the development of civilization and technological advances have meant that the strength of the environment has been increasingly mitigated by fertilizing soils, draining wetlands, irrigating farmland, building transportation routes in hard-to-reach areas, and transferring water over long distances. Since these activities involve financial outlays, richer countries can more easily afford them. Meanwhile, the WSE group was mostly represented by countries with low and very low level of economic development (the GDP of more than half did not exceed US$ 2500 per capita in 2019). The lack of adequate capital made it difficult to overcome the challenges of nature, so these countries were left only to adapt to environmental conditions. These conditions often made it difficult, if not impossible, to undertake economic activities, which consequently led to a slowdown in economic growth and development. An example of this is the unfavorable tropical and extremely dry climates of the 18 WSE (Table 7.8). This subgroup of countries recorded the lowest level of economic development, both in 2000 and in 2019, with very little growth (GDP from US$ 888 per capita to US$ 1,158 per capita).

Also, the very hot and excessively humid equatorial climate of the 54 WSE (Table 7.8) was not conducive to their economic development, as reflected in the slightly higher per capita GDP of this subgroup (GDP increased from US$ 1247 per capita to US$ 1436 per capita in 2000–2019). It is worth noting that these two subgroups: the tropical WSE and the equatorial WSE, accounted for more than 80% of the WSE group's population. They were also the subgroups with the highest rates of population growth (Table 7.8). The impact of the environment on the economies was also evident in the landforms (Table 7.9). The WSE subgroup mostly covered by

Table 7.8 WSE typology by climate zones and GDP and population changes between 2000 and 2019

No	Climate zones	Countries	Area	GDP		Population		GDP	
				2000	2019	2000	2019	2000	2019
		quantity	thousand km^2	USD million		Thousand		USD per capita	
1.	Equatorial	54	6225.3	205,754	376,642	164,976	262,352	1247	1436
2.	Tropical	18	8181.6	112,483	224,819	126,684	194,193	888	1158
3.	Subtropical	14	1062.7	82,292	176,655	45,672	65,516	1802	2696
4.	Moderate	6	1963.8	42,340	80,659	34,579	39,370	3864	4150
5.	Circumpolar	1	103.0	10,535	18,547	281	361	37,465	51,332
The WSE group in total		93	17,536.6	453,405	877,322	372,192	561,792	1218	1562

Source: Own compilation based on CIA The World Factbook

Table 7.9 WSE typology by landform and GDP and population changes between 2000 and 2019

No	Landform	Countries	Area	GDP		Population		GDP/person	
				2000	2019	2000	2019	2000	2019
		Quantity	thousand km^2	US$ million		thousand		US$ per capita	
1.	Mountainous	21	3820.4	64,115	166,315	87,293	126,260	734	1317
2.	Highlands	43	11,118.6	265,144	465,539	217,341	330,488	1220	1409
3.	Lowland	29	2597.6	124,145	245,468	67,558	105,044	1838	2337
The WSE group in total		93	17,536.6	453,405	877,322	372,192	561,792	1218	1562

Source: Own compilation based on CIA The World Factbook

mountainous terrian (21 countries) showed the lowest level of economic development (GDP increased from US$ 734 per capita to US$ 1317 per capita). In contrast, the subgroup of the lowland WSE. with areas most conducive for agriculture, transportation, industry, achieved the highest GDP growth (from US$ 1838 per capita to US$ 2337 per capita).

Regardless of the above-mentioned environmental elements that promote or hinder economic development, almost all the WSE are subject to natural disasters such as earthquakes, tsunamis, volcanic eruptions, tropical cyclones, and the El Niño phenomenon, which residents cannot control and which cause huge economic losses. They have caused tens, hundreds, or even thousands of human deaths, destruction of infrastructure, fires, landform changes, floods, and, in the case of undersea earthquakes—tsunamis. Examples from the past two decades include: the 2004 Indian Ocean floor earthquake (9.1 degrees on the Richter scale) that affected the WSE, including the Maldives and Somalia; the 2010 Haiti earthquake (7 degrees on the Richter scale), which took more than 300,000 lives; and then 2015 Nepal earthquake (7.8 degrees on the Richter scale), when nearly 9000 people were killed and more than 24,000 injured However, many more of the WSE lie in areas of high seismic activity, including Afghanistan, Armenia, Cyprus, Djibouti, East Timor, El Salvador, Fiji, Northern Macedonia, Nicaragua, Papua New Guinea, and the Solomon Islands. An example of volcanic disturbance was the eruption of the Eyjafjallajokull volcano in Iceland in 2010. At the time, volcanic ash emissions into the atmosphere caused an ash cloud to form over Europe, preventing aircraft from flying. This caused major financial losses for airlines. Tropical cyclones, known as hurricanes in the Caribbean and Atlantic Ocean and typhoons in the Pacific, are another example of natural disasters to which the WSE are regularly exposed. They form over the oceans, moving inland and bringing with them strong winds and heavy rains. Examples of hurricanes include Hurricane Georges in 1998, which hit the WSE: Antigua and Barbuda, the Bahamas, Haiti, and Saint Kitts and Nevis, causing 604 deaths and US$ 6 billion in property damage; Hurricane Felix in 2007—in Nicaragua (130 victims and U$ 720 million in damage); Hurricane Gustav in 2008—on Jamaica and Haiti (92 victims and US$ 7 billion in losses); Hurricane Sandy in 2012—on the Bahamas, Jamaica, and Haiti (107 victims and US$ 65 billion in losses); Hurricane Maria in 2017—on Dominica and Haiti (68 victims and US$ 92 billion in losses). Typhoons, on the other hand, annually hit the WSE located in the Pacific, as exemplified by Typhoon Halyan in 2013, which hit Micronesia and Palau, among others (6340 victims); Typhoon Pam in 2015—in Tuvalu, Vanuatu, and the Solomon Islands (16 victims); Typhoon Harold in 2020—in Fiji, Tonga, Vanuatu, and the Solomon Islands (31 victims).

Another threat to some of the WSE is rising ocean levels. Changes in the global climate are occurring as a result of human activity and associated excessive greenhouse gas emissions. The increase of the Earth's average temperature is contributing to the melting of glaciers near the poles and in high-altitude areas, causing global sea and ocean levels to rise. Most at risk of flooding are Kiribati, the Maldives, and Tuvalu, which the UN says are at risk of flooding by 2050. While the low level of the Maldives and Kiribati islands are due to natural geomorphological factors, Tuvalu's low levels are largely the result of human transformation. During World War II, the Americans razed the islands of Tuvalu to establish air bases, destroying the natural elevation of the land in that process. A 20 cm rise in ocean levels over the past century has left the completely flat islands in danger of disappearing beneath the surface. To prevent this, the people of Tuvalu are strengthening the coasts of the islands and reforesting them with trees and shrubs. At the same time, in the event of flooding, the Tuvalu government has signed a treaty under which the Royal New Zealand Navy undertakes to evacuate the Tuvalu people and the Tuvalu state to the Fijian island of Kioa or to the land belonging to Australia, which Tuvalu intends to buy. The effects of climate change have also begun to be felt by other WSE, prompting them to join the *Alliance of Small Island States* (AOSIS), formed in 1990. As of 2019, of 43 member countries, as many as 34 are the WSE (Antigua and Barbuda, Bahamas, Barbados, Belize, Cape Verde, Comoros, Dominica, East Timor, Fiji, Grenada, Guinea-Bissau, Guyana, Haiti, Jamaica, Kiribati, Maldives, Marshall Islands, Mauritius, Micronesia, Nauru, Palau, Papua New Guinea, Saint Kitts and Nevis, Saint Lucia, Saint Vincent and the Grenadines, Samoa, Saint Thomas and Principe, Seychelles, Solomon Islands, Suriname, Tonga, Trinidad and Tobago, Tuvalu, Vanuatu).

Global warming has also brought a reduction in rainfall, resulting in drier areas, especially in the Sahel WSE (Chad, Eritrea, Mali, Mauritania, Niger, Senegal, Somalia) and in the southern African WSE (Botswana and Namibia). This has resulted in both a reduction in water resources and cropland, and consequently a decline in food production in the WSE, which are most dependent on agriculture.

Bibliography

Domanski, J. D., Mantel-Niecko, J., & Zabek, M. (1999). *Rog Afryki. Historia i Wspolczesnosc, Wyd.* TRIO.

Furmaga, L., & Wojcicki, J. (1993). *Maly Slownik Morski.* Mitel International Ltd.

Gleik, P. H. (1996). In S. H. Schneider (Ed.), *Water Resources, Encyclopedia of Climate and Weather* (Vol. 2). Oxford University Press.

Goralczyk, W. (1957). *Szelf kontynentalny: Studium Prawnomiedzynarodowe.* Wydawnictwo Prawnicze.

Goralczyk, W. (1964). *Szerokosc morza terytorialnego i jego delimitacja.* PWN.

Kuchinski, K. (2007). In K. Kuchinski (Ed.), *Geografia.* Difin.

Mika, M. (2007). In W. Kurek (Ed.), *Turystyka Morska.* PWN.

Simmons, G. (1979). *ekologia Zasobow Naturalnych.* PWN.

CHAPTER 8

Population as Both Producer and Consumer

Consumption has always been a part of social and economic life. Looking back in history, people were first consumers of nature's goods, and then became processors and producers of products necessary for survival. Over time, development progressed, tools improved, industrialization advanced and labor productivity increased. Product surpluses emerged in some places and deficits in other (Landes, 2019), which mobilized populations to exchange goods. These processes were accompanied by advances in transportation and communication, which were preceded by development in knowledge and science. Despite environmental barriers (Meadows et al., 1972), there were seemingly unlimited opportunities for the production of goods. This led to overproduction and overconsumption in highly developed countries, as well as excessive stockpiling and waste in households. Meanwhile, the poorest countries struggled with shortages of basic necessities, including food and water. The situation in both rich and poor countries reveals that their societies' consumption patterns are far from sustainable, that is, consumption that would foster sustainable economic development. Overconsumption in wealthier countries stems from resource abundance due to high labor productivity and workforce participation, both men and women. Added to this is the age structure: the small share of the population in the pre-working age group (0–14 years), typically under 20%, is a consequence of low fertility rates. This indicates that these societies spend little on this age group. However, they must allocate

A. A. Tepe-ek, *Economic Development in the World's Smallest Economies*, https://doi.org/10.1007/978-3-031-63810-7_8

much more to those in the deactivation phase, those over 65, for healthcare, social security, pensions, etc. (Okolski, 2018). This is due to the fact that their share in the populations of highly developed countries is exceptionally high, unlike in to poor countries, where it reaches only a few percent, and life expectancy does not exceed 63 years. On the other hand, poor countries are characterized by a very high, over 40%, share of the population of children aged 0–14, which represents a big expense and burden for working people. Additionally, the percentage of working-age people in poor countries is relatively low (35–40% of the population), compared to highly developed countries (42–50% of the population). This is a result of prevailing unemployment or hidden unemployment, such as work in the *grey economy*. All this, combined with the low incomes of the population of poor countries, results in low levels of consumption, as well as low production.

The aforementioned age structure of the population, as well as the occupational structure and emigration abroad, has a significant impact on the labor market situation, and thus on the country's economy as a whole. People, being both consumers and producers, determine the possibilities for economic development. Therefore, it is important to analyze the demographic changes that are taking place, which is what governments do. However, both analyzing and forecasting these changes is a challenge, regardless of the level of socioeconomic development of countries.

Bibliography

Meadows, D., Randers, J., & Behrens, W. W., III. (1972). *Granice Wzrostu*. PWE.

Okolski, M. (2018). *Wyzwania Starzejacego sie Spoleczenstwa Polska Dzis i Jutro, Wyd*. UW.

CHAPTER 9

Demographic Change in the World's Smallest Economies Against a Global Backdrop

Demographic potential is one of the main determinants of a country's development, as human resources are the lifeblood of economies. As one well-known economist wrote: *The work of human hands and especially human minds affects the productive capacity of economies* (Kuchinski & Fierla, 2003), as well as the economic expansion of countries (Stanczyk et al., 2016). In the past, there has often been a coincidence of periods of economic boom with phases of population growth, and of periods of decadence and civilizational decline with population stagnation or decline. Many scientific disciplines have confirmed the connection between demographic conditions and economic processes. Economics has also studied the relationship between demographic development, economic growth, social development and economic progress. It considers the dynamics of population changes and its structure, as well as human resources—the population's knowledge and skills—as key elements determining economic progress. An increase in demographic potential has been viewed in two ways: as an opportunity for economic development, but also as a threat. After all, economic development only makes sense if it contributes to the gradual improvement of the population's living conditions and satisfaction of its needs (Kuchinski & Fierla, 2003). Too rapid economic growth, for example, can threaten depletion of natural resources and lead to an economic slowdown. As a result, as has occurred many times in the past, social, economic, and political conflicts can arise. It should be noted,

A. A. Teperek, *Economic Development in the World's Smallest Economies*, https://doi.org/10.1007/978-3-031-63810-7_9

however, that conflicts also erupted when economies grew more slowly than population growth. When overpopulation occurrs, it is difficult to meet basic social needs such as employment. Overpopulation is also sometimes the cause of epidemics and environmental disasters. It should be added that the phenomenon of overpopulation became a global problem in the second half of the 20th century, as global population growth had previously been very slow (Fig. 9.1).

It is assumed that when humans began to settle permanently and cultivate the land, around 8000 BC, the world was inhabited by approximately 5 million people (Fig. 9.1). The slow population growth of the global population in the following millennia was associated with high mortality rates due to famine, disease, wars that destroyed thousands of lives, and harsh living conditions. This was accompanied by a very low level of personal hygiene, stemming from a particular attitude towards cleanliness. In the Middle Ages, people lived according to the principle of a *dirty body–clean soul*, which was promoted by the church. St. Jerome admonished: *the one whom baptism has made clean does not need to bathe a second time.* On the other hand, in the following era *dry washing* was recognized, with the belief the water carries germs (Smith, 2008). It was not until the eighteenth–nineteenth centuries that social and economic changes (including technological advances in agriculture and industry) helped to improve living standards, especially in the wealhier countries of Europe and North

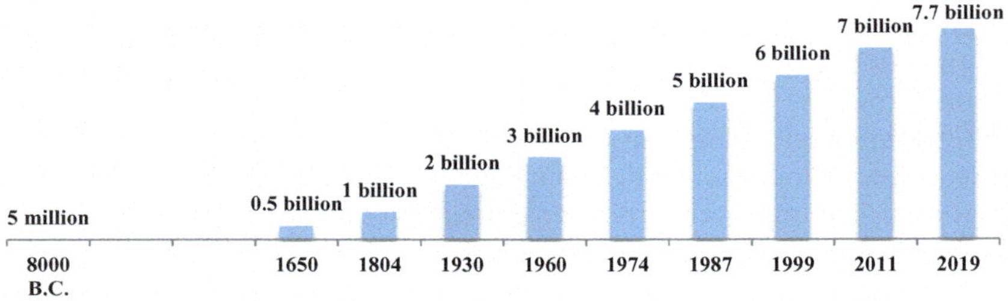

Fig. 9.1 Global population growth from 8000 BC to 2019. (Source: Own compilation based on: Worldmeter, online version: www.Worldometers.info, United Nations, Department of Economic and Social Affairs, Population Division)

America. The spread of hygiene principles and advances in medicine[1] contributed to a decline in mortality rates, which, combined with high natural increase rates, led to rapid population growth. At the turn of the twentieth century, the world population was 1.7 billion, and in the next 100 years alone, the population more than tripled, reaching 6 billion in 1999. Such dynamic population growth was lined to spatial expansion, changes in modes of production and social organization, improvements in cultivation techniques, increases in land productivity (which consequently made it possible to feed a larger population), technological advances, and developments in medical science and pharmacology.

In 2019, the world was inhabited by 7.7 billion people, 7.3% of whom were part of the WSE group. This was a significant demographic resource for the globe, especially since this share had been growing meaningfully for almost five decades (from 5.26% in 1970). It is worth noting that the global share of the group's population was much higher than the share of GDP. While the GDP remained at a similar level—about 1%—level between 1970 and 2019, the population share was not only much higher, but also increased significantly from 5.26% to 7.31% over the same period (1970–2019) (Fig. 9.2).

From the perspective of absolute numbers, between 1970 and 2019, the population of the WSE group grew almost threefold, from 193.2 million to 561.8 million (Fig. 9.3), while the global population grew twofold

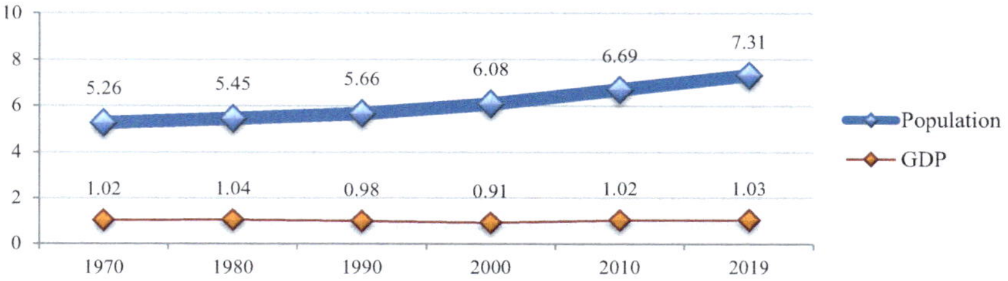

Fig. 9.2 WSE GDP and population as a global share in years 1970, 1980, 1990, 2000, 2010, 2019 (%). (Source: Own compilation based on The World Bank)

[1] It is still debatable whether the reason for population growth and overall development was due to the disappearance of epidemics in Europe, which, along with famines, had been the main regulators of growth processes from the fourteenth to the eighteenth century.

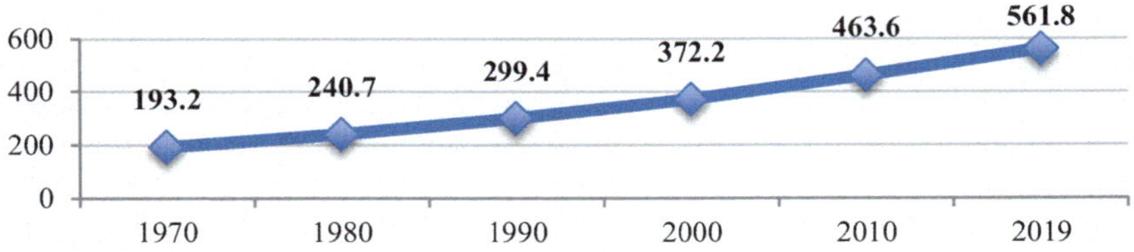

Fig. 9.3 WSE population growth from 1970 to 2019 (millions). (Source: Own compilation based on The World Bank)

(from 3682 million to 7673 million). The high rate of the WSE growth was due primarily to high fertility rates in many of the countries analyzed. Their populations grew rapidly. This was mainly true for the WSE located on the African and Asian continents.

For further analysis of the group, a typology called the *continental division* was used. This typology divides the group into six subgroups: (1) the European WSE (seven countries), which included countries located in Europe, but excluded the former republics and satellite countries of the USSR including Cyprus; (2) the Latin American WSE (17 countries), including North and South American countries; (3) the African WSE (36 countries), which includes countries within the African continent; (4) the Pacific WSE (12 countries), located in Oceania; (5) the Asian WSE (ten countries), including countries located in Asia, but excluding Cyprus and former republics and satellite countries of the USSR; (6) the Post-socialist WSE (11 countries), including former republics and satellite countries of the USSR.

Between 1970 and 2019, the African WSE subgroup recorded the largest population growth of more than 3.5 times (from 89.2 million to 320.2 million), the Pacific WSE of three times (from 3.9 million to 11.2 million), the Asian WSE of almost three times (from 54.6 million to 89.2 million), and the Latin American WSE of more than two times (from 18.3 million to 41.4 million). The Post-socialist WSE and the European WSE showed the smallest growth of less than two times (from 25.7 million to 38.5 million and from 1.2 million to 2.2 million, respectively). The population growth rate in each subgroup thus varied widely (Fig. 9.4).

This was due to a number of factors, including the different demographic past of each of the countries representing the subgroups and their different population structures, fertility rates, and, most importantly, different levels of economic development. As fertility rates declined, the rate

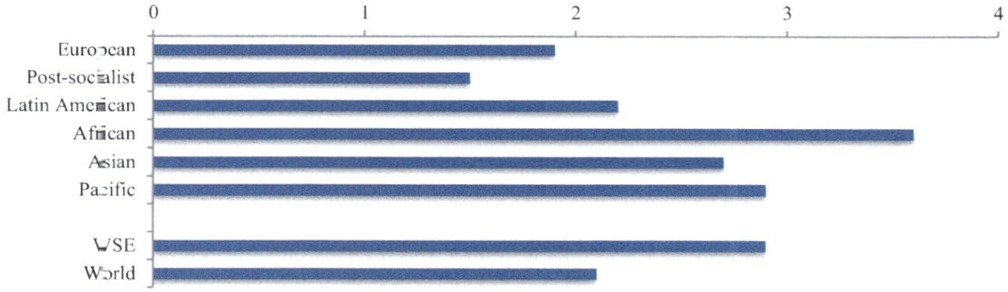

Fig. 9.4 WSE population growth by "continental division" compared to the WSE group and world from 1970 to 2019. (Source: Own compilation based on The World Bank, Population 2020)

of population growth increased (Table 9.1) as a result of higher fertility rates. This was particularly evident in the European WSE subgroup with an average GDP of US$ 36,413 per capita and a fertility rate of 1.2, as well as in the African WSE subgroup with a GDP of US$ 1046 per capita and a fertility rate of 4.2 in 2019 (Table 9.1). The consequence of the low fertility rate of European women has been depopulation trends, as population renewal only occurs when women give birth to more than two children on average. High fertility rates in the African WSE were associated with low levels of female education, lack of widespread access to contraception, lower labor force participation and women's social position. All of this contributed to the very high growth rate of African populations, which was one of the main reasons for the low growth in GDP per capita and the low growth in wealth of the societies there.

In several countries it can be observed that GDP per capita declined over the studied period from 1970 to 2019 as a result of a higher rate of population growth than GDP growth. This meant that almost all of the country's economic growth was absorbed by population growth. At the same time, the quality of life of local communities deteriorated. Examples of the African WSE where population growth was higher than GDP growth include: Liberia, with a population increase of 352% (from 1.4 million to 4.9 million) and GDP growth of 262% (from US$ 0.9 billion to US$ 2.5 billion); Madagascar with a population increase of 410% (from 6.5 million to 26.9 million) and GDP growth of 252% (from US$ 5.3 billion to US$ 13.4 billion); Mauritania with a population increase of 395% (from 1.1 million to 4.5 million) and GDP growth of 346% (from US$ 2.2 billion to US$ 7.9 billion); Somalia with a population increase of 448%

Table 9.1 WSE group by continental division

WSE subgroups	*WSE*	*Countries*	*GDP*	*Fertility*	*Growth*	
					Population	*GDP*
		Quantity	*USD per capita*	*Number of children*	*%*	
			2019		*1970–2019*	
European	Andorra, Cyprus, Iceland, Malta, Monaco, San Marino	7	36,413	1.2	1.9	6.2
Post-socialist	Albania, Armenia, Bosnia and Herzegovina, Estonia, Georgia, Kyrgyzstan, Montenegro, Moldova, Mongolia, Northern Macedonia, Tajikistan	11	4011	2.1	1.5	4.5
Latin American	Antigua and Barbuda, Bahamas, Barbados, Belize, Dominica, El Salvador, Grenada, Guyana, Haiti, Honduras, Jamaica, Nicaragua, Saint Kitts and Nevis, Saint Lucia, Saint Vincent and the Grenadines, Suriname, Trinidad and Tobago	17	3363	2.1	2.2	2.9
Pacific	Fiji, Kiribati, Marshall Islands, Micronesia, Nauru, Palau, Papua New Guinea, Samoa, Solomon Islands, Tonga, Tuvalu, Vanuatu	12	2697	3.5	2.9	4.2
African	Benin, Botswana, Burkina Faso, Burundi, Central African Republic, Cape Verde, Chad, Comoros, Congo, Djibouti, Equatorial Guinea, Eritrea, Eswatini, Gabon, The Gambia, Guinea, Guinea-Bissau, Lesotho, Liberia, Madagascar, Malawi, Mali, Mauritania, Mauritius, Mozambique, Namibia, Niger, Rwanda, Sao Thomas and Principe, Senegal, Sierra Leone, Somalia, South Sudan, Togo, Zimbabwe	36	1046	4.2	3.6	5.7
Asian	Afghanistan, Bhutan, Brunei, Cambodia, East Timor, Laos, Maldives, Nepal, North Korea, Yemen	10	920	2.6	2.7	3.8
WSE group in total		93	1562	3.1	2.9	4.5
World		193	11,059	2.4	2.1	4.4

Source: Own compilation based on The World Bank

(from 3.4 million to 15.4 million) and GDP growth of 248% (from US$ 0.5 billion to US$ 1.4 billion). It is worth noting, however, that it was not the aforementioned countries that saw the highest population growth among the entire subgroup, but Djibouti (by 610%), Niger (by 517%), The Gambia (by 506%), Chad (by 438%), which are countries that are heavily influenced by Islamic culture promoting multichild and large families. Consequently, this has contributed to economic and social backwardness while limiting the economic development potential of these countries.

Also exemplified by the African WSE was the correlation of population growth rates and the level of economic development. Countries with higher levels of economic development, such as Mauritius, with a GDP of US$ 10,893 per capita and the Seychelles with a GDP of US$ 15,049 per capita in 2019, experienced much lower population growth. In the period analyzed from 1970 to 2019, Mauritius' population grew by only 53% (from 826,000 to 1,255,000) and the Seychelles by 82% (from 54,000 to 98,000) (Table 9.2). Other examples are Lesotho (population growth of 107%) and Estwatini (population growth of 166%), which struggled for more than two decades with high mortality due to the HIV/AIDS epidemic. The scale of infection and morbidity is evidenced by the proportion of HIV/AIDS carriers, which in 2019 was 23.1% of the population in Lesotho (2nd in the world) and 27.3% of the population in Estwatini (1st in the world).

Lower rates of population growth than the African WSE subgroup between 1970 and 2019 were observed by the Latin American WSE, the Asian WSE, and the Pacific WSE subgroups, which were populated mainly by young populations with relatively high fertility rates. Each of the three subgroups included several countries where population growth exceeded GDP growth (Table 9.3). Among the Latin American WSE, these were Haiti and Nicaragua. Haiti saw a 241% increase in population (from 4.6 million to 11.2 million) and a 221% increase in GDP (from US$ 6.3 billion to US$ 14 billion), while Nicaragua saw a 272% increase in population (from 2.4 million to 6.5 million) and a 222% increase in GDP (from US$ 5.2 billion to US$ 11.5 billion). Among the Asian WSE, population grew faster than economic growth in three Muslim countries: Afghanistan, Yemen, and Brunei (Table 9.3). In Afghanistan, the population grew by 340% (from 11 million to 38 million) and GDP by 227% (from US$ 9 billion to US$ 21 billion), in Yemen, the population grew by 471% (from 6 million to 29 million) and GDP by 376% (from US$ 4 billion to US$ 18 billion), and in Brunei the population grew by 335% (from 130,000 to 433,000) and GDP by 226% (from US$ 6 billion to US$

Table 9.2 African WSE subgroup GDP and population growth between 1970 and 2019

No	*WSE*	*Population*		*GDP*		*Growth*	
		thousand		*US$ million*		*Population*	*GDP*
		1970	*2019*	*1970*	*2019*	*1970–2019*	
1	Benin	2912	11,801	2316	14,867	405	642
2	Botswana	628	2304	379	18,644	367	4916
3	Burkina Faso	5625	20,321	1533	16,708	361	1090
4	Burundi	3479	11,531	985	2399	331	244
5	Cape Verde	269	550	270	2149	205	795
6	Central African Republic	1811	4745	1199	1823	262	152
7	Chad	3644	15,947	2313	12,976	438	561
8	Comoros	230	851	293	1191	370	406
9	Congo	1327	5381	1712	11,655	405	681
10	Djibouti	160	974	773	4775	610	618
11	Eritrea	1311	3497	420	1919	267	457
12	Eswatini	431	1148	625	5532	266	885
13	Gabon	589	2173	4503	19,939	369	443
14	The Gambia	464	2348	487	1914	506	393
15	Guinea	4155	12,771	1945	11,761	307	605
16	Guinea-Bissau	705	1921	297	1221	272	412
17	Equatorial Guinea	304	1356	425	12,526	446	2950
18	Lesotho	1029	2125	360	2875	207	799
19	Liberia	1401	4937	971	2549	352	262
20	Madagascar	6576	26,969	5364	13,495	410	252
21	Malawi	4704	18,629	1431	9754	396	682
22	Mali	5949	19,658	2146	15,562	330	725
23	Mauritania	1147	4526	2299	7948	395	346
24	Mauritius	826	1266	987	13,787	153	1397
25	Mozambique	9023	30,366	1799	17,876	337	994
26	Namibia	817	2495	2798	14,383	305	514
27	Niger	4511	23,311	2533	13,127	517	518
28	Rwanda	3757	12,627	941	11,381	336	1209
29	Saint Thomas and Príncipe	75	215	62	277	288	450
30	Senegal	4258	16,296	5277	25,821	383	489
31	Seychelles	54	98	138	1469	182	1061
32	Sierra Leone	2745	7813	1308	3816	285	292
33	Somalia	3445	15,443	577	1432	448	248
34	South Sudan	3494	11,062	460	14,406	317	3132
35	Togo	2116	8082	1168	5626	382	482
36	Zimbabwe	5289	14,645	6903	17,327	277	251

Source: Own compilation based on The World Bank

Table 9.3 Latin American WSE, Asian WSE and Pacific WSE subgroups GDP and population growth from 1970 to 2019

No	*The world's smallest economies*	*Population*		*GDP*		*Growth*	
		thousand		*US$ million*		*population*	*GDP*
		1970	*2019*	*1970*	*2019*	*1970–2019*	
Latin American WSE							
1	Antigua and Barbuda	64	97	230	1525	152	663
2	Bahamas	169	389	3653	11,259	230	308
3	Barbados	239	287	2190	4621	120	211
4	Belize	122	390	232	1620	320	698
5	Dominica	71	72	105	497	101	473
6	Grenada	94	112	127	1033	119	813
7	Guyana	705	783	1452	4781	111	329
8	Haiti	4676	11,263	6332	14,023	241	221
9	Honduras	2717	9746	3558	21,843	359	614
10	Jamaica	1876	2948	8169	14,349	157	176
11	Nicaragua	2407	6546	5205	11,541	272	222
12	Saint Vincent and the Grenadines	91	111	156	759	122	487
13	Saint Kitts and Nevis	45	53	112	914	118	816
14	Saint Lucia	104	183	192	1709	176	890
15	Salvador	3673	6454	6963	23,054	176	331
16	Suriname	368	581	2090	4678	158	224
17	Trinidad and Tobago	945	1395	6486	21,071	148	325
Asian WSE							
1	Afghanistan	11,174	38,042	9591	21,809	340	227
2	Bhutan	297	763	103	2489	257	2417
3	Brunei	130	433	6209	14,007	333	226
4	Cambodia	6997	16,487	3434	20,921	236	609
5	East Timor	572	1293	280	1264	226	451
6	North Korea	14,410	25,666	6918	15,102	178	218
7	Laos	2688	7169	758	13,195	267	1741
8	Maldives	116	531	146	4501	458	3083
9	Nepal	12,075	28,609	3510	24,576	237	700
10	Yemen	6193	29,162	4900	18,415	471	376
Pacific WSE							
1	Fiji	521	890	1072	4217	171	393
2	Kiribati	51	118	122	211	231	173
3	Micronesia	61	114	91	307	187	337

(*continued*)

Table 9.3 (continued)

No	*The world's smallest economies*	*Population*		*GDP*		*Growth*	
		thousand		*US$ million*		*population*	*GDP*
		1970	*2019*	*1970*	*2019*	*1970–2019*	
4	Nauru	7	13	318	103	186	32
5	Palau	12	18	94	217	150	231
6	Papua New Guinea	2783	8776	4755	21,852	315	460
7	Samoa	143	197	310	763	138	246
8	Tonga	84	104	109	455	124	417
9	Tuvalu	6	12	11	46	200	418
10	Vanuatu	85	300	122	866	353	710
11	Marshall Islands	20	59	39	186	295	477
12	Solomon Islands	160	670	129	1172	419	909

Source: Own compilation based on The World Bank

14 billion). At the same time, the three countries were very different from each other. Afghanistan and Yemen represented the lowest level of economic development. Brunei, on the other hand, showed one of the highest levels of economic development in the world, thanks to its oil and gas exports, which brings huge revenues for its small economy. Although Brunei's higher population growth than GDP resulted in a decline in GDP per capita (from US$ 47,936 per capita to US$ 32,327 per capita between 1970 and 2019), Bruneians, with such high incomes, did not suffer the deterioration in quality of life as poor societies in Afghanistan and Yemen. The decline in Afghanistan's GDP from US$ 853 per capita to US$ 573 per capita and Yemen from US$ 791 per capita to US$ 631 per capita over the past five decades indicated deepening poverty, manifested by living in the face of hunger, in slums with prevailing conflicts.

In the Pacific WSE subgroup, two countries experienced faster population growth than GDP between 1970 and 2019: Kiribati's population grew by 230% (from 51,000 to 118,000), while its GDP increased by only 172% (from US$ 122 million to US$ 211 million). This was the result of a relatively high fertility rate (four children per one woman of childbearing age). In contrast, Nauru's higher population growth rate than GDP was the result of rapid population growth resulting from a high fertility rate (more than four children per one woman of childbearing age). Added to this was a decline in GDP related to a multiyear economic slump caused by the depletion of phosphate deposits, Nauru's major source of exports and income (21 km^2; 12,000 inhabitants), and the mismanagement of profits from their sale (corruption, unprofitable foreign investment, among other factors). As a result, Nauru's GDP fell by more than three times (from US$ 318 million to US$ 103 million), while the population increased by 92% (from 7000 to 12,000) between 1970 and 2019.

Among the subgroups: the Latin American WSE, the Asian WSE, and the Pacific WSE, there are also countries that noted very low population growth compared to GDP growth. The populations of Dominica, Grenada, Guyana, and Saint Kitts and Nevis grew by only 1% to 19% (Table 9.3). The reason for this was low fertility rates of 1.6 to 2 children per woman of childbearing age. It should also be remembered that these countries were characterized by a very large outflow of population mainly to the United States due to labor emigration. For example, in 2019, Dominica's population was 72,000, with an additional 78,000 of Dominican residents abroad. Saint Kitts and Nevis' population was 53,000, with an additional 50,000 that lived abroad. Low reproduction also characterized the Asian WSE of North Korea (1.9 children per woman of childbearing age). Faced with a totalitarian system of rule, slave labor in camps, prevailing famine, poor living conditions, poor health care, high mortality rates and low birth rates, North Korea had the lowest the natural increase rate among the subgroup, estimated at 78% (from 14.4 million to 25.6 million) between 1970 and 2019. In contrast, among the Pacific WSE, Tonga showed the lowest population growth of 24% (from 84,000 to 104,000), which, like the Latin American WSE, was associated with a high rate of labor emigration. In 2019, more than 104,000 Tongans were living in the country and 75,000 outside of it.

Demographic growth clearly declined with the higher levels of economic development of the WSE The subgroups: the Post-socialist WSE and the European WSE illustrate this (Table 9.4). Their population growth rate was more than three times lower than the GDP growth rate.

All of the European WSE experienced modest (less than 95%) population growth between 1970 and 2019 (Table 9.4), with the exception of Andorra's population, which increased more than three times (from 24,000 to 77,000) due to the influx of Spanish and French populations. A similar more than threefold increase in population growth occurred in Tajikistan (from 2930 million to 9321 million), representing the Post-socialist WSE and showing the lowest level of economic development in the subgroup. This was due to the strong influence of an Islamic culture characterized by a high fertility rate (3.6 children per woman of childbearing age). In contrast, other countries in this subgroup experienced very low population growth or even population decline, as exemplified by three

Table 9.4 European WSE and Post-socialist WSE subgroups GDP and population growth from 1970 to 2019

No	*WSE*	*Population*		*GDP*		*Growth*	
		Thousand		*US$ million*		*Population*	*GDP*
		1970	*2019*	*1970*	*2019*	*1970–2019*	
European WSE							
1	Andorra	24	77	873	3540	320	405
2	Cyprus	613	1198	3979	28,678	195	721
3	Iceland	204	361	3208	18,547	177	578
4	Liechtenstein	21	38	1423	6756	181	475
5	Malta	302	502	966	14,565	166	1508
6	Monaco	23	38	2046	8153	165	398
7	San Marino	19	33	670	1709	174	255
Post-socialist WSE							
1	Albania	2135	2854	4018	14,872	134	370
2	Armenia	2525	2958	2800	13,996	117	500
3	Bosnia and Herzegovina	3761	3301	870	20,808	88	2392
4	Montenegro	512	622	1010	5343	121	529
5	Estonia	1360	1326	6200	27,667	98	446
6	Georgia	4119	3720	10,292	18,521	90	180
7	Kyrgyzstan	2959	6456	2010	7208	218	359
8	Northern Macedonia	1720	2083	3100	11,719	121	378
9	Moldova	2445	2657	1250	9887	109	791
10	Mongolia	1278	3225	947	14,037	252	1482
11	Tajikistan	2930	9321	1860	10,450	318	562

Source: Own compilation based on The World Bank

of the Post-socialist WSE: Bosnia and Herzegovina by 12% (from 3761 million to 3301 million), Estonia by 2% (from 1360 million to 1326 million), and Georgia by 10% (from 4119 million to 3720 million). This was due to low fertility rates—less than 2 children per woman of childbearing age. In addition, in Bosnia and Herzegovina, showing 1.3, the population loss was due to war.

Low fertility rates in the European WSE and most of the Post-socialist WSE have contributed to depopulation trends. As a result, the population share of these two subgroups in the entire WSE group halved from 14% to 7% between 1970 and 2019. At the same time, the young populations of the Latin American WSE, the Pacific WSE, the Asian WSE, and the African WSE subgroups, characterized by high fertility rates, experienced rapid population growth. This was followed by an increase in the population share of

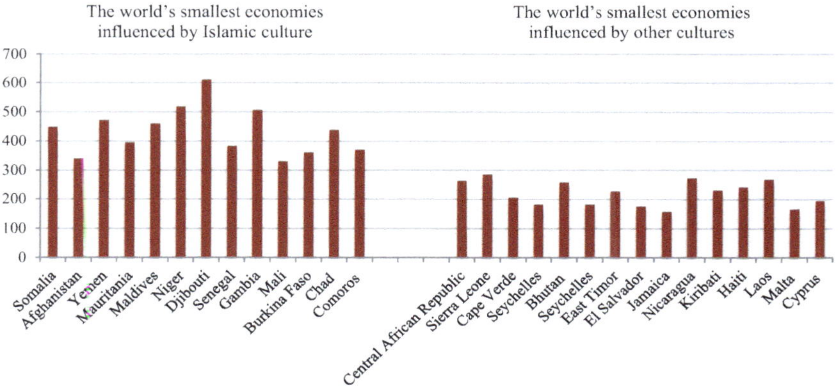

Fig. 9.5 Population growth of the WSE influenced by Islamic culture and other cultures from 1970 to 2019. (Source: Own compilation based on The World Bank)

these four combined from 86% to 93% (from 166.2 million to 521 million) in the WSE group. It should be added that the largest growth was in Islamic African and Asian countries (Fig. 9.5), with the lowest level of economic development. As a result, these countries have not been able to provide employment for their young populations, norhave they have been able to meet their basic living needs, such as food or even access to drinking water.

Worsening nutritional problems and limited access to drinking water consequently led to the deterioration of the health of the local population. This was compounded by the problem of depletion of natural resources, mainly related to overpopulation. All this resulted in economic, social, and political conflicts, and unsustainable economic growth of the WSE. In turn, the countries' rulers were unable to counter either the reduction of demographic growth or its effects. As a result, human resources were becoming a threat to economic development and social order. However, looking at it, the rapid population growth in poor countries has also had a positive side from an ecological point of view. After all, the consumption needs of the poor population are much smaller than those of the population of wealthy countries, whose societies are characterized by greater demand for consumer goods, greater consumption of natural resources, and greater environmental pollution (Kuchinski & Fierla, 2003).

Bibliography

Kuchinski, K., & Fierla, I. (2003). *Geografia Gospodarcza Swiata*. PWE.

Smith, V. (2008). *Clean: A History of Personal Hygiene and Purity*. Oxford University Press.

Stanczyk, J., Szaltys, D., & Witkowski, J. (2016). In J. Kleer & K. Prandecki (Eds.), *Potencjal Ludnosciowy Unii Europejskiej*. Komitet Prognoz Polska 2000 Plus PAN.

CHAPTER 10

Population Distribution in the World's Smallest Economies

As a result of changes in demographic potential, shaped by decreases or increases in birth, death, and migration rates, in 2019, the WSE group recorded a population of 561 million. By comparison, this was more than the population of the European Union (447 million) and about a third more than the population of South America as a whole (368 million), whose land area is almost the same as that of the group (Fig. 10.1).

In 2019, the population of the African WSE subgroup was 320.1 million. The Asian WSE subgroup had less than twice the population, 148.1 million. These two subgroups accounted for 83.4% of the WSE group's population. The remaining 16.6% resided in the Latin American WSE, the Post-socialist WSE, the Pacific WSE, and the European

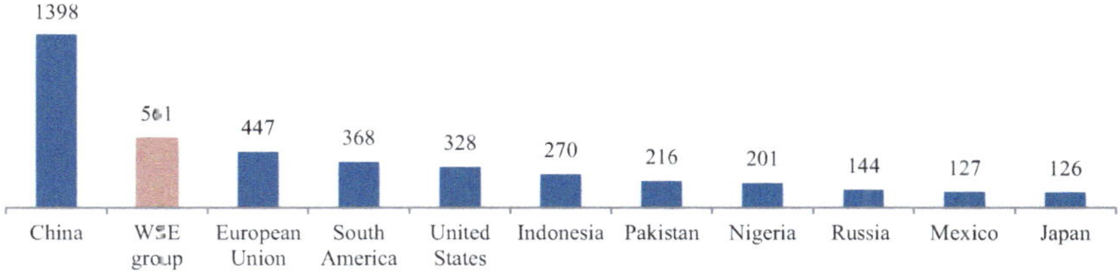

Fig. 10.1 WSE group population compared to selected countries, unions, and continents in 2019 (millions). (Source: Own compilation based on The World Bank)

A. A. Teperek, *Economic Development in the World's Smallest Economies*, https://doi.org/10.1007/978-3-031-63810-7_10

WSE. The Latin American WSE and the Post-socialist WSE were similar, with populations of 41.4 million and 38.5 million, respectively; in contrast, the Pacific WSE and the European WSE were 11.2 million and 2.2 million, respectively.

The largest differences in population proportions were observed across the WSE (Fig. 10.2), ranging from Tuvalu with a population of 11,600 to Afghanistan with a 38 million population. As many as 37 countries, or more than a third of the group, had populations of less than 1 million. Among them were 26 island countries (i.e., Dominica, Iceland, Malta, Micronesia, Nauru, and Saint Lucia), as well as European microstates (i.e., Andorra, Liechtenstein, Monaco, and San Marino) and small-area coastal countries (i.e., Belize, Brunei, Djibouti, and Montenegro).

In contrast, the 11 most populous WSE were home to almost half the population of the entire group. These are Afghanistan (38.1 million), Mozambique (30.3 million), Yemen (29.1 million), Nepal (28.6 million), Madagascar (26.9 million), North Korea (25.6 million), Niger (23.3), Burkina Faso (20.3 million), Mali (19.6 million), Malawi (18.6 million), and Cambodia (16.4 million). All these countries are located in Africa and Asia (Fig. 10.3).

The population of the most populous African and Asian subgroups (468.3 million in 2019), which together accounted for more than 83.4% of the WSE group's population, resided in 46 countries, covering 80% of the group's area (13.9 million km^2). It is worth noting that both subgroups had the lowest GDP per capita of all subgroups, at US$ 1046 per capita and US$ 920 per capita, respectively (Table 10.1).

The per capita GDP of the remaining 16.2% of the group's population (91.2 million) of the Pacific WSE, the Latin American WSE, and the Post-socialist WSE subgroups did not exceed US$ 4011 per capita, which, according to the World Bank's classification, indicates a *lower level of economic development* (Table 10.1). The international organization, defining the wealth of economies according to reported GDP per capita, listed countries of the world with (1) low *level of economic development*, (2) *lower-middle level of economic development*, (3) *upper-middle level of economic development* and (4) *high level of economic development*, in terms of per capita income. Considering this classification, it was the subgroups of the WSE that represented only (1) *low economic development* and (2) *medium-lower economic development* and there were the African WSE, the Asian WSE, the Pacific WSE, the Latin American WSE, and the Post-socialist WSE subgroups. Only the European WSE showed (4) *high level*

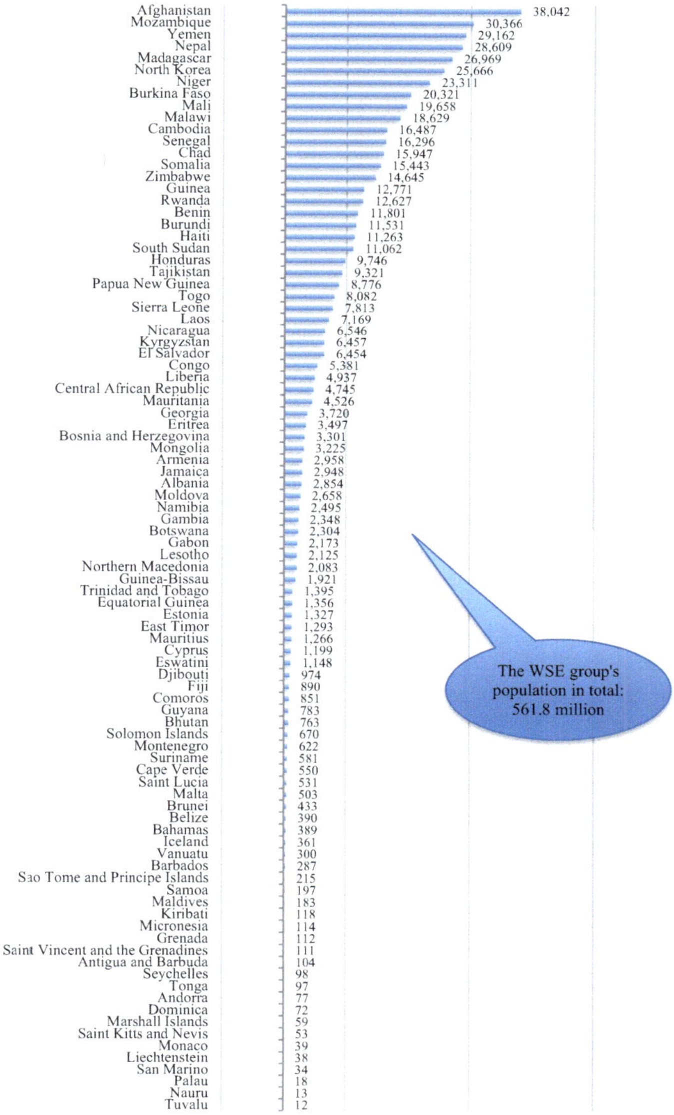

Fig. 10.2 WSE population in 2019 (thousands). (Source: Own compilation based on World Bank)

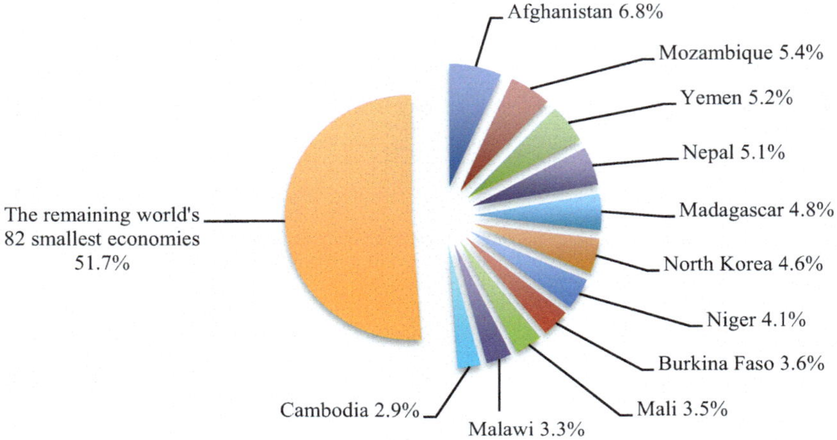

Fig. 10.3 Most Populous WSE as a share of the WSE group in 2019 (%). (Source: Own compilation based on The World Bank)

of economic development and none of the WSE subgroups represented (3) *upper-middle level of economic development*. In contrast, looking at the population, 99.4% of the group's population (559.5 million) lived in subgroups with lower than *medium-lower economic development*, and only 0.6% (2.2 million) with *high level of economic development*. This polarization indicates a huge gap in the living standards of the WSE residents. Fortunately, this polarization is not deepening, as the long-term survey shows. The share of the five poorer WSE subgroups has decreased, while the share of the richest subgroup has increased, sequentially from 99,6% to 99,4% and from 0.4% to 0.6% between 1970 and 2019, meaning that the pauperization of the WSE population is not increasing.

While many economists underline the great importance of human capital for economic growth and development, this is not borne out for most of the WSE. The qualitative aspect of the population is very important, i.e. higher levels of education and professional qualifications, which a large part of the WSE group's population, especially those with low levels of economic development, do not have, at least to a sufficient degree. It is possible to at least partially solve this problem through skillful economic and social policies of those in power. However, for this to happen, adequate leadership and financial support from countries with higher levels of economic development are essential.

Table 10.1 WSE subgroups population in relation to land area and GDP per capita in 2019

WSE subgroups	*WSE*	*Countries*	*GDP*	*Share of the WSE group*	
				Population	*Area*
		Quantity	*US$ per capita*	*%*	
European	Andorra, Cyprus, Iceland, Malta, Monaco, San Marino	7	36,413	0.4	0.6
Post-socialist	Albania, Armenia, Bosnia and Herzegovina, Montenegro, Estonia, Georgia, Kyrgyzstan, Moldova, Mongolia, North Macedonia, Tajikistan	11	4011	6.9	12.6
Latin American	Antigua and Barbuda, Bahamas, Barbados, Belize, Dominica, El Salvador, Grenada, Guyana, Haiti, Honduras, Jamaica, Nicaragua, Saint Kitts and Nevis, Saint Lucia, Saint Vincent and the Grenadines, Suriname, Trinidad and Tobago	17	3363	7.4	4.1
Pacific	Fiji, Kiribati, Marshall Islands, Micronesia, Nauru, Palau, Papua New Guinea, Samoa, Solomon Islands, Tonga, Tuvalu, Vanuatu	12	2697	2.0	3.0
African	Benin, Botswana, Burkina Faso, Burundi, Cape Verde, Central African Republic, Chad, Comoros, Congo, Djibouti, Equatorial Guinea, Eritrea, Eswatini, Gabon, The Gambia, Guinea, Guinea-Bissau, Lesotho, Liberia, Madagascar, Malawi, Mali, Mauritania, Mauritius, Mozambique, Namibia, Niger, Rwanda, Saint Thomas and Principe, Senegal, Sierra Leone, Somalia, South Sudan, Togo, Zimbabwe	36	1046	57.0	68.6
Asian	Afghanistan, Bhutan, Brunei, Cambodia, East Timor, Laos, Maldives, Nepal, North Korea, Yemen	10	920	26.4	11.0
WSE in total		93	1562	100.0	100.0

Source: Own compilation based on The World Bank

The low level of economic development of the WSE has also been linked to their low level of urbanization, as well as the social division of labor. In countries such as Afghanistan, Burundi, Cambodia, Chad, Eritrea, Eswatini, Nepal, Niger, Rwanda, South Sudan, and Tajikistan, urban residents made up only less than 30% of the total population (Fig. 10.4).

Higher urbanization rates characterize the industrialized WSE with a more developed service sector, as well as a higher degree of trade centralization (Kuchinski, 2003). In general, the higher the level of economic development of a country, the higher the level of urbanization. Therefore, the WSE with the highest percentage of urban population (above 80%) are countries with high levels of economic development (Fig. 10.5). Examples

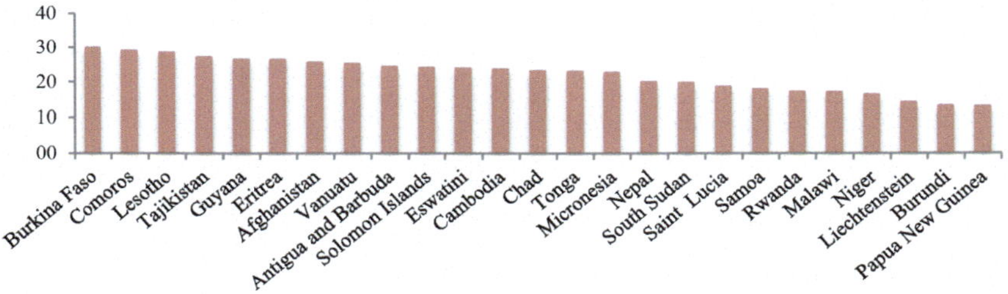

Fig. 10.4 WSE with the smallest urban population in 2019 (%). (Source: Own compilation based on The World Bank)

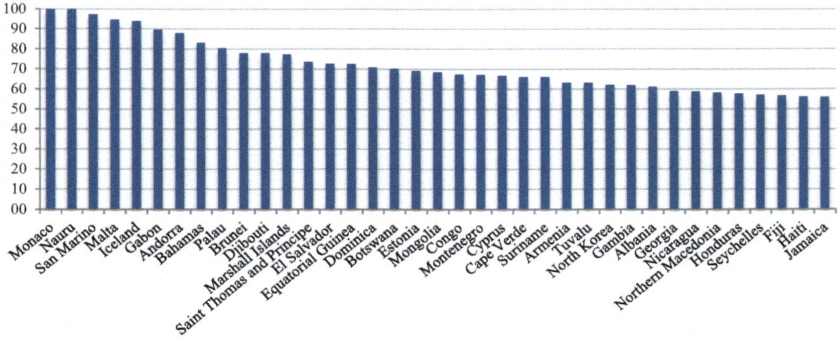

Fig. 10.5 WSE with largest urban population in 2019 (%). (Source: Own compilation based on The World Bank)

include Andorra (US$ 45,887 per capita), Iceland (US$ 51,332 per capita), Malta (US$ 28,986 per capita), Monaco (US$ 209,241 per capita), and San Marino (US$ 50,462 per capita). Monaco was the most urbanized (100%). In 2019, its 2.1 km^2 was home to more than 38,000 urban residents. Similarly, Andorra (468 km^2; 77,000 population) and San Marino (61 km^2; 33,000 population). A decisive factor in their strong urbanization is the small land area occupied. Another example is Nauru (21 km^2; 12,000 population), also with a small land area; 100% of its population is urban. In this case, strong urbanization is associated with an inability to develop areas due to open-pit phosphate mines covering almost the entire area of the country.

Intensive urbanization is also associated with intensive deforestation, as exemplified by Gabon with 89.7% of its urban population. In Gabon, equatorial forests cover 91.4% of its land area (267,000 km^2; 2.1 million inhabitants), leaving only 8.6% for agricultural land and urban centers, which are mainly concentrated in oil and gas extraction sites. In contrast, Djibouti's high 77.9% urban population share (23,000 km^2; 0.9 million people) is related to climatic conditions. The population is concentrated on the coast, as more than 90% of the country is covered by desert. Such a high percentage of urban population is also related to Djibouti's developed service sector—mainly port services. Djibouti's port serves as a key center for refueling and transshipment of international ships (an estimated 2500 vessels pass through and stop there each day) due to the country's strategic location at the crossroads of one of the world's busiest shipping routes, connecting Europe, the Far East, the Horn of Africa, and the Persian Gulf.

Cities play a very important role in the spatial concentration of the WSE's population. This is because they attract the possibility of finding better jobs and educational opportunities.

The standard of living offered by the city is much more attractive than that offered by the countryside. This is particularly evident in underdeveloped countries. Among urban centers, capitals were the most populous. In Monaco, 100% of the total population lived in the capital Monaco; in the Bahamas, 64.6% of the total population lived in the capital Nassau; in Djibouti 49.6% of the total population lived in the capital Djibouti City; in Suriname 44.1% of the total population lived in the capital Paramaribo; in the Marshall Islands 43.5% of the total population lived in the capital Majuro (Table 10.2). Additionally, the most populous capitals were Pyongyang in North Korea (3.1 million inhabitants), Kabul in Afghanistan

Table 10.2 WSE capital population in relation to total population of countries in 2019

WSE	*Capital*	*Capital population*	*Capital population as a percentage of total population*	*WSE*	*Capital*	*Capital population*	*Capital population as a percentage of total*
		Number	*%*			*Number*	*%*
Monaco	Monaco	35,986	93.0	North Korea	Pyongyang	3,144,005	12.3
Bahamas	Nassau	248,948	64.6	Bosnia and Herzegovina	Sarajevo	395,133	11.9
Djibouti	Djibouti	475,332	49.6	Mauritius	Port Louis	147,251	11.6
Suriname	Paramaribo	254,147	44.1	Guinea	Conakry	1,399,981	11.3
Marshall Islands	Majuro	25,400	43.5	Haiti	Port-au-Prince	1,235,227	11.1
Tuvalu	Fonafuti	4492	39.0	Saint Lucia	Castries	20,000	11.0
Barbados	Bridgetown	110,000	38.4	Togo	Lome	824,738	10.5
Armenia	Yerevan	1,080,487	36.6	Zimbabwe	Harare	1,487,028	10.3
Saint Vincent and the Grenadines	Kingstown	40,020	36.3	Namibia	Windhoek	252,721	10.3
Congo	Brazzaville	1,827,000	34.8	Nauru	Yaren[a]	1100	10.3
Iceland	Reykjavik	115,000	34.2	Botswana	Gaborone	225,656	10.0
Estonia	Tallinn	440,206	33.3	Fiji	Suva	84,410	9.6
Seychelles	Victoria	29,298	30.2	Solomon Islands	Honiara	59,288	9.1
Andorra	Andorra la Vella	22,884	29.7	Micronesia	Palikir	9900	8.8
Mongolia	Ulaanbaatar	907,802	28.6	Afghanistan	Kabul	3,140,853	8.4
Saint Thomas and Príncipe	Sao Tome	56,166	26.6	Salvador	San Salvador	521,366	8.1
Albania	Tirana	763,634	26.5	Honduras	Tegucigalpa	735,982	7.7

Gabon	Libreville	556,425	26.3	Equatorial Guinea	Malabo	100,677	7.7
Georgia	Tbilisi	1,044,993	26.1	Somalia	Mogadishu	1,097,133	7.3
Kiribati	Tarawa	30,000	25.9	Eswatini	Mbabane	81,594	7.2
Northern Macedonia	Skopje	521,000	25.0	Comoros	Moroni	60,200	7.2
Saint Kitts and Nevis	Basseterre	13,043	24.9	Small	Bamako	1,289,626	6.8
Guinea-Bissau	Bissau	452,640	24.1	Grenada	St. George	7500	6.7
Jamaica	Kingston	701,063	23.9	Brunei	Bandar Seri Begawan	28,135	6.6
Antigua and Barbuda	St. John's	22,679	23.6	Senegal	Dakar	1,030,594	6.5
Cape Verde	Praia	125,464	23.1	Tajikistan	Dushanbe	582,496	6.4
Cyprus	Nicosia	270,000	22.7	Madagascar	Antananarivo	1,613,375	6.1
Montenegro	Podgorica	141,854	22.6	Rwanda	Kigali	718,414	5.8
Tonga	Nukualofa	22,400	21.7	Burkina Faso	Ouagadougou	1,005,231	5.1
Liberia	Monrovia	1,010,970	21.0	Yemen	Sana'a	1,431,649	5.0
Dominica	Roseau	14,847	20.7	Malawi	Lilongwe	902,388	5.0
Samoa	Apia	39,813	20.3	Chad	N'Djamena	751,288	4.9
Eritrea	Asmara	694,000	20.1	East Timor	Dili	59,069	4.7
Maldives	Male	103,693	20.1	Belize	Belmopan	16,451	4.3
Moldova	Chisinau	794,800	19.6	Laos	Vientiane	287,579	4.1
Guyana	Georgetown	134,599	17.3	Mozambique	Maputo	1,076,689	3.7
Mauritania	Nouakchott	719,167	16.3	Nepal	Kathmandu	1,003,285	3.6
Central African Republic	Bangui	731,548	15.7	Trinidad and Tobago	Port of Spain	50,479	3.6
Nicaragua	Managua	926,883	14.3	Niger	Niamey	794,814	3.5

(*continued*)

Table 10.2 (continued)

WSE	*Capital*	*Capital population*	*Capital population as a percentage of total population*	*WSE*	*Capital*	*Capital population*	*Capital population as a percentage of total*
		Number	*%*			*Number*	*%*
Sierra Leone	Freetown	1,070,200	14.0	Papua New Guinea	Port Moresby	299,396	3.5
Liechtenstein	Vaduz	5248	13.8	South Sudan	Juba	372,410	3.4
Kyrgyzstan	Bishkek	843,240	13.4	Benin	Porto-Novo	223,552	1.9
Bhutan	Thimphu	101,259	13.4	Palau	Ngerulmud	271	1.5
San Marino	City of San Marino	4493	13.3	The Gambia	Banjul	34,828	1.5
Vanuatu	Port Vila	38,000	13.0	Malta	Valetta	6444	1.5
Lesotho	Maseru	267,652	12.7	Burundi	Gitega	41,944	0.4
Cambodia	Phnom Penh	2,011,725	12.4				

Source: Own compilation based on The World Atlas, Population of Capita Cities of the World 2021

Yaren served as Nauru's unofficial capital, because Nauru as one of two countries in the world (along with Switzerland) that does not have an official capital

(3.1 million), Phnom Penh in Cambodia (2 million), Brazzaville in Congo (1.8 million), Antananarivo in Madagascar (1.6 million), Harare in Zimbabwe (1.5 million), Sanaa in Yemen (1.4 million), Conakry in Guinea 1.4 million), Bamako in Mali (1.3 million), Port-au-Prince in Haiti (1.2 million), and Mogadishu in Somalia (1.1 million).

Bibliography

Kuchinski, K. (2003). In I. Fierla (Ed.), *Geografia Gospodarcza Swiata*. PWE.

CHAPTER 11

Population Density in the World's Smallest Economies

Population distribution is inextricably linked to population density, defined as the ratio between people and geographic space. The indicator shows the degree of concentration of the population, that is, its distribution over a certain area. The area occupied by the 93 WSE is 17,536 thousand km^2. In 2019, it was inhabited by 561,792 thousand people, so for every 1 km^2 there were an average of 31 people (for comparison, the population density in the world was 49 people per 1 km^2). As with population growth, the population density of the WSE group has nearly tripled over the past almost five decades (from 11 people per 1 km^2 in 1970).

The varying intensity of demographic development of the countries analyzed over history has affected their population densities. The Asian WSE subgroup recorded the highest rate, with 80 people per 1 km^2 (1860 thousand km^2; 148.1 million population), while the Latin American WSE was slightly lower, with 57 people per 1 km^2 (726 thousand km^2; 41.4 million population). Other subgroups, such as the African WSE (11,842 thousand km^2; 320.2 million population), the European WSE (113 thousand km^2; 2.2 million inhabitants), the Post-socialist WSE (1105 thousand km^2; 38.5 million population), and the Pacific WSE (695 thousand km^2; 11.2 million population) showed population density of 16–27 people per 1 km^2. From the point of view of the 1970–2019 period, the largest fourfold increase was observed in the African WSE and the Pacific WSE subgroups (Fig. 11.1).

A. A. Tepeřek, *Economic Development in the World's Smallest Economies*, https://doi.org/10.1007/978-3-031-63810-7_11

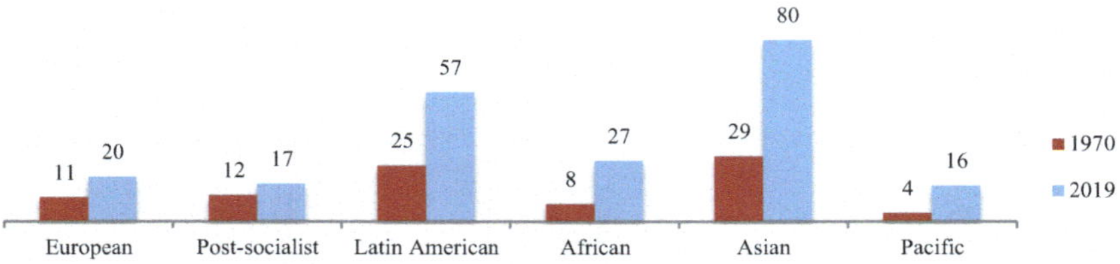

Fig. 11.1 WSE subgroups population density from 1970 to 2019 (people per 1 km^2). (Source: Own compilation based on The World Bank)

It is worth noting that in 2019, the European WSE and the African WSE subgroups recorded similar population densities of 20 and 27 people per 1 km^2, respectively. Considering the vast African desert areas (e.g., in Chad, Eritrea, Mauritania, Niger, Somalia) and the extensive areas of humid equatorial forests (e.g., in Congo, Equatorial Guinea, Gabon), which were not conducive to settlement, the similarity in population density between the African WSE and the European WSE subgroups seems inexplicable and even illogical. And yet, the European countries analyzed were characterized by very high levels of urbanization and industrialization, which would indicate a much higher population density. Iceland was the reason for this. The population density of the European WSE subgroup would have been much higher if Iceland not been among the classified countries. Most of Iceland is uninhabited due to a harsh climate, poor vegetation, soil cover and volcanic activity, which are not conductive to settlement, resulting in an average population density of just four people per 1 km^2.

The example of Iceland and its impact on the subgroup results shows that the subgroup analysis only provides a general picture of population density. Therefore, it carries the risk of drawing false conclusions. To obtain more precise results, the individual WSE were analyzed. The population densities varied widely, ranging from two people per 1 km^2 (Mongolia) to 19,482 people per 1 km^2 (Monaco) in 2019 (Table 11.1).

The highest population density, exceeding 150 people per 1 km^2, was recorded in 30 of the WSE, or one-third of the entire group (Table 11.1). Leading the way were the highly urbanized and highly developed European microstates of Malta, Monaco, and San Marino. Most of the remaining

Table 11.1 WSE population density by subgroups in 2019 (people per km²)

150 or more people per 1 km²		*50 to 149 people per 1 km²*		*49 and less people per 1 km²*	
WSE	*Population density*	*WSE*	*Population density*	*WSE*	*Population density*
	persons/km²		*persons/km²*		*persons/km²*
Monaco	19,482	Togo	149	Fiji	49
Maldives	1770	Kiribati	145	Equatorial Guinea	48
Malta	1591	Tonga	140	Madagascar	46
Barbados	666	Cape Verde	136	Montenegro	45
Mauritius	624	Cyprus	130	Djibouti	42
Nauru	599	Sierra Leone	108	Palau	39
San Marino	555	Benin	105	Mozambique	39
Rwanda	512	Armenia	99	Zimbabwe	38
Comoros	457	Albania	99	Eritrea	35
Burundi	449	Dominica	96	Kyrgyzstan	32
Tuvalu	448	Cambodia	91	Laos	30
Haiti	406	East Timor	87	Estonia	29
Grenada	326	Honduras	87	Bahamas	28
Marshall Islands	325	Senegal	85	Somalia	25
Salvador	307	Northern Macedonia	81	Vanuatu	25
Saint Lucia	295	Moldova	79	Bhutan	20
Saint Vincent and the Grenadines	284	Brunei	75	Papua New Guinea	19
Trinidad and Tobago	272	Burkina Faso	74	Niger	18
Jamaica	268	Lesotho	70	South Sudan	18
Liechtenstein	238	Samoa	69	Belize	17
The Gambia	232	Guinea-Bissau	68	Mali	16
Saint Thomas and Príncipe	224	Eswatini	67	Congo	16
Antigua and Barbuda	220	Tajikistan	65	Chad	13
North Korea	213	Bosnia and Herzegovina	64	Gabon	8

(*continued*)

Table 11.1 (continued)

150 or more people per 1 km²		*50 to 149 people per 1 km²*		*49 and less people per 1 km²*	
WSE	*Population density*	*WSE*	*Population density*	*WSE*	*Population density*
	persons/km²		*persons/km²*		*persons/km²*
Seychelles	212	Yemen	63	Central African Republic	8
Saint Kitts and Nevis	202	Afghanistan	58	Mauritania	4
Malawi	198	Georgia	53	Botswana	4
Nepal	194	Guinea	52	Guyana	4
Andorra	165	Liberia	51	Suriname	4
Micronesia	162	Nicaragua	50	Iceland	4
				Solomon Islands	3
				Namibia	3
				Mongolia	2

Source: Own compilation based on The World Bank

countries (19) were lowland islands in Latin America and Africa, ranging from 21 km² (Nauru) to 27,750 km² (Haiti).

Population densities ranging from 50 to 149 people per 1 km² in 2019 were recorded in another 30 of the WSE (Table 11.1). These WSE are larger in terms of area as well as population. Fewer were island nations, while more were continental countries, primarily located in Africa (including Burkina Faso, Eswatini, Guinea, Liberia, Lesotho, Senegal,and Sierra Leone) and Asia (including Afghanistan, Brunei, Cambodia, and Yemen). The WSE, with a population density from 50 to 149 people per km², included as many as seven countries that had socialist past, ocucupying land areas ranging from 25,713 square kilometers (North Macedonia) to 143,100 km² (Tajikistan) and populations ranging from 2,083,000 (North Macedonia) to 9,321,000 (Tajikistan).

Population densities of 49 or fewer people per km² were found in the 33 WSE (Table 11.1). Half of them are located in Africa. Many are covered by deserts (e.g., Chad, Eritrea, Mauritania, Namibia, Somalia) and/or steppes (e.g., Botswana, Mozambique, Zimbabwe), equatorial forests (e.g., Congo, Gabon, Guyana, Laos, Papua New Guinea, Solomon Islands, Suriname), or mountainous terrain (e.g., Afghanistan, Bhutan, Kyrgyzstan). Among the 33 WSE with population density of 49 or less people per km^2 were large countries whose total land area accounted for almost 80% of the group's total area. Five of these countries had area exceeding 1 million km^2 (e.g., Chad, Mali, Mauritania, Mongolia, Niger). However, their total population made up less than 40% of the WSE group's population.

Differences in population concentration and density in the WSE resulted from a number of interacting and overlapping historical, geographic (including land area and environmental features), and, most importantly, economic factors. The spatial differentiation of the WSE populations depended on the productivity of land resources, the nature, intensity of labor, productivity of economies, and the resulting ability to provide adequate living conditions for the WSE population. Cultural and social factors also played an important role, leading to areas with centuries-old civilization. All these factors contributed either to the development of population centers or to their decline. Both could have either negative or positive consequences. Excessively low population density sometimes hindered the development of countries that lack sufficient human resources relative to their natural resources, such as Mongolia (two people per km^2) or the Solomon Islands (three people per km^2). On the other hand, excessive demographic pressure brought with it environmental problems, as high population density altered the geographic environment. Its rapid increase also meant that countries were unable to feed their populations, as exemplified by Benin (fourfold increase from 26 to 105 persons per km^2), The Gambia (fivefold increase from 46 to 232 persons per km^2), Honduras (fourfold increase from 24 to 87 people per km^2), Yemen (fourfold increase from 13 to 63 people per km^2), Comoros (fourfold increasef rom 124 to 457 people per km^2), Malawi (fourfold increase from 50 to 198 people per km^2), Rwanda (fourfold increasef rom 146 to 512 people per km^2), Togo (fourfold increase from 39,149 people per km^2). The per capita agriculture area in these countries has been declining faster than their agricultural development potential, threatening to degrade agricultural resources. For example, there has been a decline in agricultural land, for example, in Benin (from 0.41 to 0.24 hectares per capita), in The Gambia (from 0.27 to 0.19 hectares per capita), in Honduras (from 0.48 to 0.10 hectares per capita), in Yemen (from 0.21 to 0.03 hectares per capita), in Comoros (from 0.28 hectares to 0.07 hectares per capita), in Malawi (from 0.38 to 0.19 hectares per capita), in Rwanda (from 0.13 to 0.09 hectares per capita) between 1970 and 2019. This decline has manifested in a reduced capacity for food self-sufficiency in these countries. Consequently, the growing threat of being unable to feed their population has disrupted their economic structure.

However, some of the WSE benefited from high population density, which provided greater human resources, both in terms of quantity and quality (i.e., specialization). These countries included those with diverse economic activities, such as Monaco (19,482 people per km^2), Malta (1591 people per km^2), San Marino (555 people per km^2), Liechtenstein (238 people per km^2), Andorra (162 people per km^2). Additionally, some countries rich in natural resources, which were extracted using labor-intensive techniques. Examples include Jamaica with bauxite mining (268 people per km^2), Nauru with phosphate extraction (599 people per km^2), and Trinidad and Tobago with oil production (272 people per km^2).

When analyzing the population density of the WSE, it is important to remember that these are only averaged indicators and do not fully reflect the actual variation in population density accross different regions within these countries. This can be obsered in the population density ratios of their capitals, which are often significantly higher than the national averages (Fig. 11.2).

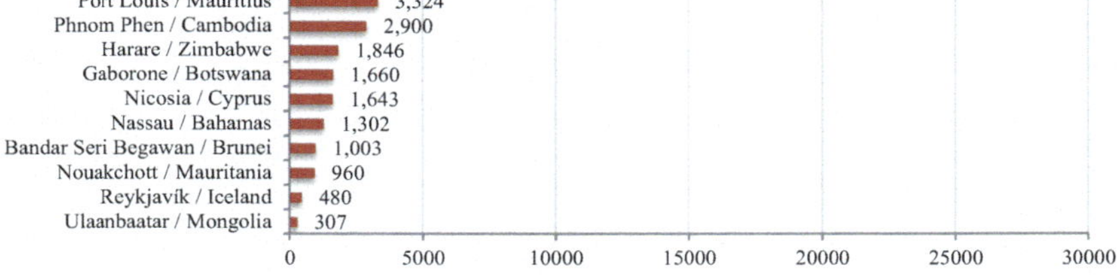

Fig. 11.2 WSE capitals population density in 2019 (persons per km^2). (Source: Own compilation based on The World Bank)

An accurate estimate of the gross population density of the WSE would require insight into the internal structure of the spatial distribution of their population. Typically, population concentrations are found in regions with favorable physiographic conditions (lowlands and plains) and areas with fertile and easy cultivable soils on flat terrain). Regions rich in water, industrialized areas (especially those with mineral resources), and locations along transportation and communication routes, particularly in coastal areas, are also commonly more densely.

CHAPTER 12

Factors Affecting the Change in Demographic Potential of the World's Smallest Economies

12.1 Natural Increase

The natural increase of the WSE and their population growth rate were primarily determined by the variations in the rate of natural increase (Fig. 12.1). These fluctuations, in turn, were influenced by changes in birth and death rates. Comparing the WSE group's natural increase rate to the global average, it was significantly higher for the WSE group—15.7‰ versus 10.4‰ for global in 2019, as well as 21.6‰ compared to 20.4‰ in 1970. However, the gas has been decreasing over time. This decline in the natural increase rate is primarily due to a reduction in both birth and death rates, with the number of deaths decreasing by half over the period (Fig. 12.2).

The significantly higher natural increase rate of the WSE group in comparison to the world indicated a low level of economic development. This was additionally illustrated by GDP per capita, which stood at US$ 1562 per capita of the WSE group and US$ 11,059 per capita of the world in 2019. Indeed, a strong correlation was observed between the rate of natural increase and the countrys' level of economic development (Fig. 12.3). As the level of economic development of the WSE increased, the rate of natural increase was decreased.

A. A. Teperek, *Economic Development in the World's Smallest Economies*, https://doi.org/10.1007/978-3-031-63810-7_12

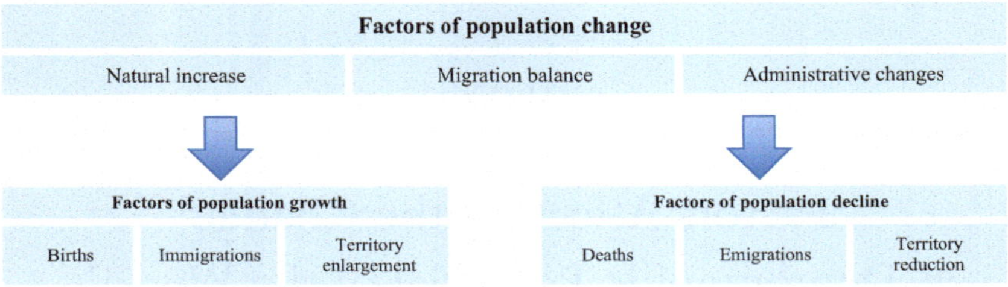

Fig. 12.1 Contributions to population change. (Source: Own compilation based on: Budner (2011))

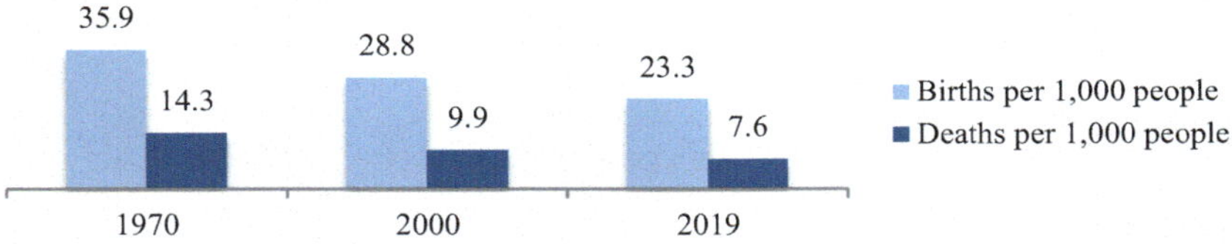

Fig. 12.2 WSE natural increase rates and its components in 1970, 2000 and 2019 (per 1000 inhabitants). (Source: Own compilation based on World Bank)

Accordingly, the lowest natural increase rates were recorded in the economically highly developed European WSE, namely, Malta (1‰ births; 8.6/1000 people and deaths 7.3/1000 people), Liechtenstein (2‰; births 9.2 and deaths 7.7), Cyprus (3‰; births 10.2 and deaths 7.1), Monaco (3‰; births 6.4 and deaths 3.2), Iceland (6‰; births 12.3 and deaths 6.3). In some countries, the natural increase rate even reached negative values, such as Andorra (-1‰; birth rate 7.0 and death rate 7.5) and San Marino (-1‰; births 8.7 and deaths 8.9). The low natural increase rate was due to low birth and death rates. In affluent, educated societies with consumerist and hedonistic lifestyles, people were more focused on accumulating material goods, which led to the adoption of a new cultural model of smaller family. The period of education lengthened, women's labor force participation increased, and the decisions about motherhood and starting a family were postponed. This shift was facilitated by widespread access to contraception and abortion rights. All these factors contributed to a simple reproduction pattern, where children merely replaced their. This trend was accompanied by a decline in mortality due to access to advanced medical care.

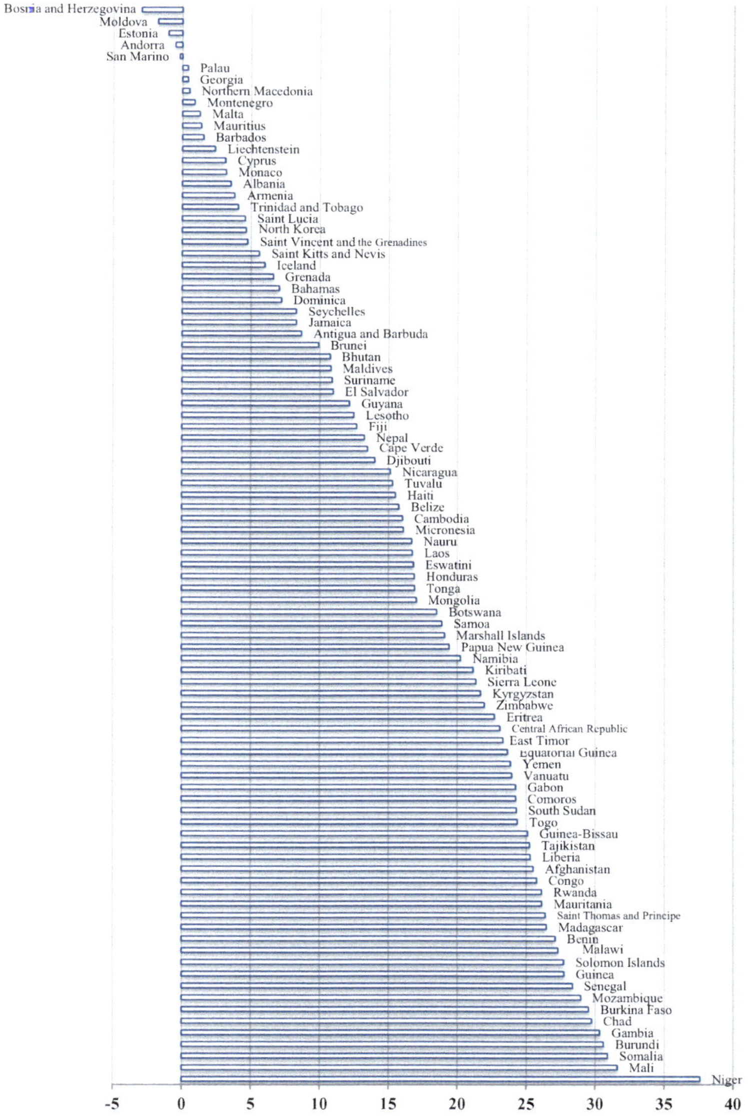

Fig. 12.3 WSE natural increase rates in 2019 (‰). (Source: Own compilation based on World Bank)

Among the WSE with the lowest natural increase rates were also the Post-socialist WSE, such as Bosnia and Herzegovina (-3‰; births 7.9 and deaths 10.9), Moldova (-2‰; births 9.9 and deaths 11.7), Estonia (-1‰; births 10.6 and deaths 11.6), Georgia (0‰; births 13.2 and deaths 12.8), North Macedonia (1‰; births 10.6 and deaths 10.1), Montenegro (1‰; births 11.7 and deaths 10.7), Albania (4‰; births 11.6 and deaths 8.1), Armenia (4‰; births 13.6 and deaths 9.8). However, their low natural increase rates were not associated with high levels of economic development but rather with lower birth rates resulting from the small numbers of the 1960s generation (i.e., the children of those born during World War II), (Philipov & Dobritz, 2004) combined with the higher death rate. The economic transformation after the collapse of the communist system was another factor. The early stages of economic transition led to widespread impoverishment of the population due to unemployment. Thousands of women of childbearing age emigrated abroad in search of work, and the uncertainty of the future discouraged them from having children. At the same time, living in Western European countries contributed to the adoption of the consumerist lifestyle, particularly the smaller family model. All of this resulted in a decline in birth rates in the Post-socialist WSE and an increase in mortality due to the over-mortality of 50- and 60-year-olds (especially men), who struggled to survive the political transition.

When discussing the Post-socialist WSE, it should be added to those previously mentioned, the two countries with the lowest level of economic development, Kyrgyzstan and Tajikistan, had high natural increase rates of 22‰ and 25‰, respectively. This was mainly due to cultural factors. Both Kyrgyzstan and Tajikistan are strongly influenced by Islamic culture (with Muslims making up more than 85% of the population), which promotes polygamy and large familes. This culture influence was reflected in the birth rates of 26.9 per 1000 people in Kyrgyzstan and 30 per 1000 people in Tajikistan in 2019. In contrast, their death rates were comparable to the rest of the Post-socialist WSE. This significant difference between birth and death rates resulted in high natural increase rates. Both Kyrgyzstan and Tajikistan were among the 37 WSE (Fig. 12.4) with the highest rates above 20‰, and the remaining countries being primarily poor African nations with GDP below US$ 900 per capita. Only Gabon (US$ 9178 per capita) and Equatorial Guinea (US$ 9238 per capita) had high levels of economic development, owning to their oil and natural gas exports. However, their high GDP per capita did not translate into

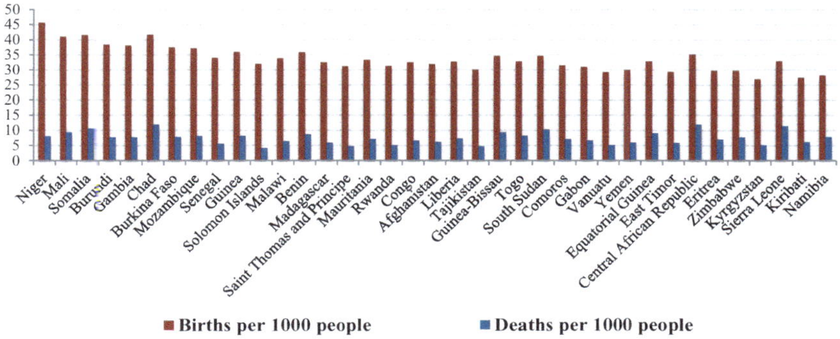

Fig. 12.4 WSE with the highest birth rates in 2019 (per 1000 inhabitants). (Source: Own compilation based on World Bank)

societal wealth, as more than 80% of the profits from raw materials sales embezzled by a narrow ruling "elite". As a result, over 60% of the population in both countries lived on less than US$ 1 a day, with limited access to education and contraception. The low levels of public awareness contributed to uncontrolled birth rates, alongside falling mortality rates (Fig. 12.4).

All the WSE experienced a decline in mortality rates. Between 1970 and 2019, countries with the highest natural increase rates (Table 12.1) saw a threefold decrease in death rates (from 21.3 to 7.5 per 1000 people). This was due to medical achievements, improved hygiene, better nutrition, and humanitarian aid. Birth rates, despite declining (from 45 per 1000 people in 1970), still remained high in most of these countries (more than 30 per 1000 population in 2019). The reason for the high birth rate were the large number of women of childbearing age and deeply ingrained cultural factors such as the use of children for labor. In addition, children were seen as future security for parents, as many elderly people had no pensions, due to the lack of pension system in poorer countries. The extended multi-child and multigenerational family model was also prevalent, particularly in countries with low levels of urbanization. This was because rural population tended to have more children than urban dwellers, largely due to lower levels of education.

The analysis of the natural increase rates confirms the thesis of dependency on the level of economic development. However, the change in natural increase rates have been variable over time and have not followed

Table 12.1 WSE with the highest birth rates and death rates in years 1970 and 2019 (per 1000 people)

No	*WSE*	*Births*		*Deaths*	
		per 1000 people			
		1970	*2019*	*1970*	*2019*
1	Niger	56.9	45.6	28.4	8.0
2	Mali	50.4	41.0	31.9	9.4
3	Somalia	46.6	41.6	23.1	10.7
4	Burundi	47.7	38.4	20.8	7.8
5	The Gambia	47.6	38.1	24.9	7.7
6	Chad	46.9	41.7	23.4	11.9
7	Burkina Faso	47.5	37.5	24.7	7.9
8	Mozambique	47.1	37.2	23.2	8.2
9	Senegal	49.9	34.0	24.7	5.6
10	Guinea	45.4	36.0	26.9	8.2
11	Solomon Islands	45.4	32.0	11.8	4.2
12	Malawi	52.1	33.7	25.5	6.4
13	Benin	46.8	35.8	23.5	8.7
14	Madagascar	48.0	32.4	20.6	5.9
15	Saint Thomas and Príncipe	41.5	31.2	12.7	4.8
16	Mauritania	46.3	33.3	15.6	7.1
17	Rwanda	49.7	31.2	20.2	5.1
18	Congo	43.9	32.4	15.3	6.6
19	Afghanistan	51.5	31.8	26.9	6.3
20	Liberia	48.6	32.7	24.9	7.4
21	Tajikistan	42.4	30.0	14.9	4.8
22	Guinea-Bissau	42.6	34.6	23.2	9.4
23	Togo	48.2	32.7	18.9	8.3
24	South Sudan	50.5	34.7	28.1	10.3
25	Comoros	45.5	31.4	19.3	7.1
26	Gabon	36.8	31.0	20.7	6.7
27	Vanuatu	42.0	29.2	12.0	5.2
28	Yemen	56.2	29.9	29.5	6.0
29	Equatorial Guinea	41.5	32.8	26.0	9.1
30	East Timor	43.1	29.3	23.1	5.9
31	Central African Republic	42.5	35.1	22.9	12.0
32	Eritrea	46.7	29.7	20.7	7.0
33	Zimbabwe	47.3	29.7	11.5	7.8
34	Kyrgyzstan	32.3	26.9	11.2	5.2
35	Sierra Leone	47.7	32.9	28.5	11.5
36	Kiribati	34.6	27.5	14.1	6.3
37	Namibia	43.0	28.2	14.5	7.9

Source: Own compilation based on World Bank

a linear pattern. This was due to the economic and demographic diversity of countries, as well as their population policies. In general, higher levels of economic development were associated with lower birth rates. Although there were times when demographic processes in neighboring countries with similar historical and cultural backgrounds played a more influential role.

The different natural increase rates among countries were closely related to the Demographic Transition Model (DTM)[1] (Demeny & McNicoll, 2003; Okolski, 1990), that the WSE have passed through (Table 12.2). Each stage of the transition, from the Preindustrial Stage of the primitive agrarian society to the Postindustrial Stage with a declining population, was characterized by specific death and birth rates. Considering the WSE group, they are currently passing through one of the stages, mostly depending on their level of economic development.

The demographic transition model[2] (Barrett et al., 1998; Duncan & Scott, 2008; Maksimowicz, 1990 begins with the Preindustrial Stage I, called the High Stationary (Table 12.2), which is characteristic of preindustrial societies that live nomadism and gathering, subsisting on hard physical labor, existing under conditions of conflicts and wars that claim many lives. These societies' dependence on natural conditions often results in food shortages; in turn, malnutrition increases vulnerability to disease. Epidemics spread, and a lack of medical knowledge limits their treatment, resulting in high mortality rates. Although a very large number of children are born, a significant proportion of them die before reaching adulthood. Accordingly, the very low natural increase rate is not due to economic growth, but rather to a very high birth rate offset by an almost equally high death rate due to famine, epidemics, and war, reaching up to 60‰. As of 2019, with the exception of a few indigenous populations living in

[1] The precursor of the demographic transition was Warren Thompson (1887–1973), who described it in the American Journal of Sociology in 1929.

[2] The demographic transition model was accompanied by the epidemiological transition model, which describes changes in the causes of death from disease during the various stages of development. The first phase was dominated by malnutrition, famine, trauma, and infectious and parasitic diseases. A characteristic of second phase was the predominance of infectious diseases affecting entire populations and parasitic diseases (especially in countries located in hot and humid climates). The subsequent third, fourth, and fifth phases were dominated by diseases of civilization, such as cardiovascular disease, diabetes, cancer, degenerative diseases (e.g., Alzheimer's, Parkinson's). However, it should be noted that this model does not take into account the HIV/AIDS and Ebola epidemics, which have significantly affected the structure of the African population in particular.

Table 12.2 WSE demographic transition stages in 2019

Demographic transition stage	*Natural increase rate*	*Description*	*WSE*
Stage I Preindustrial Stage (High stationary)	Small positive natural increase rate	Very low natural increase rate was due to high birth and death rates. The high birth rate resulted from a very high fertility rate (more than 6 children per woman of childbearing age). The high death rate was a result of famine, wars and epidemics. As a consequence, life expectancy did not exceed 45 years	Societies living in the humid equatorial forests in Congo and the subequatorial forests of Papua New Guinea
Stage II The Industrial Revolution (Early expanding)	Very rapid increase in the natural increase rate	Along with the continued high birth rate, there has been a decline in mortality due to improved living conditions, hygiene, medical achievements, control of spreading epidemics, better nutrition, and greater political stability. Life expectancy has now reached 50 years. On the other hand, the birth rate remains very high as a result of slow changes in customs, low levels of education, and, above all, a high percentage of women of childbearing age (4–5 children born per woman of childbearing age)	Afghanistan, Burkina Faso, Chad, Guinea, Mali, Mozambique, Niger, Somalia, Yemen
Stage III Post-Industrial Revolution (Late expanding)	Natural increase rate slows down	Thanks to declining birth and death rates, the natural increase rate is falling. The population continues to grow, but as the birth rate declines, the process of population growth slows down. The reason for the declining birth rate is the reduction in the number of children born (3–4 per woman of childbearing age) as a result of socioeconomic changes (increased education, awareness, and transformation of societies from rural to urban-industrial).	Belize, Benin, Botswana, Burundi, Cambodia, Cape Verde, Central African Republic, Comoros, Congo, Equatorial Guinea, El Salvador, East Timor, Eritrea, Eswatini, Fiji, Gabon, The Gambia, Guinea-Bissau, Guyana, Haiti, Honduras, Kyrgyzstan, Kiribati, Laos, Lesotho, Liberia, Malawi, Madagascar, Marshall Islands, Mauritania, Micronesia, Namibia, Nauru, Nepal, Papua New Guinea, Rwanda, Samoa, Saint Thomas and Principe, Senegal, Sierra Leone, Solomon Islands, South Sudan, Suriname, Tajikistan, Togo, Tonga, Vanuatu, Zimbabwe

Stage IV Stabilization (Low stationary)	Very low natural increase rate	Low natural increase rate is primarily due to low birth and death rates. This decline can be largely attributed to concerns about the inability to maintain a family, which is perceived as a significant challenge in the context of economic constrains. This results in simple reproduction, i.e. children quantitatively replace parents (2 for every 1 woman of childbearing age). The low mortality rate is the result of advanced medical knowledge, wider health care coverage and the age structure of the population.	Bahamas, Barbados, Bhutan, Brunei, Montenegro, Cyprus, Iceland, Jamaica, Liechtenstein, Maldives, Malta, Mauritius, Monaco, North Korea, North Macedonia, Saint Kitts and Nevis, Saint Lucia
Stage V Declining population	Zero or negative natural increase rate	Population decline, or so-called demographic regression, is caused by a steadily declining birth rate (1–2 children per woman of childbearing age), which is now lower than the death rate. Additionally, life expectancy has already reached 70 years	Andorra, Bosnia and Herzegovina, Estonia, Georgia, Moldova, Palau, San Marino

Source: Own compilation

the equatorial forests of the Congo, Central African Republic, and Papua New Guinea, none of the WSE was in Preindustrial Stage I. Although as recently as 1970, Afghanistan (birth rate 51.5 per 1000; death rate 26.9 per 1000), Yemen (birth rate 56.2; death rate 29.5), Mali (birth rate 50.4; death rate 31.9), Niger (birth rate 56.9; death rate 28.4), and South Sudan (birth rate 50.5; death rate 28.1) passed through that stage, currently, these countries are already in the Industrial Revolution Stage II (early expanding) of the demographic transition (Okolski & Fihel, 2012), (Table 3.9). It is worth mentioning that when the listed countries entered Stage II in the 1970s, highly developed WSE such as Cyprus, Iceland, Malta, and Monaco were in this stage at the turn of the twentieth century, while other developing WSE, such as Bhutan, El Salvador, Fiji, Guyana, Haiti, Honduras, Nepal, Suriname, and Tuvalu, were in this stage in the mid-twentieth century.

The transition, especially of underdeveloped countries, through Stage II involves a demographic explosion, manifested in natural increase rates exceeding 30‰ (e.g., Niger 38‰, Mali 32‰, Somalia 31‰, Burundi 31‰) due to high female fertility, high birth rates, and declining death rates. The rapid population growth occurs in a relatively short period of time due to improved living conditions, increased food production and medical development, resulting in reduced infant mortality and increased life expectancy. This is compounded by low awareness and education levels, as well as lack of knowledge about family planning methods and a young age for marriage and family formation. Cultural (especially religious) conditions also play a significant role (e.g., the perception of the extended family as a value and the practice of polygamous relationships in Islamic culture). The demographic explosion applies not only to Stage II but also to Stage III. The Post-Industrial Revolution Stage III, also called Late Expanding Stage, is observed in the WSE such as Congo, Madagascar, and Mauritania. This is a very unfavorable phenomenon, as it contributes to the impoverishment of the population, mass unemployment due to the mismatch between the labor market and the rapidly growing population, overpopulation in rural areas, and dynamic urbanization of cities, as well as the formation of slums, increased crime, hunger, and malnutrition. The decline in consumption, in turn, leads to a decrease in demand, underdevelopment of the industrial sector for highly processed and modern products, and the service sector (i.e., tourism and transportation). A lack of funds to expand basic socio-educational infrastructure leads to increased illiteracy and a shortage of healthcare. Stopping the demographic explosion is very difficult, lengthy and costly, as reducing the birth rate often involves breaking traditional and cultural (especially religious) stereotypes, which can only be achieved through education and improving the material conditions of society.

An increasing natural increase rate at the beginning of Stage III, followed by a decrease at its end, was observed in Nepal (an increase from 20‰ to 23‰ between 1970 and 2000, and a decrease from 23‰ to 13‰ between 2000 and 2019) and Papua New Guinea (an increase from 23‰ to 24‰ between 1970 and 2000, and a decrease from 24‰ to 19‰ between 2000 to 2019). Declining mortality and birth rates at the end of the period under study were the result of cultural and social changes. Education, especially for women, began to play a much greater role than in the previous Stage II. The cross section of society was also changing. Increasing life expectancy resulted in an increase in the proportion of the elderly, which was more apparent in the next Stabilization Stage IV, also known as the Low Stationary Stage. This stage is characterized by low birth rates due to low mortality, fertility, and birth rates associated with a change in the family model. The widespread knowledge of family planning, as well as knowledge of human physiology, combined with the increase in the professional aspirations of the societies in affluent countries and the focus on meeting one's own needs, has resulted in a decrease in births and the number of children per household (from 0 to 2). This process has been fostered by the financial independence of people, including the population over 65, who, thanks to pensions, are not financially dependent on their children, as was the case in Stage III. The increase in the percentage of the post-working age subgroup is also the result of medical advances and the universality of social benefits, which is the case in almost all the highly developed WSE, such as Cyprus, Iceland, Liechtenstein, Malta, Monaco, and San Marino, which are in Stage IV. Highly developed Andorra is already in the Declining Stage V of demographic regression, often referred to as the Neo-Malthusian Stage, due to its negative natural increase rate. The same applies to former socialist countries, such as Bosnia and Herzegovina (-3‰), Estonia (-1‰), and Moldova (-2‰).

It should be noted that although some of the WSE have shown high levels of economic development and relatively low rates of natural increase, they are not at Stage IV or Stage V. For example, Palau (GDP US$ 12,078 per capita; natural increase: 0‰), Saint Kitts and Nevis (GDP US$ 17,295 per capita, natural increase: 6‰), the Seychelles (GDP US$ 15,049 per capita; natural increase: 8‰), Trinidad and Tobago (GDP US$ 15,105 per capita; natural increase: 4‰). The exploitation of valuable mineral resources (e.g., in Trinidad and Tobago) or the dynamic development of tourism (e.g., in Palau, Saint Kitts and Nevis, and the Seychelles) and the high incomes earned from exports goods or services have given them only *apparent* economic development, and not comprehensive development, in terms of the whole economy, as well as civilizational development.

Neither a high natural increase rate nor a low or even negative, one was beneficial to the economic development of all the WSE. This was because it led gradual depopulation and a decline in the working-age population, threatening an economic slowdown. Changes in infrastructure were necessary: demand for schools, kindergartens and nurseries declined, while demand for hospitals, hospices, and care homes for the eldery increased. With a decline in the number of pension contributors and a rise in the number of benefit recipients in countries experiencing a demographic implosion, states incurred greater budgetary expenditures on elderly care and pension benefits, weakening the pension system further. To address this, immigrants from other countries were employed. This was usually a culturally diverse population, so host countries had to bear additional costs of adapting to the immigrants. Governments of the wealthy WSE have also undertaken various actions to stimulate demographic growth by offering economic incentives, such as discounts for multi-child families, low-interest loans for young couples, and extended maternity leave. Fortunately, these measures have led to an increase in births in many countries, such as Estonia (from 9.4 to 10.6 per 1000 people), Georgia (from 12.1 to 13.2 per 1000 people), Armenia (from 12.9 to 13.6 per 1000 people). Consequently this has resulted in an increase in the rate of natural increase, for example, in Estonia (from -4‰ to -1‰), and Monaco (from 2‰ to 3‰) between 1970 and 2019.

12.2 International Migration

In addition to population growth, the demographic process is influenced by migration movements, which are defined as the territorial movement of people to temporarily or permanently change their place of residence. Human migration has occured since ancient times, with only the scale of migrations and their spatial extent changing over time. Migration has become an important part of international economic relations, especially since the time of the great geographical discoveries, when peoples of European origin began to settle the two American continents. Subsequent migration movements occurred in stages: in the nineteenth century and early twentieth century, after the end of World War II, after the collapse of the colonial system and after the collapse of the Eastern Bloc. The increased mobility of the population, the extent of its movements, as well as the diversity of migration patterns were facilitated by the accelerated processes of globalization, along with the accompanying socioeconomic and technological changes that were part of the transnational revolution of the late twentieth century. Population movements have undergone rapid and highly complex transformations, both quantitatively and qualitatively. Migration processes have also been influenced domestic policies, national security concerns, and international agreements. New trends have emerged. The geographic structure of international migration has been changing and greater global dispersion has been observed[3] (Castles & Miller, 2004). More and more countries are becoming destinations for migration, and its impact is evident in various spheres of life, including culture, economy, and politics. The number of female migrants has increased within the overall share of migrants, making the feminization of migration a defining characteristic of population flows in the twenty-first century. A new form of youth migration has emerged, driven by the desire to study abroad (Maciejko, 2004), often combined with work and travel. The migration of retirees from wealthy countries has become common.

The primary factors influencing the spatial mobility of the population were three motives: demographic-economic, sociopolitical, and environmental. Demographic-economic migration was related to the economic condition of the country of origin. Faced with unfavorable economic conditions, residents of the poorer WSE (e.g., Armenia, Bosnia and Herzegovina, El Salvador, Georgia, Honduras, Kyrgyzstan,and Nepal) emigrated to richer countries in search of work to raise their standard of living, as well as to obtain an education and a better job. Sociopolitical factors usually involved ethnic, religious, racial, political and cultural persecution, which forced citizens to leave their country, often accepting refugee status and seek humanitarian asylum when war or conflict was present (e.g., Afghanistan, Central African Republic, Chad, East Timor, Liberia,

[3] One sociologist, Stephen Castles, saw a correlation between the directions of migration and the demand for labor and the supply of foreigners, thus distinguishing the following migration destinations: North America (the United States and Canada), the Persian Gulf countries, Southeast Asia, and Australia, and the European Union countries.

and Yemen). The third factor driving migration was the environment. Natural disasters such as hurricanes, floods, earthquakes, and volcanic eruptions, as well as droughts forced people to temporarily or permanently leave their homes (e.g., Haiti, Kiribati, Maldives, and Tuvalu) and move to another country.

Many divisions and classifications of migration can be found in the literature[4] (Skoczek, 2010; Wrony, 2006), although the basic general typology distinguishes emigration, immigration, re-emigration, deportation, repatriation. Of these, emigrations, which involves leaving home country permanently or for a certain period to another country, and immigration, which involves arriving and settling in a country permanently or for an extended period, are the most commonly analyzed. The WSE most often experienced emigration. This was related to the lower level of economic development in most of them. Their residents emigrated for work (seasonal or permanent) to richer countries. Only a few highly developed of the WSE located in Europe, such as Andorra, Cyprus, Iceland, Liechtenstein, Malta, Monaco, and San Marino, were the destinations for immigrants. However, since these were very small countries (with the exception of Iceland), they received a small number of immigrants, which together accounted for a small percentage of migrants from the entire WSE group. Therefore, further research mainly analyzed emigration from the WSE.

In 2019, a total of 47.3 million residents of the 93 WSE were in emigration, a 1.5-fold increase compared to 2000 (28.9 million). Such a large increase was related to accelerated globalization processes and the associated free movement of people, as well as the growing population of the

[4]The divisions of migration were made on the basis of migrants' qualifications, nature of migration, direction, duration, and reasons for movement. M. Skoczek made a typology of migrants according to labor qualifications, dividing them into: (a) highly skilled (transnational corporations, free professions), (b) moderately educated, (c) low-skilled or unskilled, (d) young people without work experience. J. Wrony made a division by direction (external and internal), duration of migration (daily, periodic, and permanent). He also distinguished voluntary migration (economic, health, social, religious, and forced) or forced migration (ecological, political). On the other hand, the CRONEM Center for Research on Nationalization and Multiculturalism at the University of Surrey in the UK used typologies according to migrants' migration strategies and life plans, distinguishing migrants: (a) participating in cyclical migrations lasting several months a year (so-called *storks*), (b) those leaving at one time in order to raise as much money as possible (so-called *hoarders*), (c) those staying abroad who have not yet decided to return home (so-called *seekers*), and (d) those remaining permanently abroad (so-called *settlers*).

WSE (from 372 million to 561.8 million between 2000 and 2019), which often travelled abroad in search of work. In 2019, the emigrants from the WSE accounted for 8.4% of global emigrants (up from 7.8% in 2000), which, with 272 million emigrants worldwide, meant that one in every five came from one of the 93 WSE. Considering that the population of analyzed group of countries accounted for 7.3% of the world's population and GDP only 1% of global GDP, the share of emigrant at 8.4% was quite high. This again confirms the low level of economic development of the WSE group, as the majority of their residents emigrated for labor purposes.

In 2019, emigrants from the African WSE subgroup accounted for the largest share of the group, at 37.6% (an upward trend from 32.8% in 2000). Another 26.2% were emigrants from the Asian WSE (an upward trend from 25.8% in 2000). The share of residents residing abroad from the Post-socialist WSE and the Latin America WSE was much lower, at 17.8% and 16.5%, respectively (Fig. 12.5). It is worth noting that from the WSE group perspective, all WSE subgroups have seen an increase in the share of emigrants, with only the Post-socialist WSE seeing a decrease from 22.8% to 17.8% between 2000 and 2019.

Although, emigrants from the Post-socialist WSE accounted for only one-sixth of the WSE group in 2019, this subgroup led the way per 1000 residents (from 192 per 1000 to 218 per 1000 people between 2000 and 2019). The collapse of communism and the associated changes initiated in the late 1980s and early 1990s enabled most societies in former socialist countries to travel freely. The desire to see and experience the Western world, and above all, the need to find better-paying jobs contributed to the mass emigration of the former Eastern Bloc's population, which manifested in an increase of the Post-socialist WSE subgroup's emigration rate. The Latin American WSE subgroup had a slightly lower rate than the Post-socialist WSE, with 189 emigrants per 1000 residents (an upward

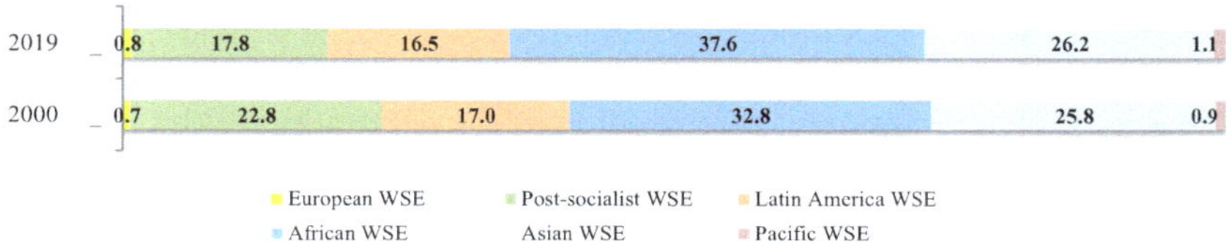

Fig. 12.5 WSE emigrants by subgroups in 2000 and 2019 (%). (Source: Own compilation based on Migration Data Portal 2019)

trend from 151 per 1000 people in 2000). The reasons of emigration were primarily economic. Residents of the African WSE and the Pacific WSE were also driven by the same motives; however, the rates of both subgroups were much lower. The low rate of the African WSE (increasing from 50 per 1000 people to 56 per 1000 people between 2000 and 2019) was due to a lack of money to cover the costs associated with travel. Despite a strong incentive to emigrate due to prevailing unemployment, the majority of residents of the African WSE subgroup were unable to afford to go abroad. It was a paradox of sorts, as the same populations and countries that could gain the most from emigration were, in fact, unable to benefit from it[5] (Hatton & Williamson, 2009). In contrast, the Pacific WSE had a low emigration rate (increasing from 33 per 1000 people to 45 per 1000 people between 2000 and 2019), primarly due to Papua New Guinea, whose population made up as much as 78% of the Pacific WSE subgroup's population. Papua New Guinea's rate was exceptionally low, with only 1 resident per 1000 Papuans. Such a low rate determined the outcome of the entire subgroup, which included 12 countries. Excluding Papua from the study yields a completely different result. The remaining 11 countries combined showed an emigration rate of 203 people per 1000 residents (up from 128 per 1000 people in 2000). The example of Papua New Guinea demonstrates how much influence a single country can have on subgroup results. Therefore, subgroup analyses should be approached with some caution. Only examination of individual countries provides more reliable results.

The largest number of emigrants, in absolute numbers, were recorded by: Afghanistan, Bosnia and Herzegovina, Burkina Faso, El Salvador, Haiti, Laos, Mali, Nepal, Somalia, South Sudan, and Yemen (Fig. 12.6). Emigrants from these eleven countries accounted for almost half of the WSE group's emigrants.

These eleven countries varied in population from 3.3 million (Bosnia and Herzegovina) to 38 million (Afghanistan) as well as in terms of their level of economic development, ranging from US$ 93 per person (Somalia) to US$ 6304 per person (Bosnia and Herzegovina). However, it was low economic development that resulted in the emigration of the population in search of work (e.g., Bosnia and Herzegovina, El Salvador, Laos, and Nepal). Sometimes sociopolitical problems (e.g., Afghanistan,

[5] This relationship, along with the concept of poverty trapping, is described by the Hatton and Williamson model, which posits that individuals are often too poor to migrate.

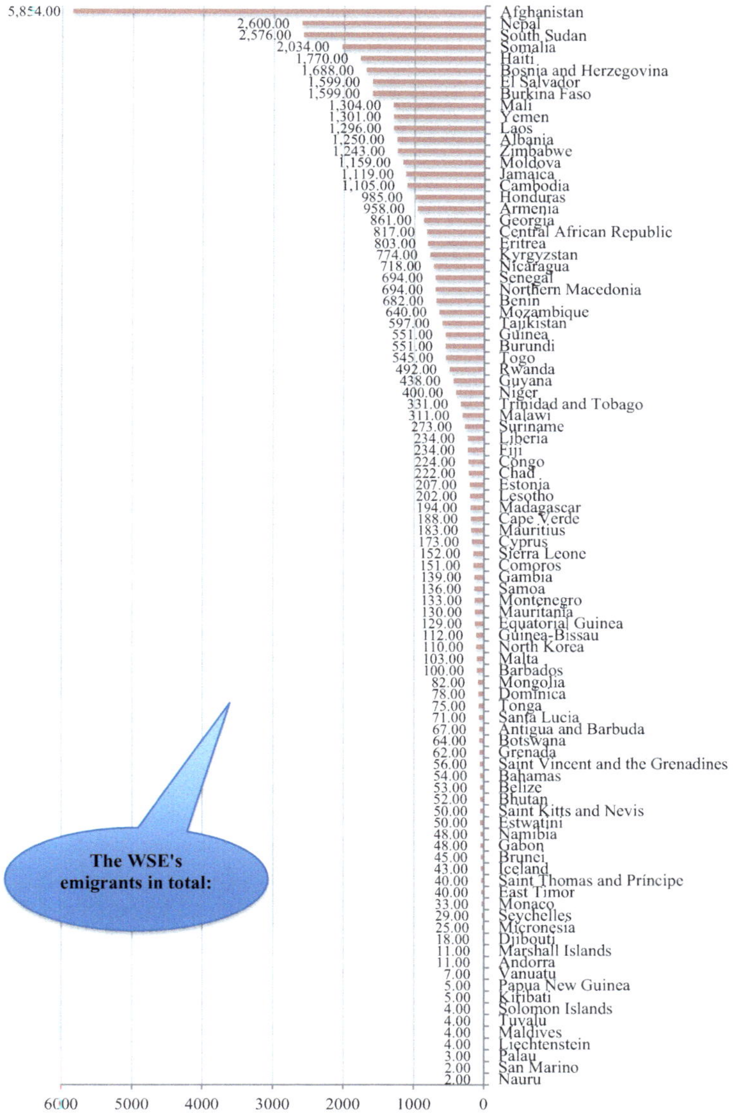

Fig. 12.6 WSE emigrants in 2019 (in thousands). (Source: Own compilation based on Migration Data Portal 2019)

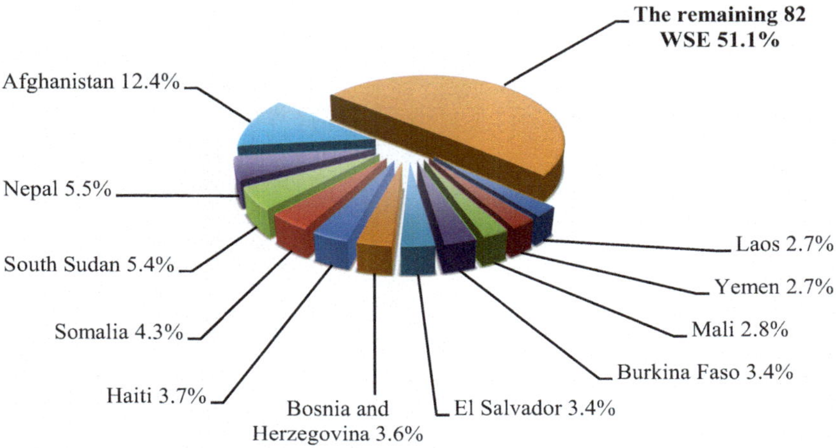

Fig. 12.7 WSE with the largest share of emigrants in the WSE group in 2019 (%). (Source: Own compilation based on Migration Data Portal 2019)

Somalia, and Yemen) or environmental issues related to droughts and water shortages (e.g., Mali) were the reason for the departures.

The other half of the WSE group's emigrants came from the remaining 82 WSE (Fig. 12.7). In 2019, the smallest number of emigrants—less than 50,000 were recorded by countries with small populations of less than 2.5 million (with Papua New Guinea, having a population of 8.7 million, being an exception). With the exception of a few, these were wealthy European countries (including Andorra, Liechtenstein, Iceland, Monaco, and San Marino), as well as countries with higher levels of economic development that export tourism services (including the Maldives, Palau, St. Kitts and Nevis, Seychelles, and Saint Thomas and Príncipe) or valuable raw materials (including Brunei, Gabon, Namibia, Nauru,and Papua New Guinea), whose residents did not need to go abroad for economic reasons.

From the perspective of the emigration rate per 1000 residents, it was Dominica that recorded the highest rate in the entire WSE group (1086 emigrants/1000 residents). It was the only country among the 93 surveyed where the number of residents living abroad was higher than the number of residents living at home (78,000 emigrants, 71,800 residents).

The reason was the difficult economic situation. Dominica was one of the less developed countries among the Latin America WSE subgroup (GDP US$ 6917 per capita), so its citizens were leaving in search of work to the neighboring United States and Canada, as well as to neighboring, wealthier Antigua and Barbuda (GDP US$ 15,704 per capita) and France and the United Kingdom, of which Dominica was a colony in the centuries past. Dominica was followed by other Caribbean countries (i.e., Antigua and Barbuda, Barbados, Grenada, Guyana, Jamaica, Saint Kitts and Nevis, Saint Vincent and the Grenadines, Santa Lucia, and Suriname), countries with a socialist past (i.e., Albania, Bosnia and Herzegovina, North Macedonia, and Moldova), the Pacific countries (i.e., Samoa, Tonga, Tuvalu), and Monaco. Their emigration rates ranged from 300 emigrants per 1000 residents to 950 emigrants per 1000 residents. The reasons for the emigration of their residents varied. Emigrants from Guyana (690 per 1000 residents), Bosnia and Herzegovina (511 per 1000 residents) and Samoa (690 per 1000 residents) left mainly for economic reasons. In contrast, the emigration rate of Antigua and Barbuda, Monaco and Saint Kitts and Nevis, the wealthier WSE (GDP above US$ 15,000 per capita), was somewhat artificial. These countries offered citizenship in exchange for investments made. As a result, wealthy residents from other countries, with significant tax burdens, made investments in the aforementioned WSE to enjoy personal and financial freedom. Despite holding passports of these countries, they usually did not live in them, which meant that demographically they were registered as emigrants. This, in turn, influenced the inflated emigration rate. On the other hand, Tuvalu's high emigration rate (343 emigrants per 1000 residences) was primarily related to the impending threat of rising ocean level and flooding of the island nation, which Tuvaluans fear (McAdam, 2010).

In contrast, the lowest emigration rate of less than 28 emigrants per 1000 inhabitants (Table 12.3) was characterized mainly populous and very poor African countries (e.g., Chad, Madagascar, Malawi, Mozambique, Niger, and Sierra Leone) with a GDP of less than US$ 850 per capita, whose citizens were not able to afford to go abroad. African mineral-exporting countries (e.g., Botswana, Gabon, and Namibia) also recorded low emigration rate. Local people did not have to look abroad for work, as mining and related industries and services provided them with jobs. Low emigration rates were also noted in "closed countries," such as North Korea (four emigrants per 1000 residents), whose regime prevented its

Table 12.3 WSE emigration against GDP per capita in 2000 and 2019

No	*WSE*	*Emigration rate*		*Emigrants' number*		*Emigrants in population*		*GDP*
		per 1000 people		*thousands*		*%*		*US$ per capita*
		2000	*2019*	*2000*	*2019*	*2000*	*2019*	*2019*
1	Dominica	718	1086	50	78	72	109	6917
2	Saint Kitts and Nevis	681	946	30	50	68	95	17,295
3	Monaco	n.a.	847	n.a.	33	0	85	209,241
4	Tonga	500	718	49	75	50	72	4355
5	Antigua and Barbuda	395	690	30	67	39	69	15,704
6	Samoa	401	690	70	136	40	69	3869
7	Guyana	308	560	230	438	31	56	6107
8	Grenada	583	554	60	62	58	55	9220
9	Bosnia and Herzegovina	392	511	1470	1688	39	51	6304
10	Saint Vincent and the Grenadines	455	506	49	56	45	51	6863
11	Suriname	446	470	210	273	45	47	8047
12	Albania	265	438	820	1250	27	44	5211
13	Moldova	205	436	600	1159	21	44	3720
14	Saint Lucia	255	388	40	71	26	39	9351
15	Jamaica	324	380	860	1119	32	38	4867
16	Barbados	306	348	83	100	31	35	16,100
17	Tuvalu	426	343	4	4	43	34	3943
18	Cape Verde	306	342	131	188	31	34	1289
19	Northern Macedonia	260	333	530	694	26	33	5625
20	Armenia	287	324	880	958	29	32	4732
21	Seychelles	197	297	16	29	20	30	15,049
22	Fiji	112	263	91	234	11	26	4739
23	El Salvador	211	248	1240	1599	21	25	3572
24	Trinidad and Tobago	245	237	310	331	24	24	15,105
25	South Sudan	55	233	341	2576	6	23	1302
26	Georgia	238	231	970	861	24	23	4978
27	Eritrea	222	230	510	803	22	23	549
28	Micronesia	186	220	20	25	19	22	2700
29	Montenegro	134	214	81	133	13	21	8590
30	Malta	n.a.	205	n.a.	103	0	20	28,976
31	Marshall Islands	79	187	4	11	8	19	3157
32	Saint Thomas and Príncipe	134	186	19	40	13	19	3908

(*continued*)

Table 12.3 (continued)

No	*WSE*	*Emigration rate*		*Emigrants' number*		*Emigrants in population*		*GDP*
		per 1000 people		*thousands*		*%*		*US$ per capita*
		2000	*2019*	*2000*	*2019*	*2000*	*2019*	*2019*
33	Laos	122	181	650	1296	12	18	1841
34	Comoros	131	177	71	151	13	18	1399
35	Central African Republic	17	172	61	817	2	17	384
36	Palau	52	167	1	3	5	17	12,078
37	Nauru	97	159	1	2	10	16	8223
38	Haiti	93	157	790	1770	9	16	1245
39	Estonia	79	156	111	207	8	16	20,856
40	Afghanistan	218	154	4540	5854	22	15	573
41	Mauritius	96	145	114	183	10	14	10,893
42	Cyprus	183	144	173	173	18	14	23,927
43	Andorra	122	143	8	11	12	14	45,887
44	Bahamas	104	139	31	54	10	14	28,909
45	Belize	194	136	48	53	19	14	4150
46	Somalia	112	132	990	2034	11	13	93
47	Kyrgyzstan	116	120	570	774	12	12	1116
48	Iceland	107	119	30	43	11	12	51,332
49	Nicaragua	102	110	515	718	10	11	1763
50	Liechtenstein	60	105	2	4	6	11	177,698
51	Brunei	120	104	40	45	12	10	32,327
52	Honduras	52	101	340	985	5	10	2241
53	Equatorial Guinea	49	95	30	129	5	10	9238
54	Lesotho	60	95	121	202	6	10	1353
55	Nepal	40	91	955	2600	4	9	859
56	Zimbabwe	26	85	310	1243	3	8	1183
57	Burkina Faso	106	79	1230	1599	11	8	822
58	Bhutan	86	68	51	52	9	7	3262
59	Cambodia	38	67	460	1105	4	7	1269
60	Togo	53	67	261	545	5	7	696
61	Mali	66	66	720	1304	7	7	792
62	Tajikistan	87	64	540	597	9	6	1121
63	The Gambia	30	59	39	139	3	6	815
64	San Marino	73	59	2	2	7	6	50,462
65	Benin	47	58	320	682	5	6	1260
66	Guinea-Bissau	51	58	61	112	5	6	636

(*continued*)

Table 12.3 (continued)

No	*WSE*	*Emigration rate*		*Emigrants' number*		*Emigrants in population*		*GDP*
		per 1000 people		*thousands*		*%*		*US$ per capita*
		2000	*2019*	*2000*	*2019*	*2000*	*2019*	*2019*
67	Burundi	54	48	342	551	5	5	208
68	Liberia	92	47	262	234	9	5	516
69	Yemen	30	45	530	1301	3	4	631
70	Eswatini	31	44	31	50	3	4	4818
71	Guinea	42	43	350	551	4	4	921
72	Kiribati	36	43	3	5	4	4	1790
73	Senegal	40	43	390	694	4	4	1584
74	Congo	41	42	129	224	4	4	2166
75	Rwanda	40	39	320	492	4	4	901
76	East Timor	171	31	151	40	17	3	978
77	Mauritania	49	29	130	130	5	3	1756
78	Botswana	18	28	30	64	2	3	8093
79	Mongolia	13	25	31	82	1	3	4353
80	Vanuatu	27	23	5	7	3	2	2887
81	Gabon	17	22	21	48	2	2	9178
82	Mozambique	36	21	640	640	4	2	589
83	Namibia	28	19	51	48	3	2	5766
84	Sierra Leone	111	19	510	152	11	2	488
85	Djibouti	10	18	7	18	1	2	4904
86	Malawi	23	17	261	311	2	2	524
87	Niger	22	17	251	400	2	2	563
88	Chad	41	14	340	222	4	1	814
89	Maldives	7	8	2	4	1	1	8477
90	Madagascar	5	7	79	194	1	1	500
91	Solomon Islands	7	6	3	4	1	1	1749
92	North Korea	3	4	71	110	0	0	588
93	Papua New Guinea	1	1	6	5	0	0	2490

Source: Own compilation based on: Migration Data Portal 2019, The total number of emigrants, online version: https://www.migrationdataportal.org/international-data?i=stock_abs_&t=2020 (accessed 2.02.21)

citizens from going abroad for many decades. Another example is Papua New Guinea (one emigrant per 1000 inhabitants), which, while politically and economically not a closed country, but is socially closed. This is because Papua New Guinea is inhabited by an isolated society that largely consists of wild tribes living on the fringes of civilization.

Also noteworthy are several countries that have experienced particularly large increase in emigration rates over nearly two decades, between 2000 and 2019. The Central African Republic experienced a more than tenfold increase (from 17 to 172 emigrants per 1000 residents). This country, one of the poorest of the WSE and the world (GDP US$ 384 per capita in 2019) has been in political and economic chaos since independence from France. It culminated in the authoritarian rule of President Francois Bozize (2003–2013), who committed genocide against hundreds of the locals. Public resentment against the ruling team led to numerous bloody conflicts, including a civil war (2004–2007) that forced more than 700,000 people to leave the country (total population: 4.7 million in 2019). Acts of genocide and conflict have also resulted in mass emigration (over 2 million) in South Sudan. As a result, South Sudan saw a more than fourfold increase in the emigration rate (from 55 to 233 emigrants per 1000 residents between 2000 and 2019). This meant that in 2019, one in five South Sudanese residents were in emigration. The same was true in Zimbabwe, where the emigration rate more than tripled (from 26 to 85 emigrants per 1000 residents in 2000–2019). Dictator Robert Mugabe, who ruled the country for three decades (1987–2017), brought Zimbabwe's economy to the brink of bankruptcy. As a consequence, more than 1 million citizens (total population: 14.6 million in 2019) had to leave the country. A large percentage of them were whites, leaving the country in fear of losing their lives, after the nationalization of white citizens' farms in 2000.[6]

In contrast to above, a decrease in the emigration rate (Fig. 12.8) was recorded in the WSE with long-running armed conflicts or wars, such as Liberia (four-year civil war in 1999–2003), Chad (civil war, fought against Sudanese-backed rebels from 2005 to 2008), East Timor (almost three-year invasion by Indonesian troops), Sierra Leone (11-year civil war in 1991–2002), after which the population returned to their homelands. As a result, Liberia saw its emigration rate drop from 92 to 47 emigrants per 1000 inhabitants, Chad from 41 to 14 emigrants per 1000 inhabitants, Sierra Leone from 111 to 19 emigrants per 1000 inhabitants, and

[6] The deprivation of farms from white citizens was a punishment imposed by R. Mugabe for the colonial injustices inflicted upon Africans. These farms were handed over to black citizens who lacked experience and knowledge necessary for effective management. Devastation and bankruptcy, as black citizens struggled to repay loans taken out from banks, which were secured against these farms as collateral. This situation ultimately led to an outbreak of hyperinflation, which reached an astounding rate of 500 billion percent.

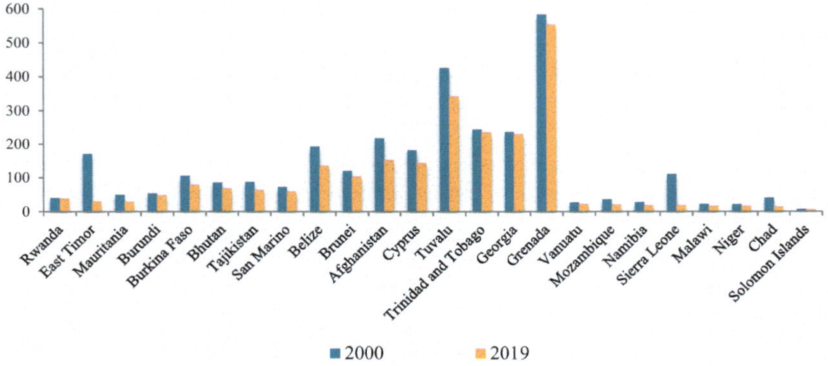

Fig. 12.8 Emigration rate in the sample WSE between 2000 and 2019 (per 1000 residents). (Source: Own compilation based on Migration Data Portal 2019)

East Timor from 171 to 31 emigrants per 1000 inhabitants between 2000 and 2019 (Fig. 12.8).

It is also worth analyzing the gender structure of expatriates. Among the group's emigrants, men dominated, with a slight advantage over women, who accounted for 49.3% of emigrants in 2019 (compared to 48.1% globally in 2019). Women accounted for more than 50% of emigrants only in 32 countries (Fig. 12.9). The highest percentage of female emigrants at 69.9%, was recorded by Nepal. It was followed by the countries with a socialist past, such as Armenia, Estonia, Georgia, Kyrgyzstan, Moldova, Montenegro, Northern Macedonia, Tajikistan, from 56.1% to 60.6% of the total. Latin American countries, including Antigua and Barbuda, Barbados, Grenada, El Salvador, Saint Lucia, and Saint Vincent and the Grenadines, were also among the WSE with a higher proportion of female emigrants (Fig. 12.9).

In contrast, the lowest percentage of female emigrants was recorded by the Maldives (12.3% of female emigrants). This was influenced by two main factors: cultural and religious norms (as Muslim societies generally exhibit lower mobility for women) and a well-developed tourism sector (66.1% of GDP) that provides significant employment opportunities for women. The same was true in the Seychelles (30% of female expatriates. Despite the country not being Muslim, it has a well-developed tourism sector. Bhutan presents another example (15.1% of female emigrants), where conservative traditions played a significant role in limiting female

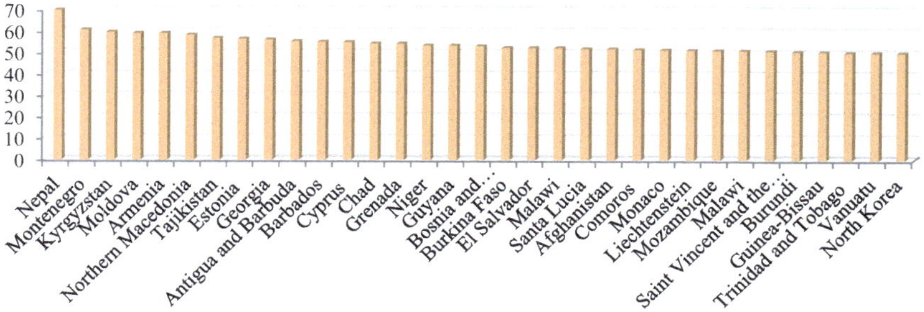

Fig. 12.9 WSE with more than 50% female emigrants in 2019 (%). (Source: Own compilation based on International Migration Report 2019)

migration. Industrialized nations like Equatorial Guinea (22.9% female emigrants), Gabon (35.7% female emigrants), Nauru (37.5% female emigrants), as well as in Papua New Guinea (39.2% female emigrants) also had relatively low proportions of female emigrants.

Looking back, there has been an increase in female emigration. Several countries within the WSE have seen significant rises in the proportion of female emigrants, such as Afghanistan (from 43.6% to 52%), Benin (from 46.4% to 52.9%), Chad (from 46.1% to 54.4%), Kyrgyzstan (from 58.2% to 59.6%), Saint Lucia (from 49.8% to 52%), Tajikistan (from 56% to 56.8%), Vanuatu (from 46.1% to 54.4%). 4%), Kyrgyzstan (from 58.2% to 59.6%), Saint Lucia (from 49.8% to 52%), Tajikistan (from 56% to 56.8%), Vanuatu (from 49.7% to 50.3%), and Zimbabwe (from 43% to 43.2%) between 2000 and 2019.

As for the median age of emigrants from the WSE, it was 35.1 years old in 2019, meaning that half of the emigrants were 35 years old or younger. The youngest emigrants came from Albania (average age 20), Samoa (23), Togo (23), Afghanistan (24), Mauritania, Niger, and Dominica (25). In contrast, the oldest emigrants were from former socialist countries, such as Estonia (average age 59), Tajikistan (54), Armenia (53), North Macedonia and Moldova (52).

The most popular geographical destinations for the WSE emigration were highly developed countries with a high level of economic potential, such as Australia, Canada, the United Kingdom, and the United States (Table 12.4).

Among the WSE, the largest number of emigrants came from the smallest economies with a GDP of less than US$ 20 billion. In general, unless

Table 12.4 WSE emigration and main geographical destinantions in 2019

WSE	*Major geographical destinations*
Afghanistan	Iran, Pakistan, Saudi Arabia, Germany
Albania	Italy, Greece, United States, North Macedonia, United Kingdom
Andorra	Spain, France, Portugal, United States
Antigua and Barbuda	United States, Canada, Guinea, United Kingdom
Armenia	Russia, Azerbaijan, United States, Ukraine, France
Bahamas	United States, Canada, United Kingdom
Barbados	United States, Canada, United Kingdom, Trinidad and Tobago
Belize	United States, Canada, Mexico, United Kingdom
Benin	Nigeria, Togo, Ivory Coast, Gabon
Bhutan	Nepal, Australia, Canada, India
Bosnia and Herzegovina	Montenegro, Germany, Austria, United States
Botswana	South Africa, Australia, United Kingdom
Brunei	Malaysia, India, Canada, Australia
Burkina Faso	Ivory Coast, Mali, Ghana, Niger
Burundi	Tanzania, Rwanda, Uganda, DRC, South Africa
Cambodia	Thailand, United States, France, Australia, Canada
Cape Verde	Angola, Portugal, United States, France, Netherlands
Central African Republic	Cameroon, DRC, Chad, Congo, France, Sudan
Chad	Sudan, Cameroon, Nigeria, South Africa
Comoros	France, Madagascar, Saudi Arabia, UAE
Congo	France, Mali, Tanzania, South Africa, Gabon
Cyprus	United Kingdom, Australia, Greece, United States
Dominica	United States, Antigua and Barbuda, Canada, France, United Kingdom
Djibouti	Canada, Ethiopia, France
East Timor	Australia, New Zealand, China, Malaysia
El Salvador	United States, Canada, Guatemala, Australia, Costa Rica, Italy
Equatorial Guinea	Gabon, Spain, Guinea, Cameroon, Congo
Eritrea	Ethiopia, Sudan, United States, Sweden, UAE
Estonia	Russia, Finland, Germany, Sweden, United States
Eswatini	South Africa, United Kingdom, Zambia
Fiji	Australia, New Zealand, United States, Canada
Gabon	Mali, France, Cameroon, Congo
The Gambia	Spain, United States, France, Germany, Guinea-Bissau
Georgia	Russia, Greece, Ukraine, Azerbaijan, Armenia, United States
Grenada	United States, Canada, Trinidad and Tobago
Guinea	Ivory Coast, Sierra Leone, Senegal, The Gambia, France

(*continued*)

Table 12.4 (continued)

WSE	*Major geographical destinations*
Guinea-Bissau	Portugal, Senegal, United States, Ivory Coast
Guyana	United States, Canada, United Kingdom, Suriname, Antigua and Barbuda
Haiti	United States, Dominican Republic, Canada, France, Bahamas
Honduras	United States, Spain, Mexico, Nicaragua, El Salvador, Belize
Iceland	Denmark, Germany, Norway, Spain
Jamaica	United States, Canada, United Kingdom, Antigua and Barbuda, Australia
Kyrgyzstan	Russia, Germany, Ukraine, Tajikistan, Azerbaijan
Kiribati	Nauru, New Zealand, United States, Marshall Islands
Laos	Thailand, United States, France, Canada
Lesotho	South Africa, Botswana, Mozambique, Zambia
Liberia	Ivory Coast, United States, Ghana, Nigeria
Liechtenstein	Switzerland, Germany, Austria
North Korea	China, Russia, South Korea
Northern Macedonia	Turkey, Italy, Australia, Switzerland
Madagascar	France, Canada, Comoros, Germany, Italy
Malawi	South Africa, Zimbabwe, Mozambique, United Kingdom, Zambia
Maldives	Sri Lanka, India, Australia, New Zealand
Mali	Ivory Coast, Nigeria, Mauritania, Niger, France
Malta	Australia, United Kingdom, Canada, Italy
Marshall Islands	United States, United States (American Samoa), Australia
Mauritania	Senegal, France, Mali, The Gambia, Guinea
Mauritius	France, United Kingdom, Australia, Canada, South Africa
Micronesia	United States, Saudi Arabia, Australia, Japan
Moldova	Russia, Italy, Romania, Ukraine, United States
Monaco	France, Italy, Greece, United States
Mongolia	South Korea, Russia, Austria, Canada, France
Montenegro	Serbia, Austria, Australia, Bosnia and Herzegovina
Mozambique	South Africa, Zimbabwe, Portugal, Malawi, Tanzania
Namibia	South Africa, Botswana, Australia, United States
Nauru	Kiribati, Fiji, Australia, New Zealand
Nepal	India, Saudi Arabia, Malaysia, Qatar, United States
Niger	Nigeria, Benin, Togo, Ivory Coast
Nicaragua	Costa Rica, United States, Spain, Canada, Panama
Palau	Australia, New Zealand Japan
Papua New Guinea	New Zealand, United States (American Samoa)
Rwanda	DRC, Uganda, Burundi, Congo, Angola, Belgium

(*continued*)

Table 12.4 (continued)

WSE	*Major geographical destinations*
Saint Kitts and Nevis	United States, Canada, United Kingdom
Saint Lucia	United States, Barbados, Canada, France
Saint Vincent and the Grenadines	United States, Canada, Barbados, Trinidad and Tobago
Samoa	New Zealand, Australia, United States (American Samoa)
Saint Thomas and Príncipe	Equatorial Guinea, Gabon, Benin, Congo
San Marino	Italy, Albania, Andorra, Algeria, Angola
Senegal	The Gambia, France, Italy, Spain, United States
Seychelles	Slovenia, Australia, Canada, South Africa
Sierra Leone	United States, United Kingdom, Liberia, Senegal
Solomon Islands	Australia, New Zealand, Bahamas, Barbados
Somalia	Kenya, Ethiopia, Yemen, United Kingdom, Libya
South Sudan	Uganda, Ethiopia, Sudan, Kenya, UAE
Suriname	The Netherlands, France, United States, Aruba
Tajikistan	Russia, Germany, Ukraine, Kazakhstan, Uzbekistan, Canada, Israel
Togo	Nigeria, Ghana, Benin, Ivory Coast, Burkina Faso
Tonga	New Zealand, United States (American Samoa), Fiji
Trinidad and Tobago	United States, Canada, United Kingdom, Australia
Tuvalu	New Zealand, United States (American Samoa), Australia
Vanuatu	Australia, United States (American Samoa)
Yemen	Saudi Arabia, UAE, Kuwait, Qatar, United States, Israel, Jordan
Zimbabwe	South Africa, United Kingdom, United States, Australia, Malawi

Source: Nomad Migration; online version: https://www.knomad.org/data/migration/immigration?tid%5B81%5D=81

emigration involved skilled professionals, it has been considered a positive phenomenon. Demographic pressure on local labor markets has decreased, leading to lower unemployment rates. Additionally, these countries were incurring less spending on benefits and social assistance. The emigration from the poorest WSE, which were in the midst of a population explosion, affected population decline. Emigrants sent remittances that not only supported their families, but also contributed to the economic development of their home countries. For example, in Tonga, remittance income constituted 37.2% of its GDP; in Lesotho, 20.8% of GDP; in Samoa, 17.2% of GDP; in The Gambia, 15.1%; in Comoros, 14.5% of GDP; in the Marshall Islands, 14.2% of GDP in 2019. For comparison, the remittance income of the entire WSE group accounted for as much as 13.7% of the group's GDP, amounting to US$ 62.4 billion. Not only did the emigration countries benefit from this process, but also the host countries employing these immigrants. Their nationality structure underwent a transformation, culture became enriched, the percentage of the working age population increased, contributing to a rejuvenation of the age structure. Emigrants gained valuable work experience, and upon returning home, they became a valuable human capital resource, saving their countries from the expense of educating them. The challenge arose when highly skilled professionals (e.g., scientists, doctors, engineers) emigrated and chose to remain abroad permanently. This brain drain had a negative impact on the economic development of many of the WSE, as the outflow of specialized human capital contributed to a slowdown in economic growth.

The phenomenon of the impact of labor migration on economic development has been studied by many researchers in the past. However, neither neoclassical theory, which treats migration as a mechanism for regulating earnings, nor modified new migration theory, which focuses on micro (household) migration, nor dual market theory, which primarily concentrates, has fully explained this phenomenon. Later studies on the relationship between migration and economic development have led to the modern trend of emphasizing the positive effects on the economies of sending countries while minimizing the negative effects (e.g., brain drain). This shift is attributed to the recognition that the migration process is guided by its own independent dynamics and it is more beneficial for the states and governments to embrace it.

The analysis of migration focused mainly on emigration, due to the fact that immigration does not play a significant role for the WSE. Given the low level of economic development, most of the WSE were not host countries, instead it was their residents who emigrated abroad in search of work. Only a few highly developed countries (e.g., Andorra, Bahamas, Estonia, Liechtenstein, Monaco, Malta) or mineral exporting nations (e.g., Brunei, Equatorial Guinea, Gabon) received emigrants. However, this was a small number from the perspective of the entire WSE group and constituted a minor share of its total migrant population.

Bibliography

Barrett, R., Kuzawa, C. W., McDade, T., & Armelagos, G. J. (1998). Emerging and Re-emerging Infectious Disease. The Third Epidemiologic Transistion. *Annual Review of Anthropology., 27*(1), 247–271.

Budner, W. (2011). Geografia Ekonomiczna. *Wspolczesne Zjawiska i Procesy, 48.*

Castles, S., & Miller, M. I. (2004). *The Age of Migration: International Population Movements in the Modern World.* Cambridge University Press.

Demeny, P., & McNicoll, G. (2003). *Encyclopedia of Population.* Macmillan Reference.

Duncan, C., & Scott, S. (2008). *Czarna Smierc. Epidemie w Europie od starozytnosci do czasow wspolczesnych.* Bellona.

Hatton, T. J., & Williamson, J. G. (2009). *Emigration in the Long Run: Evidence from Two Global Centuries* (Vol. 23).

Maciejko, A. (2004). Kobiety i Mlodziez w Migracjach (Vols. Polityka Spoleczna No 3, Wyd.). Institutu Pracy i Polityki Spolecznej.

Maksimowicz, A. (1990). In M. Okolski (Ed.), *Wzorzec Umieralnosci w Kolejnych Fazach Przejscia.* PWE.

McAdam, J. (2010). In J. McAdam (Ed.), *Disappearing States, Statelessness and the boundaries of International Law.* University of New South Wales.

Okolski, M. (1990). In M. Okolski (Ed.), *Modernizacja Spoleczenstwa a Przejscie Demografizcne.* PWE.

Okolski, M., & Fihel, A. (2012). *Demografia, Wyd.* Naukowe Scholar.

Philipov, D., & Dobritz, J. (2004). Demographic Consequences of Economic Transistion in Countries of Central and Eastern Europe. *The Population Studies, 39*, 24–57.

Skoczek, M. (2010). In A. Bakiewicz & U. Zulawska (Eds.), *Migracje Miedzynarodowe.* PWE.

Wrony, J. (2006). *Podstawy Geografii Ekonomicznej.* PWE.

CHAPTER 13

Demographic Structure of the Populations of the World's Smallest Economies

The natural and migratory movements of societies determine the distribution of the population as well as its demographic structure. Demographic structure, defined as the distribution of basic elements in the population (age groups, gender, among others), is crucial in determining the labor resources, including the supply of social, educational services. This is because the age of the population affects the size and quality of the labor force. The age structure determines consumer needs. Populations of different ages exhibit different needs, as exemplified by younger and older generations. The age structure also makes it possible to predict the consequences of population growth, both social and economic. Therefore, a thorough study of population structure, especially by age, is the basis of most demographic analyses. Today's age structure of the WSE varies widely as a result of the level of socioeconomic development of the analyzed countries and the centuries-long changes in their economies. Along with economic development, the WSE have gone through successive stages of demographic development (Table 13.1), experiencing a decline in birth and death rates and an increase in life expectancy. The consequences of this are aging populations, as seen in the most developed WSE, which are at Stages IV and V.

The highest share of people over 65 was recorded in the highly developed European WSE, ranging from 14% (Cyprus) to 35% (Monaco) in 2019 (Fig. 13.1), which has experienced a demographic implosion. This

A. A. Teperek, *Economic Development in the World's Smallest Economies*, https://doi.org/10.1007/978-3-031-63810-7_13

Table 13.1 Demographic transition stages

Demographic transition stage	*Birth rate*	*Death rate*	*Natural increase rate*	*Children per family*	*Life expectancy*	*Population*
	per 1000 people		*‰*	*Quantity*	*years*	*Age*
I	50–60	50–60	0–10	above 6	20–45	Young
II	50–60	20–30	20–30	5–6	45–50	Young
III	35–45	15–25	10–20	3–4	50–65	Mature
IV	10–20	under 15	0–10	0–2	above 65	Old
V	under 10	under 15	below 0	0–2	above 65	Old

Source: Own elaboration based on: Kop et al. (2003)

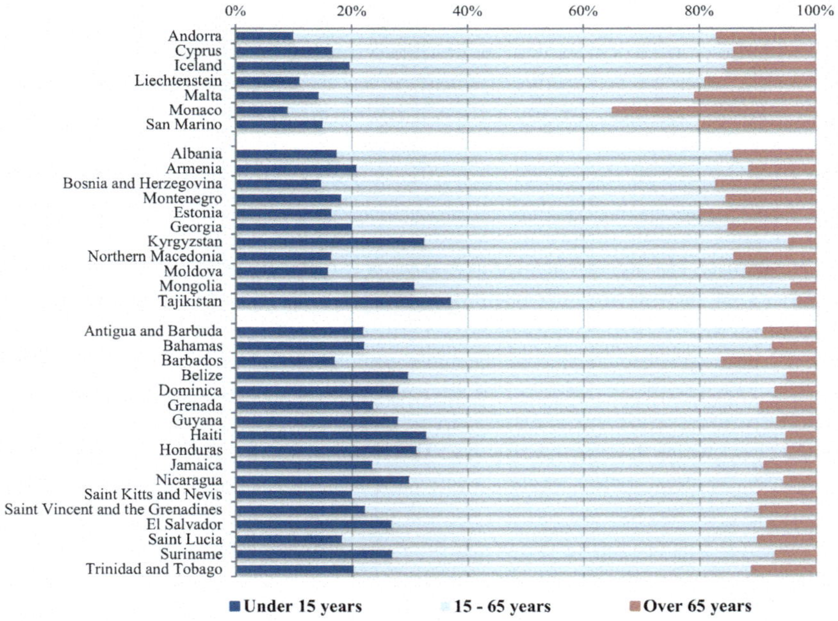

Fig. 13.1 European WSE, the Post-socialist WSE and the Latin American WSE subgroups age structure population in 2019 (%). (Source: Own compilation based on The World Bank)

followed years of steady population growth in the elderly population and declining birth rates. For example, in Cyprus from 10% to 14%; in Iceland from 9% to 15%, and in Malta from 10% to 21% of retirees between 1970 and 2019. The progressive aging of the population was associated with an increased spending on health care, social security, and pensions. At the same time, the steadily growing number of retirees in the European WSE has placed a financial burden on the working-age group of the population aged 15–64, the proportion of which has ranged from 56% (Monaco) to 73% (Andorra). The share of the working-age population increased in some countries (e.g., Cyprus from 59% to 69%, Iceland from 59% to 65%, Malta from 63% to 65%), but declined in others (e.g., Malta from 68% to 65%) between 2000 and 2019. This situation is likely to worsen in the future as a result of low natural increase rates and rising life expectancy.

Similar changes have begun to take place in the Post-socialist WSE. For example, between 2000 and 2019, the percentage of 15–64 year old in Montenegro dropped from 67% to 66%, in Estonia from 67% to 64% and in Georgia from 66% to 65%. In contrast, the poorest Kyrgyzstan and Tajikistan, which are heavily influenced by Islamic culture, saw increases (Kyrgyzstan from 60% to 63% and Tajikistan from 54% to 60%). These countries also recorded the highest percentage of children among the 11 Post-socialist WSE, accounting for more than a third of the population in 2019. The Post-socialist WSE, as in the European WSE accounted for less than a fifth of the population (Fig. 13.1). This was significantly lower than in the Latin American WSE, where the share of the under-15 subgroup was less than 24% of the population, with the exceptions of Belize, Haiti, Honduras, and Nicaragua, which were above 30%. These four countries also had the lowest percentage of people over 65 (5% in 2019). By comparison, the richer Latin American WSE, such as Barbados, El Salvador, Grenada, Saint Kitts and Nevis, Saint Vincent and the Grenadines, and Trinidad and Tobago, had twice the percentage (10%).

The results of the above analysis of dividing the populations of the European WSE, the Post-socialist WSE, and the Latin American WSE into three age subgroups: pre-production, production, and post-production confirmed the existing correlation between age structure and the level of economic development of countries. As the economic level increased, the percentage of retirees increased, while the percentage of children decreased (Fig. 13.1) due to the decline in the natural increase rate. This dependence was even more apparent when comparing the two extreme, in terms of GDP per capita, among the WSE subgroups: the European WSE (GDP

US$ 36,413 per capita), the African WSE (GDP US$ 1046 per capita), the Asian WSE (GDP US$ 920 per capita), and the Pacific WSE (GDP US$ 2697 per capita). The latter three subgroups had more than 30% of children and young people under the age of 15, which was more than double that of the European WSE subgroup (14%), which, in turn, had more than four times (20%) the proportion of those over 65 (Fig. 13.2). Such a high percentage of children and young people (especially in the African WSE exceeding 40%) was a consequence of the population explosion, a higher share of younger age groups, relatively shorter life expectancy, and premature (compared to developed countries) deaths and failure to reach retirement age. Poor health and the lack of a social security system also played a significant role.

The distribution of the population by age of the African WSE, the Asian WSE and the Pacific WSE populations gave an overall picture. Although, there were individual countries with higher levels of economic development within each age subgroup that had a population age structure similar to rich countries. For example, Mauritius and Seychelles, with GDPs of US$ 10,893 per capita and US$ 15,049 per capita, respectively, stood out from the age structure of the African WSE subgroup (Fig. 13.3). Mauritius raported only 17 children under 15, and Seychelles only 24 per 100 people. This was an exceptionally low percentage compared to the other 25 African countries in that subgroup, which rates exceeded 40% (Niger with the highest 50%). Both Mauritius and Seychelles also had the highest percentage of people of retirement age, at 12% and 8%, respectively, while in the other African countries ranged from 2 to 4% (Fig. 13.3).

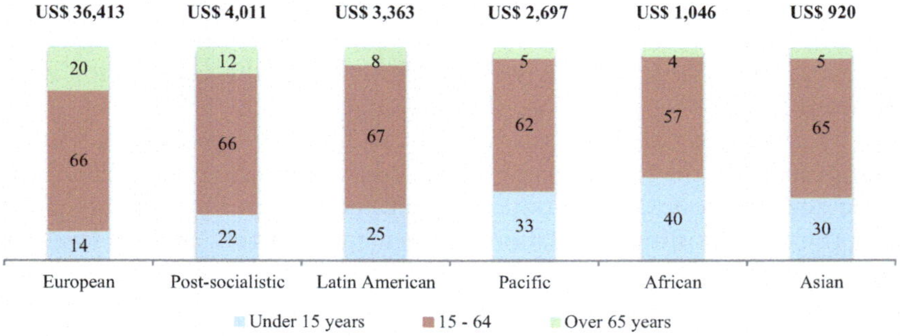

Fig. 13.2 WSE age structure population by subgroups against GDP per capita in 2019 (%). (Source: Own compilation based on The World Bank)

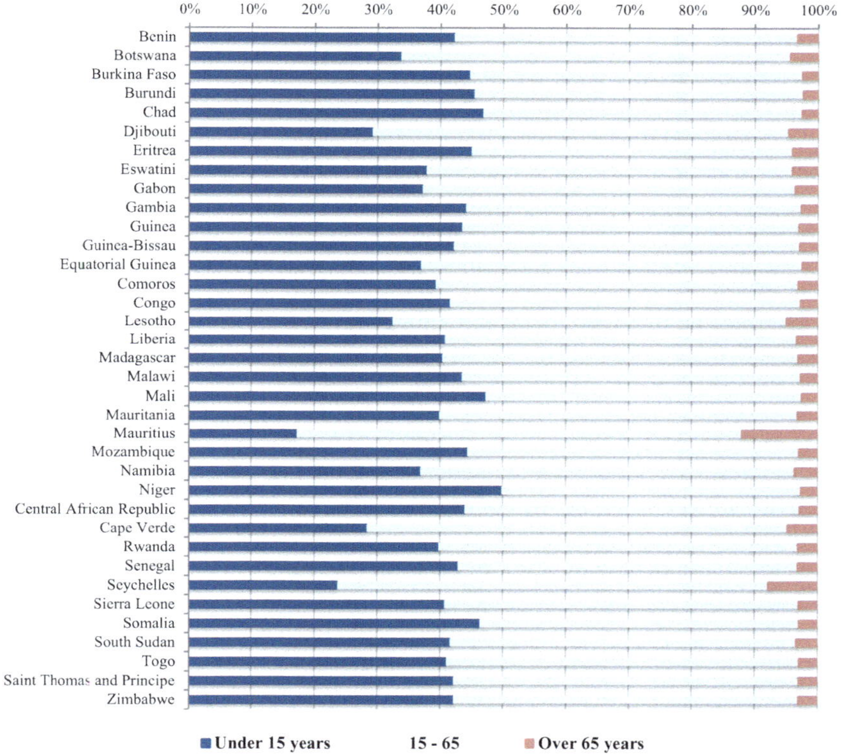

Fig. 13.3 African WSE population age structure in 2019 (%). (Source: Own compilation based on The World Bank)

While the high GDP per capita of Mauritius and Seychelles indeed translates into real socioeconomic well-being and correlates with the age structure of their populations, as seen in countries with higher levels of economic development, the high GDP of Gabon and Equatorial Guinea (US $9178 per capita and US$ 9238 per capita in 2019) does not reflect similar outcomes. The age structure of these two countries resembled that of poorer nations. The percentage of children under 15 was 37%, while the percentage of elderly over 65 ranged between 2% and 4%. This disparties is due to the unequal distribution of income, with almost 90% concentrated in a narrow ruling group, while the majority of the population remains very poor. Thus, the age structure of the population in these countries is similar to that of other improverished nations. This is illustrated by comparing Gabon and Equatorial Guinea with Saint Lucia (GDP US$ 9351 per capita) and Grenada (GDP US$ 9220 per capita), which have similar GDP per capita figures. Saint Lucia and Grenada recorded only 18% and 24%, respectively, of children under 15, and as many as 10% of those over 65. This highlights a significant difference in the age structure between these two Latin countries and Gabon and Equatorial Guinea, whose high GDP per capita figures does not accurately reflect their actual level of economic development.

Despite the high proportion of children, most African WSEs have seen a slight decline of this subgroup over the decades (e.g., Burkina Faso from 43% to 45%, Central African Republic from 40% to 44%, Chad from 43% to 47%, Gabon from 34% to 37%, The Gambia from 42% to 44%, Guinea from 41% to 43%, and Niger from 49% to 50% between 1970 and 2019). These countries were also characterized by a low percentage of elderly people over 65. Such an age structure has negative consequences for the economic development of these economies. Although a low percentage of the elderly population is not a burden on low government budgets, these countries face a huge challenge due to their millions of young human resources. They must create jobs, educate the next generation entering working age—which comes at a cost—and develop infrastructure, primarily housing. All of this involves substantial financial outlays that these economies do not possess. Failure to manage the growing labor force threatens to result in social tensions, as well as accelerated emigration to richer countries. The aforementioned wealthier countries in this African WSE subgroup have faced similar problems. In the 1970s, their share of children in the population was also very high, but over the course of several decades, it declined very rapidly: in Mauritius from 44% to 17%, in Seychelles from 44% to 24%, and in Djibouti from 45% to 29%. The decline in births was primarily related to the development of the service sector (mainly tourism or port services) and increased urbanization (78% of the population in 2019, compared to an urbanization rate of 30% in Burkina Faso and 17% in Niger). Cape Verde was another example of a large decline in the first age group of the population (from 49% to 28%). The dynamic development of tourism services has contributed to a massive influx of tourists from rich countries, who have influenced the worldview of the local population, helping to change their views on family model and the number of children they have. Year after year, the tourism sector has generated increased revenue, and the level of economic development in Cape Verde has risen (with nearly four times the economic growth between 1970 and 2019), along with improvements in education and awareness.

Like the African WSE, the Asian WSE, the Pacific WSE also noted a relatively high percentage of children, accounting for more than 30% of the population. In some cases, it was even much higher, for example in Afghanistan, children accounted for 42% of the population, and in Yemen, the figure was 39% (Fig. 13.4). This was due to high birth rates in both countries, influenced by an Islamic culture that promotes the extended family model. In contrast, Buddhist countries, such as Bhutan, Laos, as well as North Korea—officially atheist but historically heavily influenced by Buddhist culture—recorded only 20–25% child share in their populations. Among the Pacific WSE subgroup, the share of children in the Solomon Islands accounted for as much as 40% (Fig. 13.4), while in the most economically developed Palau (with GDP of US$ 12,078 per capita), the percentage was only 19%. Palau also had the highest share of people in the retirement age in that subgroup, accounting for 9% of the population.

In summary, the aging societies of the more economically developed European WSE and the Post-socialist WSE, which were in the Stage IV or

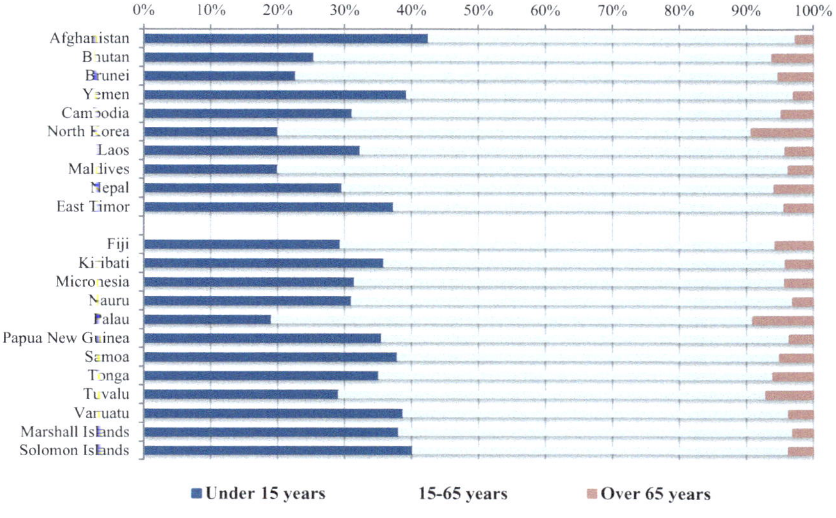

Fig. 13.4 Asian WSE and the Pacific WSE population age structure in 2019 (%). (Source: Own compilation based on The World Bank)

Stage V of demographic development, were characterized by a large and growing proportion of the elderly and a small proportion of children (Table 13.2). In contrast, the age structure of the African WSE, which were in Stage II or III of demographic development, was dominated by children under the age of 15 (Table 13.2).

As mentioned, the age structure had a very significant impact on the formation of the demographic processes of the WSE. It influences population growth and labor force resources, is crucial in determining the demand for education, health and social services, as well as affects migration. A graphical representation of the state and structure of the population is the so-called age pyramid, proposed by Gustav Sundbärg in the late nineteenth century. He distinguished three types of population structures by age, which represent the basic types of population reproduction:

a) Progressive structure (the gender and age pyramid takes the shape of an isosceles triangle), characterized by young societies with a high percentage of children as the result of a population explosion and low life expectancy.

It is found in Afghanistan, Burkina Faso, Central African Republic, Chad, Congo, The Gambia, Guinea, Liberia, Mozambique, Niger, Sierra Leone, Togo, and Zimbabwe.

b) Stagnant structure (bell-shaped pyramid), characterized by societies with equal numbers of representatives of all age subgroups and equal intensity of births and deaths.

It is found Belize, Bhutan, Fiji, Grenada, Guyana, Jamaica, Maldives, and Nepal.

c) Regressive structure (pyramid with a tapering base), characterized by old societies with declining birth rates and sometimes even an excess of deaths over births.

It is found in Andorra, Georgia, Malta, Mauritius, Monaco, Montenegro, Palau, and San Marino.

The age pyramid and the level of economic development of countries is also linked to the gender structure. Although globally the ratio of men to women is roughly equal (more boys are born, but the mortality rate

Table 13.2 WSE population age structure against GDP per capita in 1970, 2000, and 2019

No	*WSE*	*GDP*	*Pre-working age (below 15)*			*Working age (15–64)*			*Post-working age (65 years and above)*		
		US$ per capita	*%*								
		2019	*1970*	*2000*	*2019*	*1970*	*2000*	*2019*	*1970*	*2000*	*2019*
1	Monaco	209,241	n.a.	n.a.	9	n.a.	n.a.	56	n.a.	n.a.	35
2	Liechtenstein	177,698	n.a.	n.a.	11	n.a.	n.a.	70	n.a.	n.a.	19
3	Iceland	51,332	33	23	20	59	65	65	9	12	15
4	San Marino	50,462	n.a.	n.a.	15	n.a.	n.a.	65	n.a.	n.a.	20
5	Andorra	45,887	n.a.	n.a.	10	n.a.	n.a.	73	n.a.	n.a.	17
6	Brunei	32,327	43	31	23	54	67	72	4	2	5
7	Malta	28,976	27	20	14	63	68	65	10	12	21
8	Bahamas	28,909	42	29	22	54	65	70	3	5	7
9	Cyprus	23,927	31	22	17	59	67	69	10	10	14
10	Estonia	20,856	22	18	16	66	67	64	12	15	20
11	Saint Kitts and Nevis	17,295	n.a.	n.a.	20	n.a.	n.a.	70	n.a.	n.a.	10
12	Barbados	16,100	37	22	17	55	66	67	8	12	16
13	Antigua and Barbuda	15,704	45	29	22	51	65	69	4	7	9
14	Trinidad and Tobago	15,105	41	26	20	54	68	69	4	6	11
15	Seychelles	15,049	44	29	24	50	64	68	6	8	8
16	Palau	12,078	n.a.	n.a.	19	n.a.	n.a.	72	n.a.	n.a.	9
17	Mauritius	10,893	44	26	17	54	68	71	3	6	12
18	Saint Lucia	9351	50	32	18	45	60	72	5	7	10
19	Equatorial Guinea	9238	39	41	37	56	56	61	5	4	2
20	Grenada	9220	49	33	24	45	58	67	5	9	10
21	Gabon	9178	34	41	37	59	54	59	7	5	4
22	Montenegro	8590	33	21	18	60	67	66	7	12	15
23	Maldives	8477	46	40	20	51	56	76	2	4	4
24	Nauru	8223	n.a.	n.a.	31	n.a.	n.a.	66	n.a.	n.a.	3
25	Botswana	8093	48	39	34	48	58	62	4	3	4

(*continued*)

Table 13.2 (continued)

No	*WSE*	*GDP*	*Pre-working age (below 15)*			*Working age (15–64)*			*Post-working age (65 years and above)*		
		US$ per capita	*%*								
		2019	*1970*	*2000*	*2019*	*1970*	*2000*	*2019*	*1970*	*2000*	*2019*
26	Suriname	8047	48	33	27	48	62	66	4	5	7
27	Dominica	6917	n.a.	n.a.	28	n.a.	n.a.	65	n.a.	n.a.	7
28	Saint Vincent and the Grenadines	6863	50	31	22	45	62	68	5	7	10
29	Bosnia and Herzegovina	6304	35	21	15	61	68	68	4	11	17
30	Guyana	6107	47	36	28	49	60	65	4	4	7
31	Namibia	5766	43	42	37	53	55	59	4	3	4
32	Northern Macedonia	5625	34	23	16	61	67	70	5	10	14
33	Albania	5211	41	30	17	54	63	68	5	7	14
34	Georgia	4978	31	21	20	61	66	65	8	13	15
35	Djibouti	4904	45	41	29	52	56	66	2	3	5
36	Jamaica	4867	46	32	24	48	60	68	6	8	9
37	Eswatini	4818	47	43	38	50	54	58	3	3	4
38	Fiji	4739	44	35	29	54	62	65	2	3	6
39	Armenia	4732	39	26	21	55	64	68	6	10	11
40	Tonga	4355	48	38	35	49	56	59	3	6	6
41	Mongolia	4353	44	35	31	51	62	65	5	4	4
42	Belize	4150	47	41	30	49	55	65	4	4	5
43	Tuvalu	3943	n.a.	n.a.	29	n.a.	n.a.	64	n.a.	n.a.	7
44	Cape Verde	3908	49	43	28	47	52	67	4	5	5
45	Samoa	3869	51	41	38	47	55	57	2	4	5
46	Moldova	3720	32	23	16	62	67	72	6	9	12
47	Salvador	3572	46	37	27	51	58	65	3	5	8
48	Bhutan	3262	43	40	25	55	56	69	2	4	6
49	Marshall Islands	3157	n.a.	n.a.	38	n.a.	n.a.	59	n.a.	n.a.	3
50	Vanuatu	2887	45	42	39	52	55	58	3	3	4
51	Micronesia	2700	46	40	31	51	56	64	3	4	4
52	Papua New Guinea	2490	44	40	35	54	57	61	3	3	4
53	Honduras	2241	48	43	31	49	53	64	3	4	5

(*continued*)

Table 13.2 (continued)

No	*WSE*	*GDP*	*Pre-working age (below 15)*			*Working age (15–64)*			*Post-working age (65 years and above)*		
		US$ per capita	*%*								
		2019	*1970*	*2000*	*2019*	*1970*	*2000*	*2019*	*1970*	*2000*	*2019*
54	Congo	2166	44	42	42	52	55	56	3	3	3
55	Laos	1841	42	43	32	55	53	64	3	4	4
56	Kiribati	1790	45	40	36	52	57	60	3	3	4
57	Nicaragua	1763	48	40	30	49	57	65	2	4	5
58	Mauritania	1756	46	44	40	51	53	57	3	3	3
59	Solomon Islands	1749	43	42	40	53	55	56	3	3	4
60	Senegal	1584	45	45	43	53	52	54	2	3	3
61	Comoros	1399	45	44	39	52	53	58	3	3	3
62	Lesotho	1353	45	40	32	50	56	63	4	4	5
63	South Sudan	1302	43	45	42	54	52	55	3	3	3
64	Saint Thomas and Príncipe	1289	47	44	42	48	52	55	5	3	3
65	Cambodia	1269	46	42	31	52	55	64	3	3	5
66	Benin	1260	42	45	42	53	52	55	5	3	3
67	Haiti	1245	41	40	33	55	56	62	4	4	5
68	Zimbabwe	1183	49	42	42	48	55	55	3	3	3
69	Tajikistan	1121	46	43	37	49	54	60	5	4	3
70	Kyrgyzstan	1116	42	35	33	52	60	63	6	6	5
71	East Timor	978	41	45	37	57	52	58	3	3	4
72	Guinea	921	41	46	43	56	50	54	3	3	3
73	Rwanda	901	48	44	40	49	52	57	3	4	3
74	Nepal	859	41	41	30	56	55	65	3	4	6
75	Burkina Faso	822	43	47	45	54	50	53	3	3	2
76	The Gambia	815	42	47	44	56	50	53	2	3	3
77	Chad	814	43	49	47	54	48	51	4	3	2
78	Mali	792	42	47	47	55	50	50	3	3	2
79	Togo	696	45	43	41	52	54	56	3	3	3
80	Guinea-Bissau	636	40	45	42	56	52	55	4	3	3
81	Yemen	631	45	49	39	52	48	58	3	3	3
82	Mozambique	589	43	45	44	53	52	53	3	3	3
83	North Korea	588	42	26	20	55	68	71	3	6	9
84	Afghanistan	573	44	49	42	53	49	55	3	2	3
85	Niger	563	49	48	50	50	49	48	2	2	3

(*continued*)

Table 13.2 (continued)

No	*WSE*	*GDP*	*Pre-working age (below 15)*			*Working age (15–64)*			*Post-working age (65 years and above)*		
		US$ per capita	*%*								
		2019	*1970*	*2000*	*2019*	*1970*	*2000*	*2019*	*1970*	*2000*	*2019*
86	Eritrea	549	44	46	45	53	50	51	3	4	4
87	Malawi	524	44	46	43	53	51	54	3	3	3
88	Liberia	516	44	43	41	53	54	56	3	3	3
89	Madagascar	500	45	45	40	51	52	57	3	3	3
90	Sierra Leone	488	40	44	41	56	53	56	4	3	3
91	Central African Republic	384	40	43	44	55	53	53	5	4	3
92	Burundi	208	46	50	45	52	47	52	3	2	2
93	Somalia	93	43	47	46	54	50	51	3	3	3

Source: Own compilation based on The World Bank

among males is higher), in the underdeveloped WSE, the percentage of females was lower for several reasons (e.g., poor hygienic conditions, lack of professional medical care, high female mortality during frequent childbirths, and often hard physical labor). In Namibia, for example, there were 101 women for every 100 men, and 102 women in Guinea, Lesotho, Mozambique, Sierra Leone, Togo, and Zimbabwe (Fig. 13.5), compared to 105 in Iceland, 106 in Malta and San Marino, 107 in Cyprus and Andorra, and 126 in Liechtenstein (the highest in the world). With the level of economic development of the WSE, an increasing number of women can be observed, while the mortality rate of men increased due to cardiovascular diseases, cancer, depression, which emerge with the progress of civilization. At the same time, it should be noted that in the 0–15 subgroup, the gender structure is dominated by boys, which is biologically determined since they are born more often. A high proportion of women in the population also occurrs in post-socialist countries, such as Armenia, with 111 women per 100 men; Albania, with 108; Montenegro, Estonia and Tajikistan, with 107; Bosnia and Herzegovina, Georgia, Kyrgyzstan and North Macedonia, and Moldova each had 106 women per 100 men. This is due to historical and politico-economic reasons, as well as excessive male mortality caused by a large number of occupational

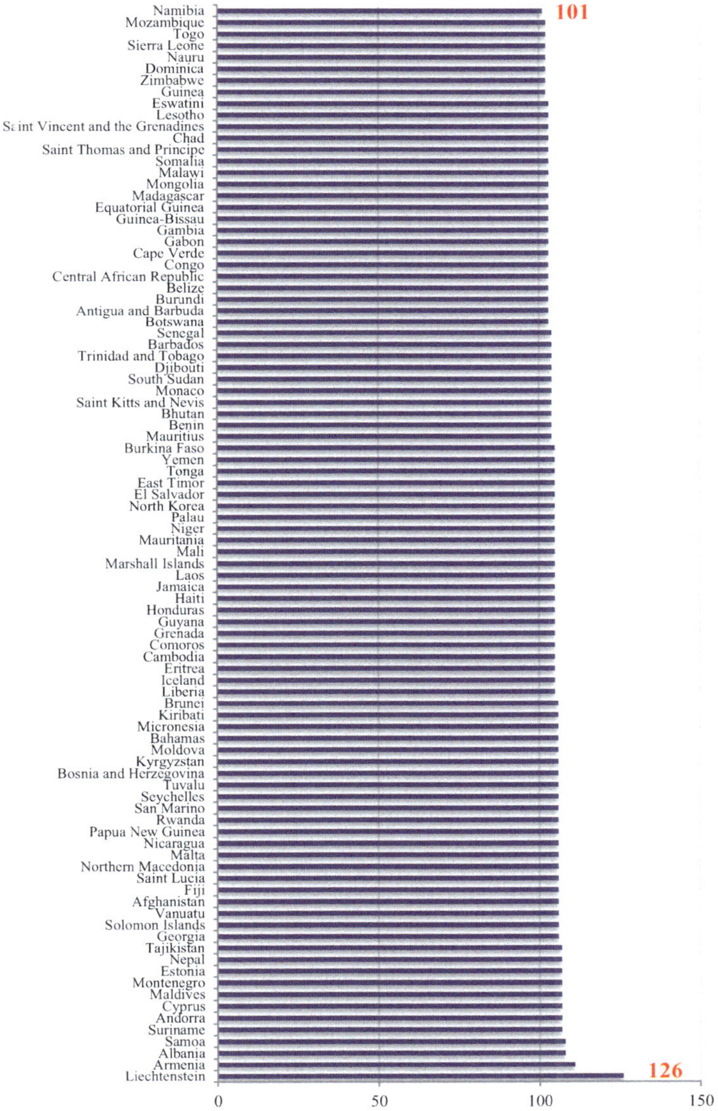

Fig. 13.5 WSE feminization rate in 2019 (per 100 men). (Source: Own compilation based on UN Data, Population by sex 2020)

accidents (in mining, metallurgy, the military), unhygienic lifestyles (such as alcoholism and compulsive smoking), greater susceptibility to disease, and relatively low levels of medical care.

Both the European WSE and the Post-socialist WSE also had the smallest number of women of childbearing age. For example, in Andorra, Cyprus, Liechtenstein, Malta, Monaco, San Marino, as well as Bosnia and Herzegovina, Moldova and North Macedonia, there was only one child per woman. In Albania, Armenia, Montenegro, Estonia, and Iceland, the ratio was less than 1.8 (Fig. 13.6). This was due to a number of reasons, including the family model (childless or with one child); the late age of marriage and the birth of the first child due to the prioritization of education, gaining a professional position, and achieving adequate material and social status; the prevalence of family planning methods and the availability of contraceptives, as well as the possibility of abortion. The societies of the very highly developed and former socialist countries are consumption-oriented. For them, having children is a barrier to achieving their goals. A secure old age does not depend on the size of the family, i.e., the number of children to support the parents, as was the case in the poorest countries. This is because the elderly are covered by social security, pension, and health care systems that allow them to live out a peaceful old age with dignity.

In contrast, the young societies of the African WSE and the Asian WSE, with a predominantly Islamic culture, were characterized by a large number of women of childbearing age, that is, between 15 and 49 (Fig. 13.6). In 2019, the highest number of children per woman of childbearing age was recorded in Niger, at seven (down from eight since 1970). In Chad, Mali, Somalia, the fertility rate was six, while in Benin, Burkina Faso, Burundi, Central African Republic, The Gambia, Guinea, Mauritania, Mozambique, Senegal, and South Sudan, there were five children per woman (Fig. 13.6). Such a high fertility rate, as mentioned, was the result of a family model (large and multigenerational) that had been perpetuated for decades, rooted in the traditions and culture of these countries. Having a large number of children increased parents' sense of financial security, as children tend to support the family. High fertility rates were also associated with a lack of contraception and abortion options, as well as generally low levels of education.

The fertility rate is one of the factors determining the age distribution of the population, and the age structure of the population depends on life expectancy. In 2019, the average life expectancy at birth in the WSE was

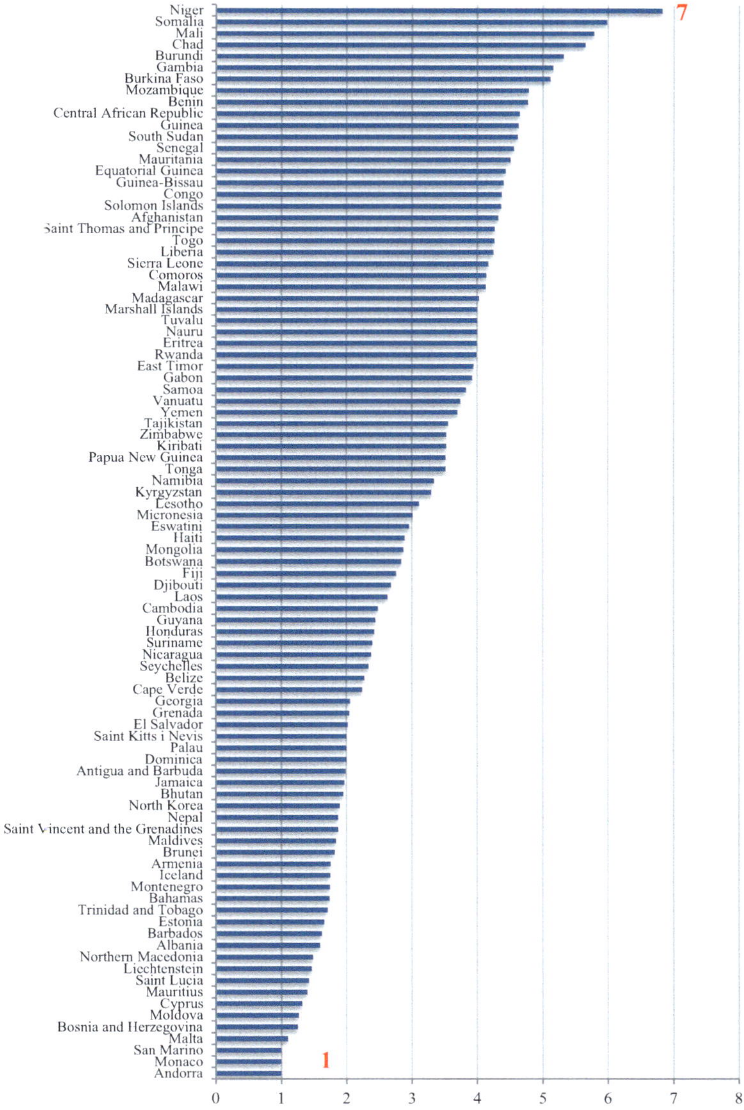

Fig. 13.6 Children number per woman in the WSE in 2019 (children per woman of reproductive age). (Source: Own compilation based on The World Bank)

69 years (compared to 73 years worldwide).[1] In the nearly five decades between 1970 and 2019, this rate increased by 17 years, more than the global increase of 14 years. The increase in life expectancy was influenced by factors such as nutrition, hygiene, development of medical services, the population's level of education, gender, and the political and economic situation. People lived the longest in the economically highly developed European WSE, such as Monaco, and San Marino, where the average life expectancy was 85 years. In Iceland, Liechtenstein, and Malta, it was 83 years, and in Andorra and Cyprus, it was 81 years (Fig. 13.7). This was associated with high levels of medical and social care, better living conditions, as well as greater self-awareness and general knowledge. Rising life expectancy has contributed to an increase in the percentage of people over 65, causing these societies to age. In contrast, residents of the African WSE, including Benin, Burkina Faso, Burundi, Central African Republic, Chad, Equatorial Guinea, Eswatini, The Gambia, Guinea, Guinea-Bissau, Lesotho, Mali, Mozambique, Namibia, Niger, Sierra Leone, South Sudan, Togo, Zimbabwe, have the shortest life expectancy. The average in these 20 countries was less than 63, with the Central African Republic was at the bottom of the list, having an average life expectancy of 53 years. All of these 20 countries struggle with low levels of hygiene, underdeveloped medical care, and a lack of a social security system.

Although, life expectancy is short in most of the African WSE, there has been a noticeable significant increase over the past nearly five decades. However, this increase has varied from country to country (Fig. 13.8) due to several factors, such as the initial life expectancy at the beginning of the period; the social policies pursued; and the rate of economic growth. The largest increase was recorded in Senegal, where life expectancy rose by 29 years (from 39 to 68 years), followed by Mali with an increase of 27 years (from 32 to 59 years), Niger by 26 years (from 36 to 62 years), Guinea (from 37 to 62 years), Liberia (from 39 to 64 years), and Malawi (from 39 to 64 years) by 25 years between 1970 and 2019.

In contrast, the smallest increase among the African WSE were observed in countries with a high average age in 1970. For example 69 years in Seychelles (up 5 years), 63 years in Mauritius (up 11 years), 57 years in Zimbabwe (up 5 years), 53 years in Namibia (up 10 years), and 51 years in Lesotho (up 4 years).

[1] In the Bronze and the Iron Ages, the average life expectancy was 18 years; at the beginning of our era, it was 22 years, and in 1800, it reached 35 years.

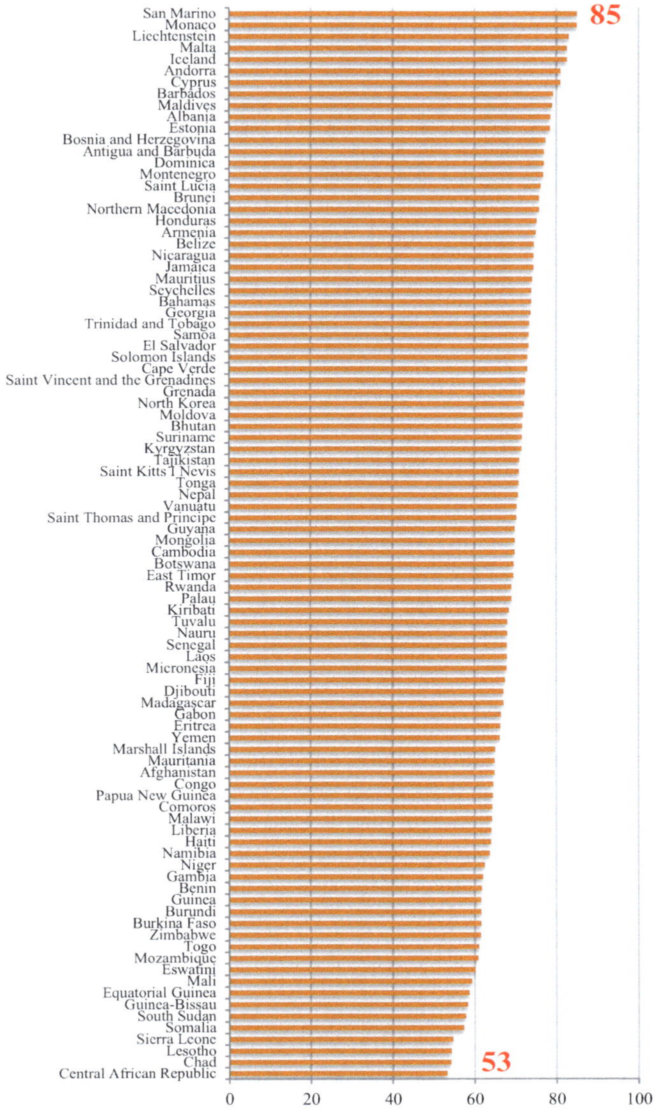

Fig. 13.7 WSE life expectancy in 2019 (years). (Source: Own compilation based on UN Data, Population median age (years) 2020)

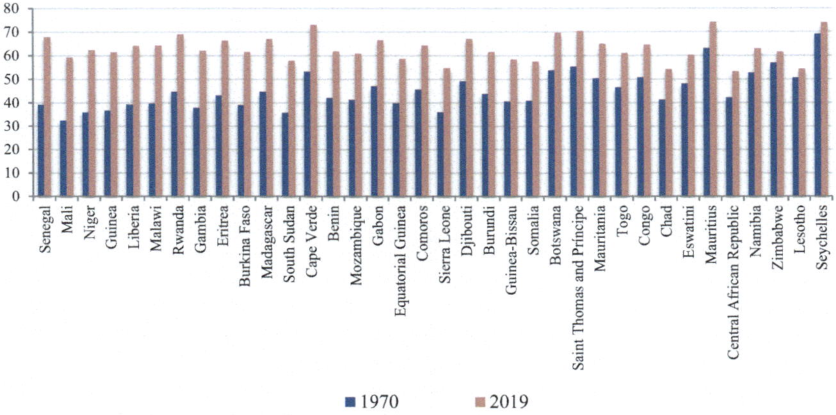

Fig. 13.8 African WSE life expectancy in 1970 and 2019 (years). (Source: Own compilation based on UN Data, Population median age (years) 2020)

Age growth in the Latin American WSE subgroup increased from 7 to 9 years (Fig. 13.9). This is exemplified by the Bahamas (from 66 to 74 years), Grenada (from 66 to 72 years), Jamaica (from 68 years to 74 years), and Trinidad and Tobago (from 65 to 74 years) between 1970 and 2019. Exceptions are economically underdeveloped countries, for example, Haiti, which saw an increase of 18 years (from 46 to 64 years) and Nicaragua, which experienced a 20 years increase (from 54 to 74 years). The Post-socialist WSE showed low growth, ranking from 5 years in economically more developed Armenia and Georgia to 17 years in economically least developed Tajikistan. The Pacific WSE displayed a similar trend, with growth ranging from 5 years in Fiji to 19 years in Papua New Guinea.

Life expectancy of the Asian WSE has increased significantly (Fig. 13.10). Between 1970 and 2019, East Timor saw an increase of 29 years (from 40 to 69 years), Nepal by 30 years (from 41 to 71 years), Bhutan by 32 years (from 40 to 72 years), and the Maldives by as much as 35 years (from 44 to 79 years). In contrast, Brunei, with the highest GDP per capita in the subgroup, experienced only a 13-year increase (from 63 to 76 years). The same trend was observed in the most economically developed European WSE, with increases ranging from 8 years in Cyprus (from 73 to 81 years) to 12 years in Malta (from 71 to 83 years).

As with life expectancy, the relationship between the level of economic and civilization development is closely related to infant mortality. A country's

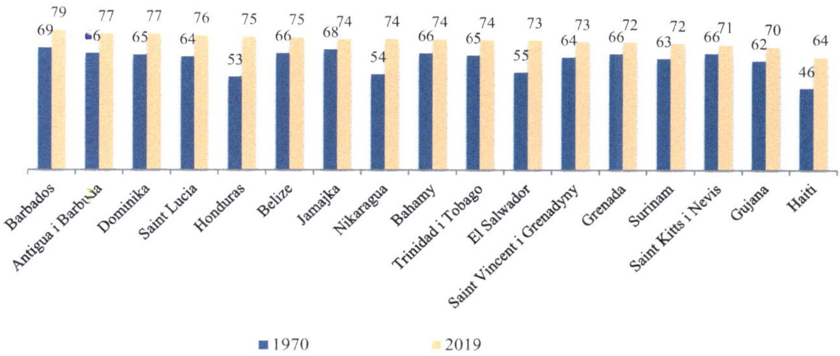

Fig. 13.9 Latin American WSE life expectancy in 1970 and 2019 (years). (Source: Own compilation based on UN Data, Population median age (years) 2020)

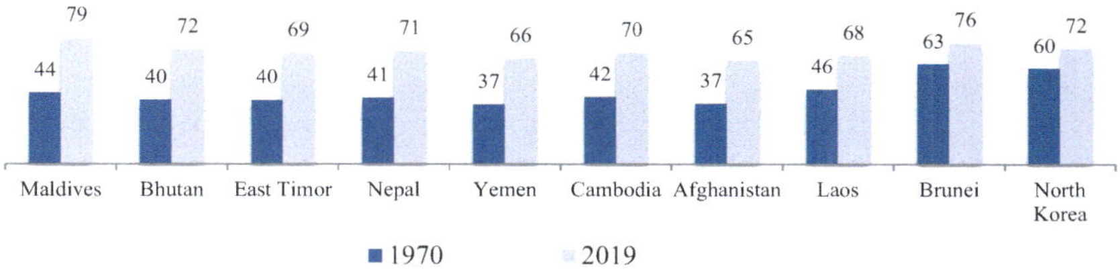

Fig. 13.10 Asian WSE life expectancy from 1970 to 2019 (years). (Source: Own compilation based on UN Data, Population median age (years) 2020)

economic underdevelopment is associated with a high infant mortality rate. As a result, the African WSE has the highest rates among the 17 largest 17 WSE. In 2019, Sierra Leone and Central African Republic recorded 81 infant deaths per 1,000 births, Somalia 74, Chad 69, Lesotho 69,[2]

[2] Lesotho's high infant death rate is linked to the HIV/AIDS epidemic (23.1% of the population in 2019—second in the world after Eswatini). According to UNICEF data, more than half of women aged 15–24 and one-third of pregnant women were infected with HIV. International aid was hampered by the prevailing situation in the country (including poverty, intergenerational sexual practices, rape of minors, unemployment caused by the closure of South African mines and Chinese textile factories, where Lesotho immigrants worked).

HIV and AIDS in Lesotho, online version: https://www.avert.org/professionals/hiv-around-world/sub-saharan-africa/lesotho.

Guinea 64, South Sudan and Liberia 62 (Fig. 13.11). According to data published by UNICEF, infants born in these countries were 50 times less likely to survive the first month of life compared to those born in the highly developed countries, where the ratio ranged from 2‰ (e.g., Cyprus, Iceland, Liechtenstein, San Marino) to 5‰ (e.g., Estonia, Montenegro). The high infant mortality rate in the underdeveloped WSE is primarily due to limited access to obstetric care for pregnant women, often exacerbated by poverty, armed conflict, and institutional inefficiency.

In the WSE like Burkina Faso, Chad, Central African Republic, Sierra Leone, Somalia, and South Sudan, more than 80% of newborn deaths were due to causes such as premature births, delivery complications and infections (e.g., pneumonia, sepsis). These daths could have been avoided with better access to clean water, disinfectants, and improved care from skilled midwives and doctors. The lack of sufficient medical professionals means that thousands of newborns are not receiving essential survival care. For example, in the undeveloped WSE like Liberia, there was only 1 doctor per 100,000 people; in Malawi, Niger and Sierra Leone 2 doctors; in Mozambique 4 doctors; in Benin, Burkina Faso, Chad, Somalia, Togo, and Saint Thomas and Principe 5 doctors. By comparison, in the highly developed WSE such as Monaco, there were 717 doctors per 100,000 inhabitants (second in the world, after Qatar), in San Marino 510 (fifth place in the world), in Andorra 400, in Iceland 398 and in Malta 349 (Fig. 13.12).

Infant mortality rates in the poorest WSE were indeed alarming; however, it is optimistic that they decreased over time (Fig. 13.13). Between 1970 and 2019, the largest decline—26-fold—occurred in the Maldives (from 172 to 7 deaths per 1000 births). Nearly eight times fewer infant deaths occurred in Nicaragua (from 116 to 14 deaths per 1000 births) and Bhutan (from 182 to 24 deaths per 1000 births), and seven times fewer in Malawi (from 204 to 31 deaths per 1000 births). The downward trend was due to improvements in living conditions, health care for pregnant women and perinatal health care. The decline indicated not only an increase in the level of health care, but also the civilization and economic development of these countries.

Demographic conditions are an important determinant of socioeconomic processes of the WSE, as people are the driving force behind economies. In 2019, the WSE group had 561 million people, more than half as many as in 2000. The increase of nearly 51% (by comparison: the global population grew by 25%) was a consequence of high natural increase.

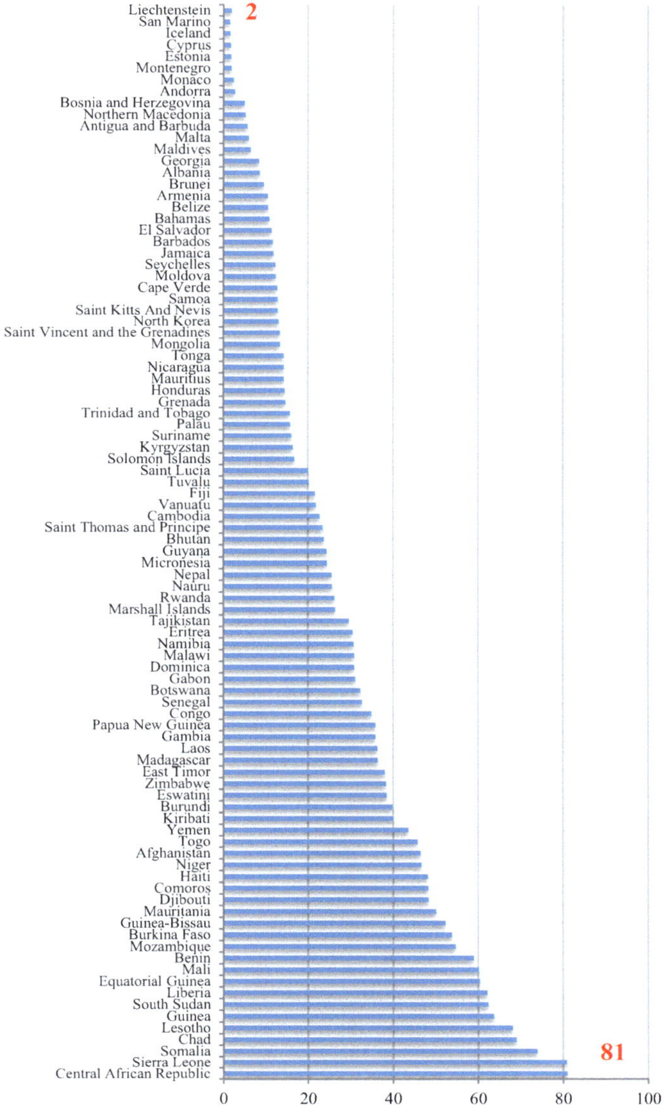

Fig. 13.11 WSE infant mortality rate in 2019 (deaths per 1000 live births). (Source: Own compilation based on The World Bank)

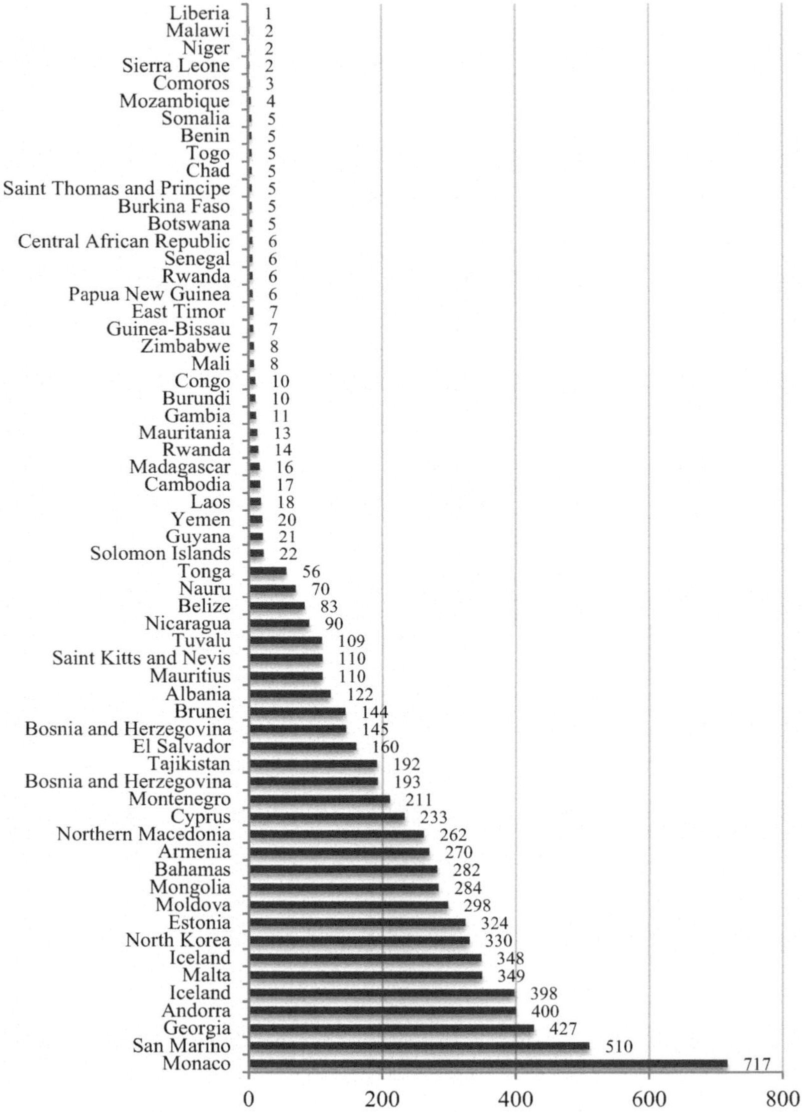

Fig. 13.12 Physicians in sample WSE in 2019 (per 100,000 population). (Source: Own compilation based on The World Bank)

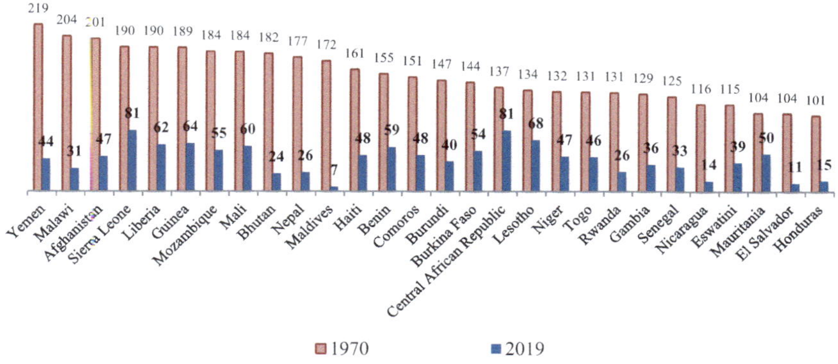

Fig. 13.13 Highest infant mortality rates among the WSE in 1970 and 2019 (deaths per 1000 live births). (Source: Own compilation based on The World Bank)

This, although reduced thanks to declines in the birth rate (from 28.8 to 23.3 per 1000 people) and death rate (9.9 to 7.6 per 1000 people), still remained quite high at 15.7‰ (much higher than the world's 10.4‰). While the WSE group had an average of three children per woman, the world average was two children. Such a high rate of the group affected not only the dynamic population growth, but also its age demographic structure. It consisted mainly of young societies with a fairly high share of people of pre-working age, at 31% and a small share of people over 65, at 7% (by comparison, globally, at 26% and 9%, respectively). It should be added that, in general, the demographic structure also depends on migration, but in the case of the WSE it was mainly due to high natural increase.

An excess of the human factor and the resulting unfavorable demographic conditions hampered economic development, causing a slowdown in economic growth. In many of the WSE with very high natural increase, the rate of human resource growth far exceeded the rate of economic development, resulting in malnutrition for a large part of the population and even starvation. There was a lack of educational and health facilities and technical infrastructure for such a large percentage of children and young people. The states were unable to provide enough jobs for the very large number of new generations. However, the unfavorable demographic conditions affected not only the WSE with high natural increase, but also those with very low or negative natural increase, which accounted for as much as one-fifth of the WSE group. Their demographic structures were characterized by aging, and an aging population means rising pensions, health care, and social security costs, as well as a declining growth in the labor pool. Thus, neither the high natural increase, nor too low natural increase was conductive to the economic development of the WSE.

Bibliography

Kop, J., Kucharska, M., & Szkurlat, E. (2003). *Geografia Spoleczno-economiczna*. PWN.

CHAPTER 14

Culture as a Differentiating Factor of the World's Smallest Economies

Culture is one of the main factors determining the level of economic development. Cultural conditions are the basis for the formation of ethics, attitudes to life, and motivate societies to work and act for economic development. However, it happens that culture is a barrier to economic development and even a source of serious conflicts that prevent the functioning and development of the economy. Therefore, the study of the cultures of the WSE is very important.

In order to analyze the cultural potential, it is first necessary to clarify the concept of *culture*. The word culture comes from the Latin *cultura agris* (Eng. *agriculture*) and the later *cultura mentis* (Eng. *cultivation of the mind*) (Cynarski, 2003). There are many definitions of *culture*, ranging from succinct ones, such as: a *characteristic way of life of a particular people, a way of life* (Kluckhohn, 1949) to enumerative ones that state that culture is *the totality, which includes knowledge, beliefs, arts, morals, laws, customs and other skills acquired by a person, who is a member of society* (Taylor, 1911). Some definitions are descriptive, while others are evaluative. Some emphasize what is inherited; others emphasize what is new. Some speak only of processes and activities related to work or leisure. Others, on the other hand, take into account what constitutes the sum total of creations passed from generation to generation, which sociologist Jan Szczepański expressed as *the totality of products of human activity,*

A. A. Teperek, *Economic Development in the World's Smallest Economies*, https://doi.org/10.1007/978-3-031-63810-7_14

tangible and intangible, values and recognized ways of behavior, objectified and accepted in some communities, passed on to other communities and to subsequent generations (Szczepanski, 1963).

The problem with a unified interpretation of the concept of *culture* stems from the fact that the interpreter is a participant in culture and, remaining in this position, is unable to gain distance from it and objectively define it. Moreover, culture is such an ambiguous and extensive phenomenon that it is impossible to give it a single, consistent definition, as the German philosopher Johan Herder pointed out as early as the eighteenth century, writing: *There is nothing more indefinite than the word culture* (Herder, 1962).

Despite the lack of a clear definition of the term "culture", almost all interpretations take into account certain elements, such as that it is not a characteristic of the individual, but of society. This is because an isolated individual, relying on his own skills and the natural resources available to him, is incapable of producing culture on his own, being deprived of a multigenerational heritage. For its creation, a human collective requires the transmission of acquired experience from one generation to the next, as one author pointed out: *a conscious, socially transmitted heritage of creations, knowledge, values and normative expectations (...)* (Goodman, 1997). This multigenerational creation of culture was the basis for the progress of civilization, as well as the changes took place (Hausner & Karwinska, 2013).

There are many cultures in the world, although some are broader in scope and refer to many societies that share the same lifestyle and use the same or similar language. Using the typology of political scientist Samuel P. Huntington, who went down in history as the founder of the theory of dividing the world into major civilizations based on cultures, a classification of the 93 WSE was made. Taking into account elements such as religious, linguistic and ethnic similarities, the WSE were divided into eight subgroups (Fig. 14.1).

The WSE subgroups cover very different areas, ranging from 158,000 km^2 (the Western WSE) to 7,727,000 km^2 (the Islamic WSE). They also have very different populations, ranging from 3.5 million (the Western WSE) to 208.2 million (the Islamic WSE) in 2019. The most numerous, in terms of the number of countries classified, is the African WSE (24 countries), with a population of 180.1 million, about one-third of the total population of the WSE group. The area occupied by this subgroup (5,497,000 km^2) is almost one-third of the total area of the whole

Cultural subgroups	WSE	Countries Quantity	Area 1000 km²	Population 1000
AFRICAN				
A subgroup consists of countries located south of the Sahara, or in so-called Black Africa, characterized by great ethnic diversity (mainly negroid race: Negroes, Bushmen, Pygmies, Masai) and religious (local animistic religions with widespread belief in sorcery, magic and superstition); strong attachment to tradition (love of dance, living in harmony with nature); structural diversity (tribalism with kings and chiefs at the head, in addition to state structures); political instability, often ending in religious, ethnic wars; overpopulation; high mortality from wars, disease, natural disasters; high share of the agriculture sector in GDP and employment; low level of economic development.	Benin, Botswana, Burundi, Cape Verde, Central African Republic, Congo, Equatorial Guinea, Eritrea, Eswatini, Gabon, Guinea-Bissau, Lesotho, Liberia, Madagascar, Malawi, Mauritius, Mozambique, Namibia, Rwanda, Saint Thomas and Principe, Seychelles, South Sudan, Togo, Zimbabwe	24	5,486.0	180,155
LATIN AMERICAN				
A subgroup consists of countries inhabited by mixed races: Europeanid (conquistadors, immigrants), American mongoid (Indians), mixed varieties (Métis, Mulattoes) and negroid (slaves). It is characterized by a rich Ibero-American culture with roots dating back to Spanish colonization with the dominance of the Spanish language and the Latin Church (mainly Catholicism with influences of folk beliefs and elements of Indian culture); attachment to tradition (strong faith combined with rituals, love of music and dance); high stratification among the population due to historical conditions (landowners are usually descendants of white people who came from Europe during the Spanish-Portuguese colonization).	Antigua and Barbuda, Bahamas, Barbados, Belize, Dominica, El Salvador, Grenada, Guyana, Haiti, Honduras, Jamaica, Nicaragua, Saint Kitts and Nevis, Saint Lucia, Saint Vincent and the Grenadines, Suriname, Trinidad and Tobago	17	726.8	41,409
ISLAMIC				
This subgroup consists of racially and ethnically diverse countries, inhabited mainly by negroid and mongoid races; mainly Arabic-speaking; under the strong influence of the Islamic religion, to which the economy, politics and private life of the population are subordinated (including strict Sharia law restricts women's participation in public, political and economic life; moral strictness prevails; governance in the form of authoritarian regimes that violate the civil rights of the population).	Afghanistan, Brunei, Burkina Faso, Chad, Comoros, Djibouti, Gambia, Guinea, Maldives, Mali, Mauritania, Niger, Senegal, Sierra Leone, Somalia, Yemen	16	7,727.1	208,251
PACIFIC				
This subgroup consists of countries with a high degree of racial diversity (indigenous Polynesian negroid race mixed with immigrants who arrived during colonialism), with Polynesian and English languages predominant; characterized by a strong commitment to culture, rituals and traditions (strong belief in the forces of nature and living in harmony with nature depicted in local handicrafts and dot paintings depicting landscapes and animals).	East Timor, Fiji, Kiribati, Marshall Islands, Micronesia, Nauru, Palau, Papua New Guinea, Samoa, Solomon Islands, Tonga, Tuvalu, Vanuatu	13	542.9	12,562
SLAVIC-ORTHODOX				
This subgroup consists mainly of Orthodox countries, characterized by a strong cult of power and leadership (a remnant of the communist era); close relations between state and church authority; and a highly stratified society (rich oligarchs and a poor majority of the population).	Albania, Armenia, Bosnia and Herzegovina, Montenegro, Georgia, Kyrgyzstan, Moldova, Northern Macedonia, Tajikistan	9	595.8	33,974
WESTERN (EUROPEAN)				
This subgroup consists of democratic states that were founded on Christian values, despite the manifestation of religion in secular form; they are characterized by openness to man as an individual, respect for the individual and human rights, personal freedom; their identity is strengthened by the existence of the European Union.	Andorra, Cyprus, Estonia, Iceland, Liechtenstein, Malta, Monaco, San Marino	8	158.4	3,577
BUDDHIST				
The subgroup consists of countries whose values are based on a Buddhist philosophical and ethical system that promotes the belief in transience, reincarnation, inner development, harmony, wisdom and the pursuit of nirvana considered the main goal of life through meditation, self-improvement and non-attachment to matter.	Bhutan, Cambodia, Laos, Mongolia, North Korea[30]	5	2,140.8	53,310
HINDU				
The subgroup consists of countries whose societies believe in multiple gods, the wandering of souls, karma and destiny, and reincarnation, and thus believe that the goal is to gain merit during one's lifetime in order to achieve a higher state of existence in the next incarnation; the belief prohibits the killing of living beings (mainly cows, considered the mother of hosts) and the consumption of beef; societies are characterized by a strong caste divide, resulting in social inequality and discrimination based on origin.	Nepal	1	147.1	28,608
WSE group in total:		93	17,536.6	561,792

Fig. 14.1 WSE typology based on cultural similarities. (Source: Own compilation based on: Cynarski (2003); Huntington (2007); The World Bank)

group (Fig. 14.1). Fewer countries are influenced by Islamic culture (16 countries), although the Islamic WSE subgroup occupies a much larger area (7,727,000 km^2) and is constrained by a larger population (208.2 million). A similar number of the WSE (17 countries) are influenced by Latin American culture, although the area of this subgroup is more than four times smaller than that of the Islamic WSE subgroup (Fig. 14.1). A population similar to that of the Latin American WSE subgroup (41.4 million) was recorded by the Buddhist WSE subgroup (53.3 million), which is almost three times larger in area. The remaining WSE subgroups cover smaller areas and were less populous. The Western WSE subgroup (3.5 million) and the Hindu WSE subgroup have similar areas (158,400 km^2 and 147,100 km^2, respectively), but the population of the Hindu WSE was almost nine times larger in 2019.

The main factor that determines the cultural divide is the difference in religion. It is mainly religion that gives distinct identity (Dziemidok, 2000) to each of the WSE subgroups, while significantly impacting their economic development.

Bibliography

Cynarski, W. J. (2003). *Globalizacja a Spotkanie Kultur*. Wyd UR.

Dziemidok, B. (2000). Tozsamosc narodowa a sztuka i nowe media w epoce globalizacji [in:] Kultura Wspolczesna i media. Kultura i Spoleczenstwo, Wyd. *PAN, XLVI*(1), 57–71.

Goodman, N. (1997). *Wstep do Socjologii*. Wydawnictwo Zysk i S-ka.

Hausner, I., & Karwinska, A. (2013). In J. Purchla (Ed.), *Kultura a rozwoj*. Narodowe Centrum Kultury.

Herder, J. G. (1962). *Mysli o Filozofii Dziejow*. T1.

Huntington, S. P. (2007). *Zderzenie Cywilizacji i Nowy Ksztalt Ladu Swiatowego* (Vol. Wyd 9). WWL Muza.

Kluckhohn, C. (1949). *Mirror for Man*. Whittlesey House.

Szczepanski, J. (1963). *Elementy Pojecia Socjologii*. PWN.

Taylor, F. (1911). *Principles of Scientific Management*. Harper & Brothers.

CHAPTER 15

Religious Diversity of the World's Smallest Economies

Religion has always played a very important role in human history. It has shaped the basis of life, as well as the value system of its adherents (Luhmann, 1998). It has influenced the development of culture and art, as well as the social and economic relations of countries and regions. It is estimated that there are between 5000 and 10,000 religions (Gorski, 2007) and beliefs in the world today. The world religions with the largest number of adherents are Christianity, Islam, Buddhism, and Hinduism. These are also the dominant religions in the WSE.

Christianity is the dominant religion among the populations of the Latin American WSE, the Pacific WSE, and the Western (European) WSE subgroups. Christianity is also largely dominant in the African WSE, although tribal folk religions are also very popular there. Christianity is popular in the Slavic-Orthodox WSE, with the exception of Albania, Kyrgyzstan, and Tajikistan, where mostly Islam is practiced. However, these three countries were classified into the Slavic-Orthodox WSE subgroup due to historical, systemic, economic, and cultural similarities. The WSE with a predominance of Islamic adherents were included in the Islamic WSE subgroup, Buddhist adherents in the Buddhist WSE subgroup, and Hindu adherents in the Hindu WSE subgroup.

From the perspective of the entire population living in the WSE group, the largest percentages identified as followers of Christianity (40.2%). The proportion of Muslims was slightly lower (37.9%). Hindus (4.9%) and

A. A. Teperek, *Economic Development in the World's Smallest Economies*, https://doi.org/10.1007/978-3-031-63810-7_15

Buddhists (4.5%) and followers of tribal religions (4.7%) made up similar shares of the WSE population, though they were outnumbered by atheists (7.3%).

Compared with the global religious structure, the percentages of adherents to Christianity and Islam were higher in the WSE group than in the world overall (Fig. 15.1).

The Christian religion is derived from Judaism and is funded on the belief of existing one God, manifested in the three persons of the Trinity: God the Father, God the Son, and the Holy Spirit. It emphasizes salvation and eternal life through the resurrection of Jesus Christ—the Messiah. The holy book of Christianity is the Bible, which includes the Old Testament (adopted from Judaism) and the New Testament, detailing the life and work of Jesus and his disciples. In the WSE, Christianity was professed by 40.2% of population, amounting to over 225 million people, it was the dominant religion in 64 surveyed countries (Fig. 15.2), where Christians constituted more than 50% of adherents. These countries were primarily located in the Americas (17 of 17 of the WSE), Oceania (12 of 12 of the WSE), and Europe (10 of 12 of the WSE).

Among the three major branches of Christianity, which differ in their worship of Mary, saints, relics, church organization, and clerical celibacy (Table 15.1), Protestants represented the largest share with 44.9% of Christians. Catholics accounted for a slightly smaller percentage, at 41.1%, while Orthodox Christians made up the smallest share, at 6.6%. The remaining 2.1% belonged to other Christian denominations. By comparison, worldwide percentages are different, with Catholics at 50.1%, Protestants at 36.7%, and Orthodox at 11.9%. This indicates a significantly higher percentage of Protestants and Orthodox in the WSE group than in the world as a whole.

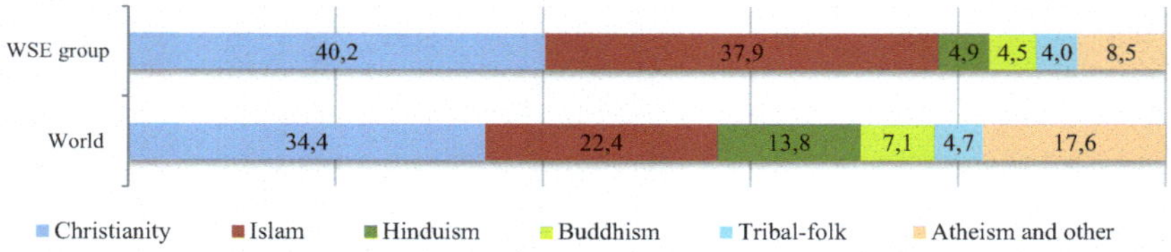

Fig. 15.1 WSE major religions compared to the world in 2019 (% of population). (Source: Teperek, Odmiennosci Kulturowe a Poziom Rozwoju Panstw o Malym Potencjale Ekonomicznym (2020))

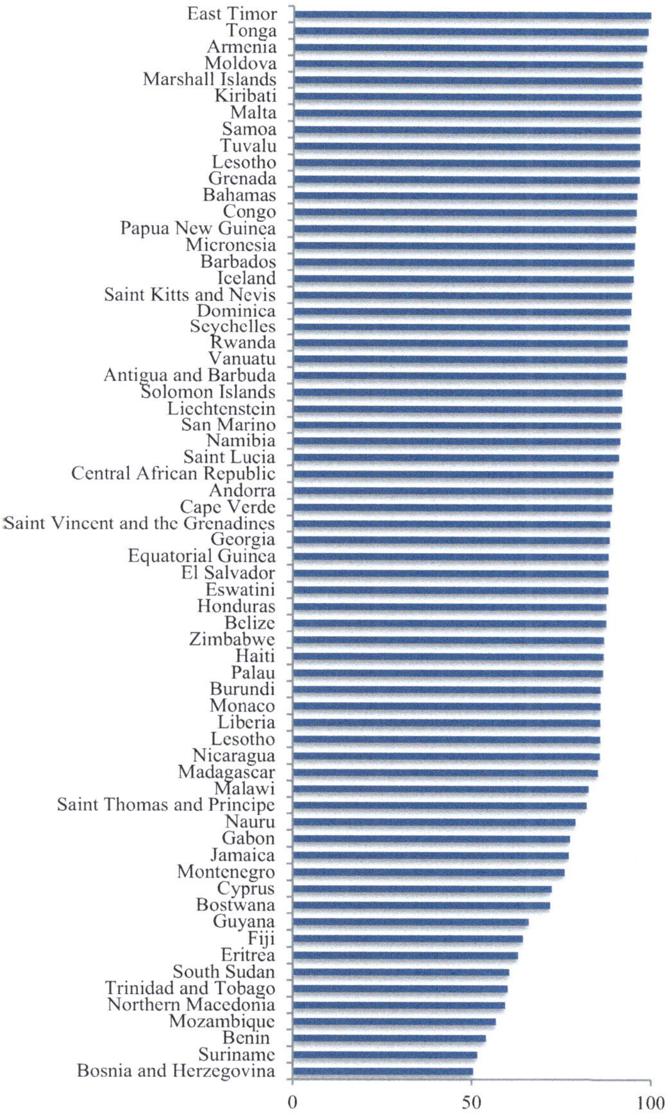

Fig. 15.2 WSE with predominantly Christian adherents (% of population). (Source: Own work based on CIA Factbook)

Table 15.1 Major Christian denominations

Catholic	*Protestant*	*Orthodox*
Latin, Greek Catholic, Old Catholic • acknowledges the seven sacraments • believes in the Immaculate Mary as the Mother of God • the Church is one, universal and apostolic • the head of the Church is the Pope • the organization of the Church includes archdioceses, dioceses, deaneries, parishes • celibacy is obligatory • particularly meritorious to the Church are beatified or canonized • an important role is played by male and female religious orders	Pentecostals, Evangelicals, Anglicans, Lutherans, Baptists • arose after the great schism in the Catholic Church during the Reformation in the sixteenth century • acknowledges the Bible as the only source of faith • does not recognize the authority of the Pope • the only mediator between God and the believer is Jesus Christ • do not recognize the worship of the Virgin Mary and the saints, holy places, relics, images, indulgences, the transubstantiation of bread into the flesh and wine into the blood of Jesus Christ	Eastern churches including Orthodox churches • arose from Catholicism as a result of the so-called Eastern Schism in 1054 after the separation of the Byzantine Church • does not accept Catholic dogmas, such as the origin of the Holy Spirit, the primacy of the apostle Peter over the other apostles, the primacy of the Pope, purgatory, the Immaculate Conception and the Assumption of Mary. • no celibacy except for bishops • has no single head • divided into dioceses and parishes

Source: Own compilation based on: Beyer (2005); Marthaler (1994)

Protestants accounted for more than 50% of adherents in 29 countries with the highest percentages in: Tuvalu (95% of the population), Barbados (88%), Saint Kitts and Nevis (84%), Eswatini (82%), Saint Vincent and the Grenadines (82%), Antigua and Barbuda (81%), the Bahamas (80%), Vanuatu (78%), Zimbabwe (76%), Iceland (75%), Liberia (75%). Catholics dominated in 28 of the WSE, also accounting for more than 50% of the population. They were most numerous in: East Timor (97%), Malta (96%), San Marino (91%), Andorra (85%), Seychelles (83%),

Monaco (82%), Equatorial Guinea (81%), Cape Verde (79%), Liechtenstein (76%). Orthodox Christians made up more than 50% of the population in 7 of the WSE, primarily in those with a socialist systemic past, including: Moldova (95% of the population), Georgia (87%), Armenia (83%), Montenegro (72%), and Cyprus (66%).

After Christianity, the second most popular religion in the WSE is Islam, representing 37.9% of the population in this group). Islam was founded by Muhammad, considered the greatest prophet, in the seventh century AD. It is based on the monotheistic belief in one God, Allah. The main branches of Islam, include Sufism (e.g., in Afghanistan) and Shiism (e.g., in Yemen) (Abrahamian, 1989). The obligations of followers are outlinked in the Qur'an, which serves as the fundation for universally binding law (Sharia). Followers of Islam adhere to five principles: public profession of faith in God (shahada), whose messenger is Muhammad; recitation of prayers five times a day while facing Mecca; observance of fasting during Ramadan; giving alms (zakat) to the poor, typically 2.5% of income; and making a pilgrimage to Al-Kaba in Mecca (Gade, 2007). The largest percentage of Muslims (over 90% of the population) reside in the WSE such as Afghanistan, Djibouti, The Gambia, Mali, Mauritania, Niger, Senegal, Somalia, Tajikistan, and Yemen (Fig. 15.3).

Buddhism is practiced by 4.5% of population the WSE group. It is both a religion and a philosophical system, founded in the sixth century BC by Siddhartha Gautama, known as the Buddha (Heim, 2007). Adherents of Buddhism neither deny nor affirm the existence of God, instead, they accept the existence of an infinite number of worlds inhabited by humans, animals, gods, and demons. Buddhism emphasizes the belief in reincarnation and the law of cause and effect (karma). It is based on the Four Noble Truths taught by the Buddha, and the Eightfold Path, which

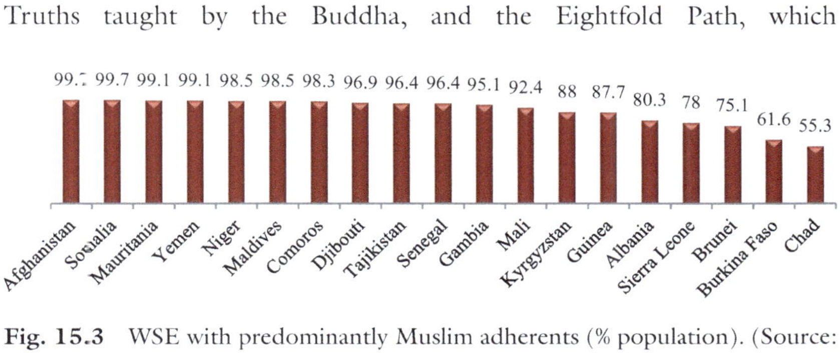

Fig. 15.3 WSE with predominantly Muslim adherents (% population). (Source: Own compilation based on: (Teperek, Odmiennosci Kulturowe a Poziom Rozwoju Panstw o Malym Potencjale Ekonomicznym, 2020, p. 100)

outlines Buddhism's set of precepts aimed at achieving liberation, peace, cessation of suffering, knowledge, enlightenment and nirvana. Most Buddhists live in the WSE such as: Cambodia (83%), Bhutan (75%), Laos (66%). In Mongolia, Buddhists make up more than half of the population (55.1%). Unofficial statistics suggest that 12.3% of North Koreans follow Buddhism, albeit in a modified form called Chondoism. A small percentage of Buddhists also reside in Nepal (10%) and Brunei (9%).

A slightly larger proportion of the WSE population—4.9%—adhere to Hinduism. Like Buddhists, Hindus believe in reincarnation for the continuous improvement of the soul, and in karma. The polytheistic religion teaches that God, or Brahmna manifests as many deities, including Siwa, Brahma, Vishnu Hindus. The sacred scriptures of Hinduism include the Shastras, Vedas, Upanishads, and the epics of the Ramayana and Mahabharata. The largest percentage of Hindus live in Nepal (81% of the population). They also make up nearly half of the population in Mauritius (49%) and about a quarter in Fiji (27%) and Bhutan (22%).

Similar to Hinduism and Buddhism, a comparable percentage of the WSE population adheres to tribal religions, accounting for 4.7% of the group's population. These beliefs are characterized by the worship of spirits, ancestors, and various rituals performed by chiefs, priests, diviners, and witches. Oral traditions passed down from generation to generation, play an important role fin the lives of tribal people. The largest percentage of followers of tribal and folk religions are found in the WSE located in Africa, including Togo (36% of the population), South Sudan (33%), Guinea-Bissau (31%), Benin (18%), Burkina Faso (15%), and Mozambique (7%).

Bibliography

Abrahamian, E. (1989). *Radical Islam: The Iranian Mujahedin.* Tauris.

Beyer, P. (2005). Religia i Globalizacja, Zakl. Wyd. NOMOS, 191–218.

Gade, A. M. (2007). In J. Corrigan (Ed.), *Islam: The Oxford Handbook of Religion and Emotion.* Oxford University Press.

Heim, M. (2007). In J. Corrigan (Ed.), *The Oxford Handbook of Religion and Emotion.* Oxford University Press.

Gorski, K. J. (2007). *Spotkami z religiami.* Ksiegarnia Sw. Jacka.

Luhmann, N. (1998). *Funkcja Religii, Zak. Wyd.* NOMOS.

Marthaler, B. (1994). *Introducing the Catechism of the Catholic Church, Traditional Themes and Contemporary Issues.* Paulist Press.

Teperek, A. A. (2020). *Odmiennosci Kulturowe a Poziom Rozwoju Panstw o Malym Potencjale Ekonomicznym* (Vol. 4). Kwartalnik Kolegium Ekonomiczno-Spolecznego, Studia i Praca.

CHAPTER 16

Linguistic Heterogeneity in the World's Smallest Economies

Along with religion, language is a fundamental cultural characteristic. Throughout history, languages have played a special role in the formation of nations, performing functions that go beyond ethnicity, as carriers of information and culture between nations. They unite the inhabitants of an area and give them a sense of distinctiveness. The ability to communicate in the same language is a prerequisite for a country's economic growth and development, as well as for its economic relations with other countries. In contrast, linguistic heterogeneity, combined with cultural diversity, has been an obstacle to the economic expansion of many underdeveloped countries, limiting their economic growth.

As of 2019, there were 7097 languages in the world. Both globally and in the WSE group, the largest number of languages is spoken by the people of Papua New Guinea (830 languages). In second place is the Congo, whose people communicate in 215 languages. Although many of these are officially recognized, taught in schools, and used in formal documents, they are not official languages. In both Congo and the majority of the colonized WSE, the official languages are those of the former colonial powers. For example, French is the official language in Burkina Faso, Mali, and Senegal; English is the official language in Gabon, The Gambia, Malta, Trinidad and Tobago; Portuguese is the official language in Cape Verde, Mozambique; Spanish is the official language in El Salvador;

A. A. Tokarek, *Economic Development in the World's Smallest Economies*, https://doi.org/10.1007/978-3-031-63810-7_16

and Dutch is the official language in Suriname. Some of the WSE have one official language (57 countries) or two official languages (26 countries), or even three official languages (10 countries) (Table 16.1), which are specified in their constitutions and government documents and have legal status in their territories (Rykiel, 2006).

Many of the WSE have the same official languages: English, French, Arabic, Portuguese, and Spanish. However, most of them (60 countries) use their own official language, specific to them, for example Afghanistan—Persian, Botswana—Tswana, Lesotho—Sotho, Nauru—Nauruan, North Korea—Korean, Samoa—Samoan, Somalia—Somali (Table 16.1). It is worth noting that English, French, Arabic, Portuguese, or Spanish are almost always among the official languages of the WSE that have two or three official languages. The exceptions are Afghanistan, Bosnia and Herzegovina, Cyprus, Eritrea, Kyrgyzstan.

English, the most popular language, is officially spoken in the 38 WSE and by nearly one-fifth of the WSE group's population (100 million people in 2019). In practice, however, English is used by a much larger number of people due to its global prevalence in external communication. For this reason, it is often referred to as the first language of mankind, as it has the greatest impact on trade and business relations, technology, politics, diplomacy, and mass culture.

Although, French is an official language in almost half as many of the WSE (22 countries) as English (38 countries), it is spoken by more than twice as many people (206 million people) as English (100 million people). In contrast, Portuguese and Spanish, used as official languages, are spoken by 35 million and 24 million people, respectively, totaly almost as many as those who speak Arabic (70 million) (Table 16.2).

The French WSE, the Arabic WSE, and the Portuguese WSE subgroups had the highest population growth of more than 70% between 2000 and 2019. At the same time, these three language subgroups had the lowest GDP growth per capita, while the English and Spanish WSE subgroups had the highest GDP growth (Fig. 16.1).

In contrast, the Portuguese subgroup experienced the largest increase in GDP (more than three times) (from US$ 10.7 billion to US$ 35.3 billion between 2000 and 2019) (Table 16.2). This is mainly due to a nearly fourfold increase in GDP (from US$ 3.3 billion to US$ 12.5 billion) in Equatorial Guinea and a 3.5-fold increase in GDP (from US$ 5.1 billion to US$ 17.8 billion) in Mozambique. On the other hand, the Arabic language WSE subgroup experienced the smallest growth (from US$

Table 16.1 Official languages in the WSE

No	*The world's smallest economies*	*Official languages*		
		1st language	*2nd language*	*3rd language*
1	Andorra	Catalan	Spanish	French
2	Bosnia and Herzegovina	Serbian	Croatian	Bosnian
3	Fiji	English	Fijian	Fijian Hindi
4	Equatorial Guinea	Spanish	French	Portuguese
5	Palau	English	Palau	Japanese
6	Papua New Guinea	English	tok pisin	hiri motu
7	Rwanda	French	English	Rwanda
8	Seychelles	English	French	Seychelles Creole
9	Togo	French	kabiye	Ewe
10	Vanuatu	bislama	French	English
11	Afghanistan	Pushto	Persian (dari)	
12	Botswana	English	Tswana	
13	Burundi	French	Rundi	
14	Cyprus	Greek	Turkish	
15	Chad	French	Arabic	
16	Haiti	French	Creole (Haitian)	
17	Chambers	French	Arabic	
18	Central African Republic	French	Sango	
19	Tonga	Tongy	English	
20	Djibouti	French	Arabic	
21	Eritrea	Arabic	Tigrinia	
22	Jamaica	English	Creole (Jamaican)	
23	Kiribati	English	Kiribati	
24	Kyrgyzstan	Kyrgyz	Russian	
25	Lesotho	English	Sotho	
26	Madagascar	French	Malagasy	
27	Malawi	English	Chicheva	
28	Malta	Maltese	English	
29	Namibia	English	Afrikaans	
30	Nauru	English	Nauruan	
31	Samoa	English	Samoan	
32	Somalia	Omalian	Arabic	
33	Swaziland	English	Siswati	
34	East Timor	Portuguese	Tetum	
35	Tuvalu	English	Tuvalu	

(*continued*)

Table 16.1 (continued)

No	*The world's smallest economies*	*Official languages*		
		1st language	*2nd language*	*3rd language*
36	Marshall Islands	English	Marshal	
37	Albania	Albanian		
38	Antigua and Barbuda	English		
39	Armenia	Armenian		
40	Bahamas	English		
41	Barbados	English		
42	Belize	English		
43	Benin	French		
44	Bhutan	Jongkha		
45	Brunei	Malay		
46	Burkina Faso	French		
47	Montenegro	Montenegrin		
48	Dominica	English		
49	Estonia	Estonian		
50	Eswatini	English		
51	Gabon	English		
52	The Gambia	English		
53	Grenada	English		
54	Georgia	Georgian		
55	Guyana	English		
56	Guinea	French		
57	Guinea-Bissau	Portuguese		
58	Honduras	Spanish		
59	Iceland	Icelandic		
60	Yemen	Arabic		
61	Cambodia	Khmer		
62	Congo	French		
63	North Korea	Korean		
64	Laos	Lao		
65	Liechtenstein	German		
66	Northern Macedonia	Macedonian		
67	Maldives	Maldivian		
68	Small	French		
69	Mauritania	Arabic		
70	Mauritius	English		
71	Micronesia	English		
72	Moldova	Moldavian		
73	Monaco	French		
74	Mongolia	Mongolian		

(*continued*)

Table 16.1 (continued)

No	*The world's smallest economies*	*Official languages*		
		1st language	*2nd language*	*3rd language*
75	Mozambique	Portuguese		
76	Nepal	Nepali		
77	Niger	French		
78	Nicaragua	Spanish		
79	Salvador	Spanish		
80	San Marino	Italian		
81	Senegal	French		
82	Sierra Leone	English		
83	Saint Kitts and Nevis	English		
84	Saint Lucia	English		
85	Saint Vincent and the Grenadines	English		
86	South Sudan	English		
87	Suriname	Dutch		
88	Tajikistan	Tajik		
89	Trinidad and Tobago	English		
90	Solomon Islands	English		
91	Saint Thomas and Príncipe	Portuguese		
92	Cape Verde	Portuguese		
93	Zimbabwe	English		

Source: Own compilation based on: Hilary and Kelly (2012)

32.1 billion to US$ 48.6 billion). As a result of slower GDP growth (by 51%) than population growth (by 72%), the subgroup experienced a decline in GDP per capita (from US$ 787 to US$ 691 from 2000 to 2019) (Fig. 16.1).

The ability to speak the official colloquial language—often referred to as the *liaison* language (Kuchinski, 2003)—such as Arabic in Islamic countries or Russian in the former republics of the USSR (even though Arabic and Russian are not the official languages in these countries), or even one's mother tongue or native language, which is a person's first language (the language in which it thinks, dreams, prays, counts, swears, and with which it identifies) (Lipinska, 2003), does not necessary imply the ability to read and write. Many residents of the WSE struggle with Illiteracy, which limits their active participation in social life, not to mention economic activities. In 2019, there were 187.8 million illiterate

Table 16.2 Most popular official languages in the WSE in 2019

Official languages in the WSE	*WSE*	*Area*	*Population*			*GDP*		
			2000	*2019*	*2000–2019*	*2000*	*2019*	*2000–2019*
	Number	*thousand km²*	*Thousand*		*%*	*USD million*		*%*
ENGLISH								
Antigua and Barbuda, Bahamas, Barbados, Belize, Botswana, Dominica, Eswatini, Fiji, The Gambia, Grenada, Guyana, Jamaica, Kiribati, Lesotho, Liberia, Malawi, Malta, Marshall Islands, Mauritius, Micronesia, Namibia, Nauru, Palau, Papua New Guinea, Rwanda, Saint Kitts and Nevis, Saint Lucia, Saint Vincent and the Grenadines, Samoa, Seychelles, Sierra Leone, Solomon Islands, South Sudan, Tonga, Trinidad and Tobago, Tuvalu, Vanuatu, Zimbabwe	38	3631	67,900	100,089	47	130,561	226,934	74
FRENCH								
Andorra, Benin, Burkina Faso, Burundi, Central African Republic, Chad, Comoros, Congo, Djibouti, Equatorial Guinea, Gabon, Guinea, Haiti, Madagascar, Mali, Monaco, Niger, Rwanda, Senegal, Seychelles, Togo, Vanuatu	22	6647	120,839	206,570	71	103,45	223,682	110
ARABSKI								
Chad, Comoros, Djibouti, Eritrea, Mauritania, Somalia, Yemen	7	3622	40,819	70,981	72	32,131	48,655	51
PORTUGAL								
Guinea-Bissau, Equatorial Guinea, Mozambique, Cape Verde, East Timor, Saint Thomas and Príncipe	6	883	20,974	35,701	70	10,795	35,313	327
SPAIN								
Andorra, El Salvador, Equatorial Guinea, Honduras, Nicaragua	5	292	18,203	24,178	33	38,381	72,504	87

Source: Own compilation based on: Teperek (2020); The World Bank

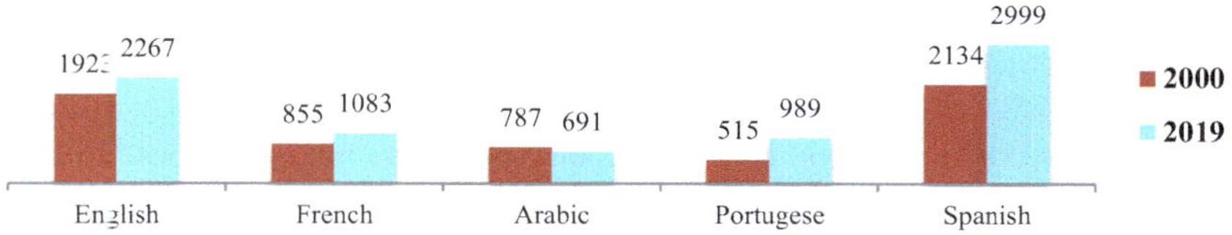

Fig. 16.1 WSE by official languages and GDP per capita change between 2000 and 2019. (USD per capita). (Source: Own compilation based on The World Bank)

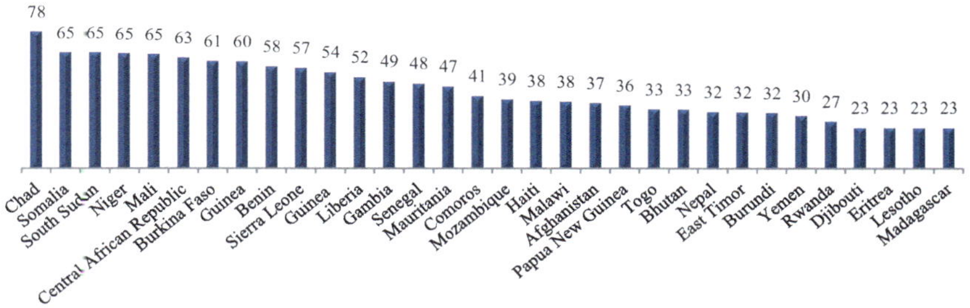

Fig. 16.2 WSE with the highest percentage of illiteracy in 2019 (%). (Source: Own compilation based on The World Bank)

people in the WSE, accounting for 34.4% of the group's population. In comparison, the global illiteracy rate stood at 13.5%, highlighting not only the low educational level within the WSE, but also indicating the very low level of economic development. Among the illiterate population in the WSE, women represented a significantly higher percentage at 66%, while men accounted for only 34%. The highest percentages of illiterates were recorded in Niger (77.7%), Somalia (65.5%), South Sudan (65.5%), Niger (65%), Mali (64.5%), Central African Republic (62.6%), Burkina Faso (60.7%), Guinea (60.4%), among others, with women outnumbering men in each of these countries. Notably, the top 16 of the WSE with the highest percentages of illiteracy are impoverished African nations (Fig. 16.2).

Despite the still high rate of illiteracy in many of the WSE, the percentage of illiterate individuals has declined over the past two decades, thanks to investments in education. The progress is clearly reflected in the group's indicators. Between 2000 and 2019, the illiteracy rate decreased from 38%

to 33.4%. Consequently, the number of literate individuals in the WSE increased from 230.7 million to 373.9 million.

An analysis of the WSE group revealed that despite the decline in illiteracy, a third of the population (187.8 million of the 561 million in 2019) still lacked the ability to read, write and perform basic mathematical operations. This issue is particularly prevalent among the African population. Steadily increasing financial support from international organizations, such as UNESCO and highly developed countries have contributed to improvements in literacy rates (e.g., in Benin from 34.7% to 42.4%; Eswatini from 81.7% to 88.4%; The Gambia from 36.8% to 50.8%; Mali from 26.2% to 35.5%; Niger from 14.4% to 35%; Sierra Leone from 34.8% to 43.2%; Togo from 53.2% to 66.5% between 2000 and 2019). However, completely eradicating illiteracy remains a challenge. Given the high rate of population growth, meeting basic needs often takes precedence, relegating education funding to a secondary priority. Consequently, many of the WSE face a shortage of skilled workers, which hinders their economic development.

Bibliography

Hilary, F., & Kelly, M. (2012). *Languages at War: Policies and Practices of Language Contacts in Conflicts*. Palgrave Macmillan.

Kuchinski, K. (2003). In I. Fierla (Ed.), *Geografia Gospodarcza Swiata*. PWE.

Lipinska, E. (2003). *Jezyk Ojczysty, JezykObcy, Jezyk Drugi*. Wstep do Badan Dwujezycznosci, Wyd. UJ.

Rykiel, Z. (2006). *Podstawy Geografii Politycnej*. PWE.

Teperek, A. A. (2020). *Odmiennosci Kulturowe a Poziom Rozwoju Panstw o Malym Potencjale Ekonomicznym* (Vol. 4). Kwartalnik Kolegium Ekonomiczno-Spolecznego, Studia i Praca.

CHAPTER 17

Cultural Determinants, and the Level of Economic Development of the World's Smallest Economies

Both the religions professed and the languages spoken are fundamental exponents of the cultural characteristics of the WSE. Speaking a common language facilitates the maintenance of economic ties with wider world, while religions shape ethical and moral values, influencing societal consciousness, politics, and economics. One of the authors expressed the impact of culture on a multitude of facets of human existence, stating: "a study of economic history reveals a clear influence of culture on almost every aspect of economic development" (Landes, 2003). Culture also plays a crucial role in shaping societies' attitudes toward work. The German sociologist Max Weber argued that Christian values, especially Protestant ones, promote a strong work ethic, while simultaneously propelling economic growth (Weber, 2010). This hypothesis was also confirmed by economist Horst Feldmann, who conducted research in 80 countries around the world under the influence of different religions (Feldmann, 2007). Countries with predominantly Protestant population exhibited labour force participation rates that were 6% higher (11% higher for women) than those influenced by other Christian denominations, and significantly higher than in countries with a different religious affiliations. The theories put forth by Weber and Feldmann are also reflected in the WSE. The Western (European) subgroup, comprising Christian countries that are predominantly Protestant or shaped by Protestantism, where

A. A. Teperek, *Economic Development in the World's Smallest Economies*, https://doi.org/10.1007/978-3-031-63810-7_17

religion is still alive but in a secular form, exhibited the highest level of economic development in 2019, at US$ 30,643 per capita (Table 17.1). Protestants espouse a commitment to democratic principles, the rule of law and gender equality. (Elias, 1980), and place the greatest emphasis on the value of freedom, including economic freedom. These values encourage entrepreneurship, self-initiative, and protect privacy. Consequently, the Christian WSE, particularly those influenced by Protestantism (e.g., in Iceland), have achieved very high economic levels. This success is evident not only in economic indicators such as high GDP per capita, a high value of exports and imports per capita, a high share of services in GDP creation, and high spending on high technology, but also in social indicators, including low illiteracy, a high level of education, urbanization, and demographic indicators such as low natural increase rate, and a high rate of population aging. (Teperek, 2020).

Unlike Western culture, which acts as a catalyst for high levels of economic development in Western WSE, African, Islamic, Buddhist, and Hindu cultures have not similarly stimulated the economies of the African WSE, the Islamic WSE, the Buddhist WSE, and the Hindu WSE. By 2019, the populations of these four subgroups accounted for as much as 84% of the total WSE population, an increase from 79% in 2000 (Table 17.1). This growth resulted primarily from rapid population increases, especially in the WSE influenced by African and Islamic cultures, which grew by 61% and 77%, respectively, between 2000 and 2019. Unfortunately, the population growth was not accompanied by such rapid economic growth, resulting in a modest increase, in the already very low GDP per capita, in African WSE by 24% (from US$ 893 per capita to US$ 1108 per capita) and in Islamic WSE by 14% (from US$ 817 per capita to US$ 931 per capita) between 2000 and 2019 (Table 17.1). Low levels of economic development are associated with high rates of natural increase and fertility, which are influenced by cultural factors and low levels of education. In the African WSE, the family unit is regarded as the most important social value, with having many children seen as a sign the status. Furthermore, it serves a practical purpose. This is due to the fact that children are employed as labourers or as additional hands for physical labour in agriculture settings. Similarly, Islamic culture, characterized by polygamy, embraces a multi-child family model, the number of wives and children is associated with the father's strength and wealth. The very low socioeconomic level of the Islamic WSE subgroup (GDP US$ 931 per capita in 2019) can also be attributed cultural and religious factors. The economic development is

Table 17.1 WSE by cultural division in 2019

WSE subgroups	*WSE*	*Dominant religion*	*Dominant official language*		*Area*	*Population*		*GDP*		*GDP*	
						2000	*2019*	*2000*	*2019*	*2000*	*2019*
	quantity		*Official languages*	*Countries' number*	*thousands km²*	*Thousands*		*US$ million*		*US$ /person*	
African	24	Christianity, Tribal religions	English	11	5486.4	112,223	180,155	100,252	199,698	893	1108
			French	8							
			Portuguese	4							
			Arabic	1							
Latin American	17	Christianity	English	12	726.8	32,445	41,351	91,829	139,432	2830	3372
			Spanish	3							
			French	1							
			Dutch	1							
Islamic	16	Islam	French	8	7727.1	117,656	208,251	96,126	193,788	817	931
			Arabic	5							
			Maldivian	1							
			Persian	1							
			Malay	1							
Pacific	13	Christianity	English	12	542.9	8694	12,562	15,690	31,659	1805	2520
			Portuguese	1							
Slavic-Orthodox	9	Christianity Islam	Albanian	1	595.8	30,665	33,974	49,243	112,807	1606	3320
			Armenian	1							
			Croatian	1							
			Montenegrin	1							
			Georgian	1							
			Russian	1							
			Macedonian	1							
			Moldavian	1							
			Tajik	1							

(*continued*)

Table 17.1 (continued)

WSE subgroups	*WSE*	*Dominant religion*	*Dominant official language*		*Area*	*Population*		*GDP*		*GDP*	
						2000	*2019*	*2000*	*2019*	*2000*	*2019*
	quantity		*Official languages*	*Countries' number*	*thousands km^2*	*Thousands*		*US$ million*		*US$ /person*	
Western (European)	8	Christianity	French	2	158.4	3169	3577	63,552	109,614	20,050	30,643
			Greek	1							
			Estonian	1							
			Icelandic	1							
			English	1							
			Hairs	1							
Buddhist	5	Buddhism	Jongkha	1	2140.8	43,396	53,310	25,811	65,745	595	1233
			Khmer	1							
			Korean	1							
			Laotian	1							
			Mongolian	1							
Hindu	1	Hinduism	Nepalese	1	147.1	23,941	28,608	10,899	24,575	455	859
WSE group in total	93			93	17,536.6	372,192	561,792	453,405	877,322	1218	1562

Source: Own compilation based on: Teperek (2020); The World Bank

largely limited by the influence of Qur'anic religious law (Sharia) on the economy, politics, and the private lives of individuals. The tenets of the faith shape daily routines, including the observance if five daily prayers and fasting from dawn until sunset during Ramadan. The religion prohibits the consumption of pork, which has led to the absence of pig farming in the Islamic WSE. It prohibit the consumption of alcohol and its production. Additionally, women are restricted from working and exercising various professions. Although the principles of Quranic law do not support the adoption of progressive norms seen in highly developed economies—partly due to the very low levels of education and high rates of illiteracy—Islamic countries have a relatively well-developed system of cashless transactions (using checks, bills of exchange, etc.), which originated from the religious prohibition of usury. This can be seen as a kind of progress. It is also worth noting that, in the distant past, Islam contributed to the spread of the decimal system and the development of sciences such as astronomy, mathematics, and physics. The achievements established the fundation for the revitalisation of European civilization.

In addition to the above factors, conflicts—often religiously motivated—have been a major cause of slowing down the economic development in the Islamic WSE, as well as in the African WSE. Examples include: the long-running conflict between the Mujahideen, the Taliban, and the government army in Afghanistan; the civil war in Mali between separatists, the Tuaregs, and Islamists linked to al-Qaeda. In addition to religious conflicts, ethnic conflicts have often erupted in the Islamic WSE as well as in the African WSE, dating back to colonial times. Colonizers drew artificial boundaries, dividing populations that were culturally cohesive—ethnically and linguistically—believing in the same deities and sharing the same hierarchy of values. The result was numerous conflicts, often lasting decades, that weakened the economies. Examples include Afghanistan (GDP decline of 18% from 1980 to 1990 and 39% from 1990 to 2000), Liberia (GDP decline of 66% from 1980 to 1990), Mauritania (GDP decline of 22% from 1970 to 1980), Sierra Leone (GDP decline of 54% from 1990 to 2000), Somalia (GDP decline of 23% from 1990 to 2000), and South Sudan (GDP decline of 17% from 2010 to 2018).

An analysis of the economies of the Buddhist WSE and the Hindu WSE subgroups (Table 17.1) shows that the Buddhist and Hindu traditions have not served as an inspiration for accelerated economic development, largely due to the strong influence of religion—or rather, professed philosophy—on economics and politics. The practiced principle of Ahinsa, or non-violence towards living beings, has contributed to the growth of vegetarianism in Bhutan, Cambodia, Laos, Nepal, and consequently to an increase in the share of crops as well as the agricultural sector in GDP creation. The belief in reincarnation hinders the development of animal husbandry and limits pig farming in the Buddhist WSE and the Hindu WSE. In turn, the worship of the cow as a *sacred animal* prevents the vast cattle population from being economically exploited. In addition, cattle interfere communication, transportation, cleanliness, and grazing. Economic development in Hinduism is also hampered by the caste system, which prohibits certain occupations for members of specific castes. This results in socioeconomic disparities within societies, social discrimination and low levels of education among a large part of the population. Buddhism, on the other hand, preaches modesty, obedience, and the pursuit of Nirvana as the main goal of life. It rejects wealth, fame, pride, and success, which has a negative impact on economic development. Although the Buddhist WSE subgroup had a very low level of economic development, its growth is the highest among the eight WSE cultural subgroups analyzed. Between 2000 and 2019, its GDP per capita increased more than doubled (from US$ 595 per capita to US$ 1233 per capita). The Slavic-Orthodox WSE subgroup came in second with a slightly lower two-fold increase (from US$ 1606 per capita to US$ 3320 per capita). Such a large increase in both subgroups was mainly due to the rapid economic development of the three WSE: Cambodia, Laos and Mongolia. Cambodia experienced up to fourfold GDP growth, with only 35% population growth, while Laos and Mongolia experienced 3.5-fold economic growth, with about 25% population growth. This was associated with political–economic transformation, openness to the world and the influx of foreign capital. In contrast, the cultural subgroups with the highest level of economic development (Table 4.4), namely, the Western (European) WSE (GDP growth from US$ 20,050 per capita to US$ 30,643 per capita) and the lowest level of economic development, namely the Islamic WSE (GDP growth from US$ 817 per capita to US$ 931 per capita), showed the lowest growth. The Western (European) WSE subgroup already had a high level of economic development at the beginning of the period, so the increase from that high level was small. The Islamic WSE subgroup, on the other hand, included very poor countries (with the exception of Brunei and the Maldives) that have been sinking into poverty for years.

Cultural conditions were undoubtedly one of the main factors influencing both the level of economic development and the dynamics of economic development in most of the WSE, but there were exceptions in each subgroup. For example, in the African WSE: Burundi, with a GDP per capita of only US$ 208, and Equatorial Guinea, with almost 50 times more, US$ 9238 per capita in 2019; in the Islamic WSE: Somalia, with a GDP per capita of only US$ 93 and Brunei, with a GDP per capita of US$ 32,327; in the Latin American WSE: Haiti, with a GDP per capita of US$ 1245 and Trinidad and Tobago, with a GDP per capita of US$ 15,105. It should be noted, however, that the richest of these countries became wealthy in a relatively short period of time, primarily due to the export of their natural resources (oil and gas). Their rapid economic growth, supported by high incomes, did not close the gap separating them from North American or Western European countries. As a result, these countries remained economically backward.

Despite cultural separateness, recent decades have witnessed the mixing and diffusion of cultures, as a result of accelerated globalization processes that have brought economic and political connections and dependencies (Orlowska, 2002). Communicative and technological transgressions of spatial boundaries have contributed to a sense of accessibility to the most remote regions of the world. Previously isolated societies, cultures, and economies have begun to form links and relationships with one another, leading to a gradual transformation of cultures. Xenophobia and parochialism have weakened, and been replaced by a greater acceptance of otherness and tolerance of other traditions and cultures. However, this positive process has also been accompanied by negative consequences. Direct interpersonal contact has slowly disappeared, largely replaced by virtual communication, which did not allow for mutual understanding and transmission to the same extent as face-to-face encounters. Cultural uniqueness and authenticity have been replaced by uniformity (Jawlowska, 2004), which one of the authors described as follows: *Man moves from place to place, dresses similarly, eats similarly, and uses similar facilities of civilization and technology, such as hotels, airports, banks, offices, supermarkets, and so on. His consciousness has a cosmopolitan dimension, because the global has displaced the local (..)* (Skoczynski, 2004). Despite the overall global unification, cultural conditions still play a major role. They mobilize societies in Western economies (e.g., Andorra, Cyprus, Liechtenstein, Iceland, Malta), bringing them long-term economic benefits, while the traditional principles of Buddhist (e.g., Bhutan, Laos), Hindu (Nepal), African (e.g., Benin, Burundi, Madagascar, Togo), and Islamic (e.g., Afghanistan, Chad, Comoros, The Gambia, Yemen) cultures slow down economic development. Economic development is also hampered by conflicts, or internal disintegration, leading to the disintegration of political and economic structures (e.g., in the former Yugoslavia, which led to the creation of the WSE: Bosnia and Herzegovina, Montenegro, and North Macedonia, among others), which are also driven by cultural differences. In turn, common cultural roots motivate countries to create organizations, such as the European Economic Area, which has contributed to the economic growth of its member states (including the WSE of Cyprus, Iceland, Liechtenstein, Malta). Thus, cultural influences have brought both opportunities and threats. However, it should be remembered that cultural conditions are only one of the factors influencing the economic development of the WSE, in addition to the natural and demographic conditions analyzed in the previous chapters, as well as many others.

Bibliography

Elias, N. (1980). *Przemiany obyczajow w cywilizacji Zachodu*. PWN.

Jawlowska, A. (2004). In S. Amsterdamski (Ed.), *Globalizacja i Swiadomosc Globalna : Globalizacja i co dalej? Wyd.* IFIS PAN.

Feldmann, H. (2007, October 17). Protestantism, Labor Force Participation and Employment Across Countries, Online Version:. Retrieved from Wiley Online Library: https://onlinelibrary.wiley.com/doi/full/10.1111/j.1536-7150.2007.00540.x

Landes, D. S. (2003). In L. E. Harrison, S. P. Huntington, & S. Dymczyk (Eds.), *Kultura Przesadza Prawie o Wszystkim*. Zysk i S-ka.

Orlowska, R. (2002). In K. Zoladkiewicz (Ed.), *Globalizacja i Regionalizacja w Gospodarce Swiatowej*. PWE.

Skoczynski, J. (2004). In B. Szlachta (Ed.), *Kultura*. Slownik Spoleczny, Wyd. WAM.

Teperek, A. A. (2020). *Odmiennosci Kulturowe a Poziom Rozwoju Panstw o Malym Potencjale Ekonomicznym* (Vol. 4). Kwartalnik Kolegium Ekonomiczno-Spolecznego, Studia i Praca.

Weber, M. (2010). *Etyka Protestancka a Duch Kapitalizmu*. Wydawnictwo Aletheia.

Summary

Although the world's smallest economies constitute a large and diverse group of countries, they do not occupy a significant place on the geopolitical and economic map of the world due to their small economic potential. This group's share of global GDP has remained at just 1% with small deviations of a few tenths of a percent since the 1970 survey. However, it is worth noting that the group's share of other economic indicators has significantly increased. This can be seen even in the short period from 2000 to 2019, as the group's share of global trade increased in both exports of goods and services (from 0.9% to 1.4%) and imports (from 1.1% to 1.8%). The share of foreign direct investment also increased, both in inflows (from 0.8% to 3.2%) and outflows (from 0.1% to 1.7%) of global trade. The analyzed group of countries experienced an increase in foreign tourists, resulting in a rise in their share of global tourist arrivals (from 4.2% to 5.4%), as well as an increase in tourism revenues (from 2.7% to 3.1%). These figures demonstrate the group's growing participation in the global flow of goods, services, capital, and people, indicating greater integration with the world economy. All of this was made possible by the conditions of the world's smallest economies, particularly their environmental, demographic, and cultural factors.

Although the importance of geographic location is increasingly marginalized in today's globalized world, it still plays a crucial role. Location in the global space, particularly by the sea and geographic proximity to the

A. A. Teperek, *Economic Development in the World's Smallest Economies*, https://doi.org/10.1007/978-3-031-63810-7

markets of wealthy countries, enables the world's smallest economies to develop foreign trade more intensively. International trade, in turn, is based on the sale of goods that are derived from the natural environment. This is what enables development and agricultural production, determining livestock breeding, and providing resources of raw materials that can be exported. This is made possible by the transportation network, both water and land, which also depends on the environment. Additionally, environmental advantages promote the development of tourism, which is a primary source of income for many of the world's smallest economies. The natural environment has also been a determinant of settlement boundaries. However, the impact of the natural environment on the development of the analyzed countries was significant. While nature could facilitate and accelerate economic development, it could also delay or even prevent it. Most of the world's smallest economies (55 out of 93) are located in a hot equatorial climate that is favorable for tourism development. However, this climate also poses threats in the form of disastrous typhoons in the Pacific and hurricanes in the Atlantic Ocean. As a result, the economies of Caribbean and Pacific countries suffer multiple damages every year. The impact of climate change is evident in natural vegetation formations, particularly in forests, which are essential for economies and cover more than half of the area in one-third of the world's smallest economies. Climatic and vegetation conditions influence the nature and rate of soil-forming processes. As a result, soils with average production potential and very low fertility have formed in most of the world's smallest economies, making them unsuitable for agriculture. Consequently, the proportion of arable land in almost two-thirds of the analyzed countries is less than 10%, significantly limiting food production. This is further influenced by the unfavorable relief of most of the world's smallest economies, with over two-thirds of them covered in mountains and highlands. Such terrain hinders not only agriculture but also transportation and mining industries. The depletion of raw materials and their difficult availability have led to exploitation of the seas and oceans. Direct access to these resources is available to 67 coastal countries, which also have vast areas of maritime Exclusive Economic Zone, providing them with many benefits from sea-related activities. These examples demonstrate the significant influence of the environment on the economic development of the world's smallest economies. However, it is important to consider the significant impact of the human factor. Population growth dynamics and demographic structure can greatly influence opportunities and directions for the economic development. From 2000 to 2019, the group experienced nearly 51% population growth, primarily due to a high natural increase. This sustained natural increase rate of 15.7‰ in 2019 was attributed to the group's low level of economic development, with a per capita income of only US$ 1562 per capita. The growth in GDP per capita was limited by the rapidly growing population in most of the world's smallest economies. This has led to low standard of living of the population, insufficient housing, poor infrastructure, low levels of education and healthcare, a shortage of skilled labor mostly due to mass migration to wealthier countries, high unemployment rates, rising tensions due to the limited opportunities to improve the population's quality of life, as well as general slow economic growth caused by overpopulation. Examining this from another perspective, many of the world's smallest economies possess a significant pre-working and working-age labor pool that, while currently a hindrance to economic growth, represents an opportunity for human capital development. However, this necessitates initiatives to enhance labor force participation, primarily through financial investments in education, job creation, and infrastructure development. While this is a formidable challenge for governments, it is possible given the group's continued economic growth (nearly doubling of GDP over the period 2000–2019) and greater capacity to provide skilled human resources. Undoubtedly, cultural change, particularly in countries that are heavily influenced by tradition and religion, would be a great facilitator in this process. For these cultures to be more of a source of inspiration for accelerated economic development would require changes in the way of thinking about progress through education, as well as changes in the principles around which economic activity operates, without which progress is impossible, and without which, economic development is also impossible. As in the case of countries with Western culture, which is characterized by the strongest work ethic of all the eight cultures analyzed. The characteristics of Western culture proved to be the most developmentally stimulating, as evidenced by the highest level of economic development of the world's smallest economies under its influence. Meanwhile, Islamic, African, Hindu, Buddhist cultures have not proven so inspiring, as evidenced by the low level of economic development of the world's smallest economies, influenced by these cultures.

It is important to remember that in addition to natural, demographic, and cultural factors, numerous historical, political, social, and above all, economic factors influence the economic development of the world's smallest economies. These include a stable macroeconomic and political environment, transparent and effective government institutions, sufficient infrastructure, and an adequate healthcare system. Therefore, when analyzing the level of development of the world's smallest economies, it is imperative to examine each of them individually.

On-line Publications

CIA The World Factbook, https://www.cia.gov/the-world-factbook

Cruise Industry News, Annual Report 2021, https://www.cruiseindustrynews.com/store/product/annual-reports/2021-cruise-industry-news-annual-report/

FAO, World Food and Agriculture – Statistical Yearbook 2020.

Feldmann H., Protestantism, Labor Force Participation, and Employment Across Countries, https://core.ac.uk/download/pdf/1583323.pdf

International Migration Report 2019, https://www.un.org/en/development/desa/population/migration/publications/migrationreport/docs/MigrationReport2019_Highlights.pdf

Knomad Migration, https://www.knomad.org/data/migration/immigration?tid%5B81%5D=81

Migration Data Portal 2019, The total numer of emigrants, https://www.migrationdataportal.org/international-data?i=stock_abs_&t=2020

OECD, Agriculture land, https://data.oecd.org/agrland/agricultural-land.htm

OECD.Stat, Surface water 2015, https://stats.oecd.org/Index.aspx?DataSetCode=SURFACE_WATER

The World Bank, https://data.worldbank.org

United Nations, Department of Economic and Social Affairs, Population Division.

United Nations, List of SIDS, https://www.un.org/ohrlls/content/list-sids

A. A. Teperek, *Economic Development in the World's Smallest Economies*, https://doi.org/10.1007/978-3-031-63810-7

UN Data, Population Division, World Population prospects 2020, https://population.un.org/wpp/

UNCTAD, Martime Transport Services and Infrastructure Supply, Review of Martime Transport 2020.

World merchant fleet and top shipowning countries (2020), INFOMARITIME.eu, https://stats.unctad.org/handbook/MaritimeTransport/MerchantFleet.html

World Meteorological Organization's World Weather & Climate Extrem, https://wmo.asu.edu

Worldmeter, www.Worldometers.info, United Nations, Department of Economic and Social Affairs, Population Division.

World Lake Database, International Lake Environment Commitee Fundation; OECD.Stat, Surface water, Permanent water 2015.

Bibliography Listed

1. Abrahamian E., Radical Islam: The Iranian Mujahedin, Tauris, London 1989.
2. Apollo M., The true accessibility of mountaineering: The case of the High Himalaya, Journal of Outdoor Recreation and Tourism, Vol. 17, 2017.
3. Arango J., Explaining migration: a critical view, International Social Journal, No 52, 2000.
4. Bachvarov M., Suliborski A., Kompendium wiedzy geografii politycznej i geopolityce, PWN, Warsaw 2003.
5. Barrett R., Kuzawa C.W., McDade T., Armelagos G.J., Emerging and re-emerging infectious disease. The third epidemiologic transition, Annual Review of Anthropology, Vol. 27, No. 1, 1998.
6. Bauman Z., Globalizacja. I co z tego dla ludzi wynika, PIW, Warsaw 2000.
7. Beard J. S., A Note on Gallery Forests, Ecology, 36 (2), 1955.
8. Beyer P., Religia i globalizacja, Zakł. Wyd. NOMOS, Carcow 2005.
9. Budner W., Geografia ekonomiczna. Współczesne zjawiska i procesy, WUE, Poznań 2011.
10. Castles S., Miller M.I., The Age of Migration: International Population Movements in the Modern World, Cambridge 2004.
11. Coyle D., GDP: A Brief but Affectionate History exciting history, Princeton University Press, Princeton, NJ, 2015.

A. A. Teperek, *Economic Development in the World's Smallest Economies*, https://doi.org/10.1007/978-3-031-63810-7

12. Cox C.B., Field R., Ladle R. J., Moore P. D., Biogeography. An Ecological and Evolutionary Approach, John Wiley & Sons Inc., New Jersey 2016.
13. Cynarski W. J., Globalizacja a spotkanie kultur, Wyd. UR, Rzeszów 2003.
14. Demeny P., G. McNicoll, Encyclopedia of population, Macmillan Reference, New York 2003.
15. Domański P., Dżibuti, [in:] J. Mantel-Niećko, M. Ząbek (ed.), Róg Afryki. Historia i współczesność, Wyd. Trio, Warsaw 1999.
16. Duncan Ch., Scott S., Czarna Śmierć. Epidemie w Europie od starożytności do czasów współczesnych, Bellona, Warsaw 2008.
17. Dziemidok B., Tożsamość narodowa a sztuka i nowe media w epoce globalizacji [in:] Kultura współczesna i media, Kultura i Społeczeństwo, Wyd. PAN, No 1, Warsaw, 2000.
18. Elias N., Przemiany obyczajów w cywilizacji Zachodu, PWN, Warsaw 1980.
19. Furmaga L., Wójcicki J., Mały słownik morski, Mitel International Ltd., Gdynia 1993.
20. Frydrych M., Kobojek S., Rdzany Z., Geografia Świata, SBM, Warsaw 2016.
21. Gade A.M., Islam [in:] J. Corrigan (ed.), The Oxford Handbook of Religion and Emotion, Oxford University Press, Oxford 2007.
22. Gleik P.H., Water resources [in:] S.H. Schneider (ed.), Encyclopedia of Climate and Weather, Vol 2, Oxford University Press, New York 1996.
23. Goodman N., Wstęp do socjologii, Wydawnictwo Zysk i S-ka, Poznań 1997.
24. Góralczyk W., Obszary morskie i ich delimitacja, Wydawnictwo UW, Warsaw 1993.
25. Góralczyk W., Szerokość morza terytorialnego i jego delimitacja, PWN, Warsaw 1964.
26. Góralczyk W., Szelf kontynentalny: studium prawnomiędzynarodowe, Wydawnictwo Prawnicze, Warsaw 1957.
27. Hatton T. J., Williamson J.G., Emigration in the Long Run: Evidence from Two Global Centuries, Asian Pacific Economic Literature, Vol. 23 (2) 2009.
28. Hausner I., A Karwińska, J. Purchla (ed), Kultura a rozwój, Narodowe Centrum Kultury, Warsaw 2013.

29. Heim M., Buddhism, [in:] J. Corrigan (ed.), The Oxford Handbook of Religion and Emotion, Oxford University Press, Oxford 2007.
30. Herder J.G., Myśli o filozofii dziejów, T.1, Warsaw 1962.
31. Hilary F., Kelly M., Languages at War: Policies and Practices of Language Contacts in Conflict, Palgrave Macmillan, 2012.
32. Huntington S.P., Zderzenie cywilizacji i nowy kształt ładu światowego, Wyd. 9, WWL Muza, Warsaw 2007.
33. Jawłowska A., Globalizacja i świadomość globalna, [in:] S. Amsterdamski (ed.), Globalizacja i co dalej?, Wyd. IFiS PAN, Warsaw 2004.
34. Kempny M. (ed.), Konsumpcja – istotny wymiar globalizacji kulturowej, Wyd. IFiS PAN, Warsaw 2005.
35. Kluckhohn C., Mirror for Man, Whittlesey House, New York 1949.
36. Kop J., Kucharska M., Szkurłat E., Geografia społeczno-ekonomiczna, PWN, Warsaw 2003.
37. Kranz-Szurek M., kultura lokalna a globalizacja kulturowa – próba oceny zjawiska, Rocznik Nauk Społecznych, T. 4 (40), No 2, 2012.
38. Ks. Górski, J., Spotkanie z religiami, Księgarnia Św. Jacka, Katowice 2007.
39. Kuciński K. (ed.), Geografia, Difin, Warsaw 2007.
40. Kuciński K., Ludność [in:] I. Fierla, Geografia gospodarcza świata, PWE, Warsaw 2003.
41. Landes D.S., Kultura przesadza prawie o wszystkim [in:] L.E. Harrison, S.P. Huntington, Kultura ma znaczenie, (ed.), tłum. S. Dymczyk, Zysk i S-ka, Poznań 2003.
42. Lipińska E., Język ojczysty, język obcy, język drugi. Wstęp do badań dwujęzyczności, Wyd. UJ, Cracow 2003.
43. Luhmann N., Funkcja religii, Zak. Wyd. Nomos, Cracow 1998.
44. Łabno G., Ekologia, Słownik encyklopedyczny, Wyd. Europa, Warsaw 2006.
45. Maciejko A., Kobiety i młodzież w migracjach, Polityka Społeczna No 3, Wyd. Instytutu Pracy i Polityki Społecznej, Warsaw 2004.
46. Maksimowicz A., Wzorzec umieralności w kolejnych fazach przejścia, [in:] M. Okólski (ed.), Teoria przejścia demograficznego, PWE, Warsaw 1990.
47. Marthaler B, Introducing the Catechism of the Catholic Church, Traditional Themes and Contemporary Issues, Paulist Press, NY 1994.

48. Massey D.S., Arango J., Hugo G., Kouaouci A., Pallegrino A., Taylor J.E., Theories of international migration: review and appraisal. Population and Development Review, Vol. 19, 1993.
49. Mączyńska E., Refleksje na kanwie książki Diane Coyle pt. PKB: krótka lecz emocjonująca historia, PWN, Warsaw 2018 [in:] E. Mączyńska, S. Owsiak, Biuletyn PTE No 3 (86), August 2019.
50. Meadows D., Meadows D., Randers J., Behrens III W. W., Granice wzrostu, PWE, Warsaw 1972.
51. McAdam J., Disappearing states, statelessness and the boundaries of international law [in:] J. McAdam (ed.) Climate Change and Displacement: Multidisciplinary Perspectives, Oxford 2010.
52. Mika M., Turystyka morska, [in:] W. Kurek (ed.), Turystyka, PWN, Warsaw 2007.
53. Okołowicz W., Klimatologia ogólna, PWN, Warsaw 1969.
54. Okólski M., Modernizacja społeczeństwa a przejście demograficzne, [in:] M. Okólski (ed.), Teoria przejścia demograficznego, PWE, Warsaw 1990.
55. Okólski M. (ed.), Wyzwania starzejącego się społeczeństwa Polska dziś i jutro, Wyd. UW, Warsaw 2018.
56. Okólski M., Fihel A., Demografia, Wyd. Naukowe Scholar, Warsaw 2012.
57. Orłowska R., Żołądkiewicz K. (ed.), Globalizacja i regionalizacja w gospodarce światowej, PWE, Warsaw 2002.
58. Otok S., Geografia polityczna, PWN, Warsaw 2012.
59. Philipov D., Dobritz J., Demographic Consequences of economic transition in countries of central and eastern Europe, The Population Studies, No 39, 2004.
60. Piore M.J., Labor Market Segmentation: To What Paradigm Does It Belong? American Economic Review, Vol. 73, No 2.
61. Podbielkowski Z., Szata roślinna Ziemi, Wyd. Kurpisz, Poznań 1997.
62. Radomski A., Gasińsk M., Elementy oceanologii. Wprowadzenie do środowisk morskich, Wydawnictwo UJ, Cracow 2004,
63. Ratnasekera L., Buddhism and Christianity in Dialogue, Dialogue and Universalism, No 4, pp. 81-88.
64. Rykiel Z., Podstawy geografii politycznej, PWE, Warsaw 2006.
65. Sedlacek T., Orrell D., Zmierzch homo economicus, Rozmowa z R. Chłupatym, Studio Emka, Warsaw 2012.
66. Simmons G., Ekologia zasobów naturalnych, PWN, Warsaw 1979.

67. Skoczek M., Migracje międzynarodowe, [in:] A. Bąkiewicz, U. Żuławska, Rozwój w dobie globalizacji, PWE, Warsaw 2010.
68. Skoczyński J., Kultura, [in:] B. Szlachta (ed..), Słownik społeczny, Wyd. WAM, Cracow 2004.
69. Smith V., Clean: A History of Personal Hygiene and Purity, Oxford University Press, Oxford 2008.
70. Stańczyk J., Szałtys D., Witkowski J., Potencjał ludnościowy Unii Europejskiej, [in:] J. Kleer, K. Prandecki, Ekonomiczna pozycja Europy w świecie, Wyd. Komitet Prognoz Polska 2000 Plus PAN, Warsaw 2016.
71. Stiglitz J. E., Fitoussi J.-P., Durand M., Beyong GDP, Measuring What Counts for Economic and Social Performance, OECD, Paris 2019.
72. Szaflarski J. (ed.), Słownik Geografii Świata, Wiedza Powszechna, Warsaw 1977.
73. Szczepański J., Elementy pojęcia socjologii, PWN, Warsaw 1963.
74. Taylor F., Principles of Scientific Management, Harper & Brothers, New York-London 1911.
75. Teperek A.A., Odmienności kulturowe a poziom rozwoju państw o małym potencjale ekonomicznym, Kwartalnik Kolegium Ekonomiczno-Społecznego, Studia i praca, No 4 (40), Warsaw 2020.
76. The World Atlas, Population of Capita Cities of the World 2021.
77. Todaro M.P., Internal migration in developing countries, International Labour Office, Geneva 1976.
78. Trzcińska B., Różnice i podobieństwa. Zróżnicowanie przyrodnicze. [in:] K. Kuciński (ed.) Geografia, Difin, Warsaw 2007.
79. Weber M., Etyka protestancka a duch kapitalizmu. Wydawnictwo Aletheia, Warsaw 2010.
80. Wrony J., Podstawy geografii ekonomicznej, PWE, Warsaw 2006.

Index[1]

[1] Note: Page numbers followed by 'n' refer to notes.

A. A. Teperek, *Economic Development in the World's Smallest Economies*, https://doi.org/10.1007/978-3-031-63810-7

B

C

R

S

T

U

V

W

Y

Z

The manufacturer's authorised representative in the EU is Springer Nature Customer Service Centre GmbH, Europaplatz 3, 69115 Heidelberg, Germany. If you have any concerns regarding our products, please contact ProductSafety@springernature.com

Printed and bound by CPI Group (UK) Ltd, Croydon, CR0 4YY
01/10/2026
02225964-0001